Criminal Justice

Criminal Justice

The Essentials

SECOND EDITION

STEVEN P. LAB
Bowling Green State University

MARIAN R. WILLIAMS
Appalachian State University

JEFFERSON E. HOLCOMB
Appalachian State University

MELISSA W. BUREK
Bowling Green State University

WILLIAM R. KING
Sam Houston State University

MICHAEL E. BUERGER
Bowling Green State University

New York   Oxford

OXFORD UNIVERSITY PRESS

2011

Oxford University Press, Inc., publishes works that further Oxford University's objective of excellence in research, scholarship, and education.

Oxford   New York
Auckland   Cape   Town   Dar es Salaam   Hong Kong   Karachi
Kuala Lumpur   Madrid   Melbourne   Mexico City   Nairobi
New Delhi   Shanghai   Taipei   Toronto

With offices in
Argentina   Austria   Brazil   Chile   Czech Republic   France   Greece
Guatemala   Hungary   Italy   Japan   Poland   Portugal   Singapore
South Korea   Switzerland   Thailand   Turkey   Ukraine   Vietnam

Copyright © 2011, 2008 by Oxford University Press, Inc.

Published by Oxford University Press, Inc.
198 Madison Avenue, New York, New York 10016

http://www.oup.com

Oxford is a registered trademark of Oxford University Press

ISBN: 978-0-19-973719-2

Printing number: 9 8 7 6 5 4 3 2 1

Printed in the United States of America
on acid-free paper

CONTENTS

PREFACE

Any time a publisher asks an author to prepare a new edition of a book it is a welcome request. While the cynical person may think it is welcome because of royalties a book may bring, the real excitement comes from knowing your work is finding acceptance among your peers. This is the case now.

When we first set out to write this book it was with a couple of ideas in mind. First, we wanted to prepare something that was not just another tome on criminal justice. Intro books have become almost encyclopedic, encompassing everything including the prison sink. We knew from experience that most students do not read all of that material, and some actually do not read any of it after looking at the first chapter. There is just too much to absorb. Second, we know that most instructors do not intend for their students to master everything that comes in those encyclopedic books anyway, so what is the purpose of all that material? Finally, we watched as the cost of textbooks escalated out of sight. Many students simply cannot afford to pay for those large textbooks. Our solution was to try and write a concise, valuable introductory text that students could afford and read in its entirety in the course of a single academic term. The fact that we have been asked to write a second edition suggests that our efforts have been at least somewhat successful.

CHANGES TO THE SECOND EDITION

While the book follows the same basic format and goals, this second edition has been improved in several ways. First, we have taken the many comments we received from readers and have attempted to incorporate those thoughts into each chapter. Of course, not all the comments have found their way into the book, but we have attempted to make changes where appropriate, without changing the basic tenor of the work. Second, we have succumbed (to some degree) to the calls for adding more figures and tables. We have been selective in what we have added. Third, like all new editions we have updated all the data so that the book is as accurate as possible. Fourth, we added chapter outlines as requested by many readers. Fifth, we have converted/eliminated all of the study breaks in favor of "critical thinking" exercises. This was done at the behest of several commentators who thought students simply ignored the breaks but would benefit more from exercises that could be more easily incorporated into classroom discussions. Last, at the request of our reviewers, we added a brief chapter to summarize and conclude the book.

Hopefully you will find this edition as valuable as the last (and maybe even more valuable). It is indeed a pleasure to know that our work has found acceptance in the field and we thank you for that honor. We would also like to thank the reviewers who formally commented on the manuscript for Oxford University Press: Sarah Bacon, Florida State University; Lindsey J. Bertomen, Hartnell College; Dean Dabney, Georgia State University; Alan Harland, Temple University; Thomas R. O'Connor, Austin Peay State University; Alissa Pollitz Worden, University at Albany–SUNY; Quint Thurman, Texas State University–San Marcos.

By all means feel free to continue to send us feedback on the book. As long as we can remain true to the original goal of an inexpensive alternative to introductory tomes, we will strive to meet your needs.

Steven P. Lab

CHAPTER 1

Crime, Criminal Justice, and Policy

INTRODUCTION

Crime remains a considerable problem in most societies. Since the inception of the first codified law (the Code of Hammurabi) around 1900 BC, the response to crime has garnered considerable attention from societies (Lab 2004). This chapter introduces some fundamental concepts concerning crime and criminal justice policy. First, crime and deviance are reviewed. Policy, the method by which problems are addressed, and then the notion of criminal justice policy are discussed. The chapter then moves on to the different and sometimes contradictory philosophies of criminal justice (the Classical and Positivist schools, and retribution, deterrence, rehabilitation, incapacitation). The chapter then returns to the notion of crime and reviews the three primary methods of measuring crime. Next the chapters addresses different competing tensions in the criminal justice system, such as the tension between due process and crime control in processing, discretion, and four decision points in the system. Finally, the chapter concludes with a review of some recent trends in criminal justice.

WHAT IS CRIME?

Understanding crime is best begun with a discussion of a concept called **deviance**. Deviance refers to human behaviors or actions that are considered by others to be wrong, bad, or inappropriate. Some inappropriate acts are relatively minor, such as spitting on the sidewalk, while others, such as killing a person, are seen as being seriously deviant. Not all deviant acts are illegal. For example, in most places it is not illegal for men to wear women's clothing in public, but a man in a dress will usually draw stares and scorn from onlookers.

Deviance is location, time, person, and event specific, meaning that some behaviors could be considered normal or deviant depending on the circumstances. For example, it is considered normal to yell at a football game, but deviant to yell in a library. This simply means that deviance is more than just a particular act; the person committing the act, the surrounding events, the time, and the location all help others define if someone's behavior should be deemed deviant.

Societies rely upon something called **informal social control** to influence people's behavior. Examples of informal social control include staring, scorn, the cold shoulder, shunning, and telling people that they are doing something wrong. Indeed, societies rely very heavily upon informal social control to keep people in conformity. Some agents of informal social control include parents, schoolteachers, employers, classmates, and fellow employees.

Some deviant acts are too serious to be managed via informal social control. These examples of serious deviance are prohibited by societies with written laws. These laws state the prohibited deviant behaviors, the circumstances that make such behaviors illegal, and the possible punishment for violating them. For example, it is not illegal to kill another person in self-defense, but it is illegal to do so with premeditation. Laws are generally written and approved by elected legislators at either the federal or state level. Local governments (such as towns and cities) may also pass their own laws. Crimes can be classified as either **mala in se** or **mala prohibita**. Mala in se acts such as murder, robbery, and rape are viewed as inherently evil and are thus often classified as serious crimes. Mala prohibita acts are less serious offenses such as underage drinking, speeding, and disturbing the peace. Mala prohibita acts are still considered crimes, but they are not viewed as inherently bad, only as behaviors that should be prohibited by law. A law is usually classified as either a **felony**, which is a serious breach of law usually carrying a penalty of more than one year in prison, or a **misdemeanor**, a less serious crime usually carrying a sentence of less than one year in prison. When someone engages in an illegal act, and the conditions of the act are not excused by a law, that person has broken the law and thus committed a crime.

Critical Thinking Exercise

Some simple societies rely exclusively upon informal social control and have no written laws or criminal justice system. What are some benefits of this system for these simple societies? What are some of the problems such societies encounter by only using informal social control?

CRIMINAL JUSTICE SYSTEM POLICY

The criminal justice system engages in policy on a daily basis. From arrest policy to prosecution policy to sentencing policy, the system engages in practices to deal with crime. Throughout the history of the criminal justice system, various policies have been supported more than others, and the justification behind these policies also varies over time.

What Is Policy?

Public policy is "*A relatively stable, purposive course of action followed by an actor or set of actors in dealing with a problem or matter of concern.* This definition focuses on what is actually done instead of what is only proposed or intended; differentiates a policy from a decision . . . ; and views policy as something that unfolds over time" (Anderson 2003, 2, emphasis in original). Simply, if crime is a problem, the criminal justice system and its policies represent society's response to that problem.

Historically, criminal justice policy, or lack thereof, first centered on revenge on the part of the victim. In Europe, between the collapse of the Roman Empire and 600 AD, it was common for individuals and families to act as their own criminal justice systems (Johnson and Wolfe 1996). These societies tried to rely upon informal social control to keep order. If a person was harmed by another, however, the victim had to seek his or her own justice, often violently. This system was called blood feud and vengeance. If a person was killed, the victim's family had to seek justice from the offender or the offender's family. Since the government was not involved in this system of justice, there was very little criminal justice policy.

The victim-centered system of justice did not work well, so the primitive system of blood feuds was replaced by governmental control of justice. Under governmental control of justice, the government assumes the role of deciding what behaviors are considered illegal, who are considered offenders and victims, and what the punishments are. As a result, when a law is broken and a crime is committed, the government acts as the victim, as it is the government's law that has been violated.

Public policies are created at different levels of government. At the highest level are policies created by the federal government, which apply to the federal criminal justice system, but could also apply to state and local systems. These are macrolevel policies. An example of a macrolevel policy is the Clean Air Act, passed in 1990 by the U.S. Congress. Under the Clean Air Act, the federal government sets standards for air quality and states are required to develop State Implementation Plans to carry out the provisions of the act with regard to controlling pollution. Although the states take the lead in developing plans to maintain air quality standards, the federal government has enforcement responsibility if, for example, a factory is spewing too many pollutants into the air.

Public policies at the local level, called microlevel policies, are also used to change criminal justice. Using the example of the Clean Air Act, all states must abide by the requirements set forth by the federal government, but states are allowed to impose tougher standards for pollution than the federal government requires. As a result, one state may have higher air quality standards than another.

Policies are created at different levels of government, but policies can be created by governmental entities other than federal and state legislatures. The judicial branch creates policy by issuing court rulings, and the executive branch creates policy through executive orders. Within each of these branches, various agencies are able to create policies that are far-reaching or that apply only to the agency at hand. For instance, the Ohio Public Defender Commission outlines standards and guidelines that must be followed for its public defenders. At the local level, some towns and cities create their own policies, such as local ordinances banning loud car stereos. Finally, individual criminal justice organizations like jails and prisons create their own internal policies, such as visitation requirements.

Critical Thinking Exercise

Some policies are more effective in achieving their intended results than are others. What attributes do you think make criminal justice policies successful? What are the characteristics of unsuccessful criminal justice policies?

CRIMINAL JUSTICE SYSTEM PHILOSOPHY

Initially, the relationship between policy and crime sounds simple. Crime is a problem, so society chooses how to solve the problem. Unfortunately, combating crime is not so simple. Part of this complication is caused by differences in society's philosophies about what the criminal justice system *should* do. Because society is not unanimous in how it should respond to crime, criminal justice policy becomes more complicated. In some instances, certain criminal justice organizations will implement one type of policy, while other agencies will adopt other policies. Sometimes these policies compete with or contradict each other. Part of this complication is due to different philosophies of criminal justice.

The Classical School

The **Classical school** of criminal justice stemmed from the mid-eighteenth-century writings of Cesare Beccaria. Beccaria promoted a philosophy of human behavior and crime that argued that humans possess free will, are rational, and make choices about how to behave. Human behavior is influenced by each person's weighing of the costs of an action and the benefits he or she expects to receive. For example, someone contemplating robbery will weigh the possible rewards (getting money) against the possible costs (arrest and imprisonment) and decide whether to rob or not rob.

The Classical school promoted a number of reforms to eighteenth-century criminal justice policy. Beccaria argued that punishments should be harsh enough to deter potential offenders, but not overly punitive or cruel. Laws should be clearly written in advance and should specify the punishments for each crime. Mitigating factors, such as the criminal's personality, social circumstances, or financial need, should not be weighed by a judge or jury. Simply, the law should be applied evenly to everyone who breaks it.

The Positivist School

The **Positivist school** of criminal justice developed after the Classical view was established. Positivists claim that human behavior is influenced by conditions and situations external to individuals. Human behavior is determined by outside forces that are beyond the control of individuals. Things such as poverty and abusive parenting influence the likelihood that a child will grow up poor and abusive as well. The law would likely hold little deterrent value for this child, since he or she may have learned that this is the only way to behave.

Positivists contend that the solutions to crime lay not in stricter laws, but in improving the social conditions that cause crime. Thus, crime can best be combated by eliminating poverty, providing opportunity, improving parenting, or reducing contact with delinquent peers. Positivists disagree about the exact causes of crime, however, so their particular prescriptions for attacking the roots of crime differ. For example, some theorists claim that blocked economic opportunities lead some people to commit crime, so increasing the chances for economic advancement will decrease crime. In contrast, other theorists believe that crime is learned by watching and mimicking other delinquent people, so crime could be lessened by reducing exposure to these delinquent peers.

The Classical and Positivist schools provide a general overview of the potential causes and solutions to crime. Although some solutions involve an overhaul of social conditions, most come in the form of punishment. There is disagreement, however, over why, how, and to what extent punishment should be used. These disagreements are illustrated in four punishment philosophies: retribution, deterrence, rehabilitation, and incapacitation.

Retribution

Retribution is a philosophy based on the belief that criminals should be punished because they have violated the law. Thus, the criminal justice system exists to punish wrongdoers. Punishment should be commensurate with the harm committed by the criminal (an "eye for an eye"), which is in accord with the beliefs of those who follow the Classical school. Retribution, however, does not punish in order to prevent potential criminals from committing crime. Rather, advocates of retribution argue that punishment is the proper and just thing for a society to do, regardless of its effectiveness in preventing crime. This is sometimes called deserts, or **just deserts.**

Retribution assumes that a crime has been committed and that the offender has been discovered. Once the offender is found, he or she must be punished. Retributivists favor the use of incarceration as a way to punish offenders. Lesser punishments such as probation and policies such as plea bargaining may not result in the punishment fitting the crime. Retributivists also favor the use of capital punishment, in accordance with the "eye for an eye" edict.

Deterrence

Like retribution, **deterrence** believes that offenders should be punished; however, punishment should have some other goal besides just deserts. Deterrence contends that punishments should prevent crime by making potential offenders aware of the costs of crime. In effect, potential offenders will know that punishment will ensue if a crime is committed; thus, they will refrain from engaging in crime. Deterrence argues that the costs of crime outweigh its benefits. This belief is also drawn from the Classical school.

There are two types of deterrence: specific and general. **Specific deterrence** refers to the deterring effect of punishing a particular offender. For example, a juvenile punished for skipping school will not skip again, for he or she will remember the punishment received the first time. **General deterrence** keeps people from committing crime by showing them, through the experiences of other punished criminals, that crime does not pay. For example, fellow students at the truant's school will probably not skip school in the future if they have learned of the punishment received by their friend for skipping. Thus, a person does not need to be punished firsthand in order to be deterred.

Deterrence appears to work best when the punishment is *certain, severe* and *quickly applied*. Offenders must be punished every time they commit a crime (*certainty*). Furthermore, the punishment must be averse enough to make punishment outweigh the benefits or fruits of the crime (*severity*). Finally, the punishment must be inflicted soon after the crime is committed (sometimes called *celerity*).

A system dedicated to deterrence would try to maximize these three elements via policy. A deterrent system would first find ways to increase the rate at which crimes are reported and offenders are caught. This might involve policies requiring that crime victims report their victimizations to authorities. A deterrent system would also have to ensure that the severity of punishment was painful enough to outweigh the benefits of crime. This could result in an abolition of plea bargains, which result in more lenient punishments for offenders. Finally, the system would value speedy processing of suspects. There should be little delay between arrest, trial, and punishment.

Deterrence also entails policies and laws that limit the discretion of workers in the criminal justice system. Simply, the law should apply evenly to everyone, no matter what their status, gender, or other nonlegal factors. A system based on deterrence would have to ensure that all offenders are arrested, that suspects cannot plea bargain, and that sentences are fixed and fully served.

Rehabilitation

Rehabilitation does not advocate punishing criminals, but rather seeks to prevent crime by rectifying individual problems that are thought to be responsible for the criminal behavior.

Rehabilitation views criminals as "broken" and seeks to "repair" them by reformation and treatment. Rehabilitation occurs with individuals who have already committed a crime and this philosophy assumes that criminals can be reformed. Once reformed, criminals will no longer engage in crime. Examples of rehabilitation include drug treatment, mental health counseling, and job training.

A system devoted to rehabilitation would try to maximize the reformation of offenders without focusing on punishment or deterrence. Thus, prisons and jails would be structured to be more therapeutic and would offer drug and alcohol treatment, job skills training, and therapy for inmates. Rehabilitation might be furthered by laws requiring that all offenders receive treatment.

Rehabilitation also requires some flexibility in the criminal justice system, for rehabilitation involves an individual focus. Each offender should be held in prison or jail or kept under supervision in the community until he or she is rehabilitated. Some offenders will be quickly rehabilitated while others will require long periods of treatment. This individual focus requires differential sentences and even sentencing offenders guilty of the same crime to sentences of different lengths. The staff of correctional facilities should also have a voice in deciding when an offender is rehabilitated and can be released. Rehabilitation would also entail the use of community supervision of offenders, where offenders are allowed to live in the community, but must report to probation or parole officers. Keeping offenders in the community while still treating them might assist in their rehabilitation and reintegration into society.

Incapacitation

Incapacitation argues that the role of the criminal justice system is to separate or segregate criminals from the rest of society in order to protect society. If known criminals are removed from society, there should be less crime. Unlike retribution, incapacitation does not see segregation as a form of punishment. Rather, incapacitation is designed to keep offenders away from society. Incapacitation also differs from rehabilitation in that it does not necessarily advocate treating offenders.

Incapacitation comes with its own policy implications. First, it entails an emphasis on using secure facilities, such as prisons and jails, rather than community corrections like probation. This is not to say that community corrections cannot be used as part of incapacitation; rather, pure incapacitation would emphasize physical segregation. This segregation restrains offenders from engaging in further criminal activity. Incapacitation is the goal behind laws such as habitual-offender and "three-strikes" laws that incarcerate individuals for an extensive amount of time if they continue to commit offenses. The idea is that previous punishment (if any) was not sufficient to deter or reform the offenders, so the system must resort to keeping them away from society for a long time in order to prevent further crime.

Critical Thinking Exercise

Each of these philosophies entails its own policy, to impel criminal justice employees to adhere to the policy's intent. Choose one of the philosophies above and write a policy designed to implement that philosophy at a particular step of the criminal justice process (that is, to be implemented by the police, courts, or corrections). If you find this task easy, try writing a policy that satisfies the dictates of two or three of these philosophies. Do you find this to be easy or difficult?

MEASURING CRIME

Defining crime is relatively easy when compared to the task of measuring crime, but crime is central to the existence of any criminal justice system, and measuring crime accurately is important. Accurate measures of crime are important because these measures give us better insights into the nature and extent of crime. For instance, we can determine if crime is increasing or if certain types of crime are becoming less common. Further, measuring crime lets us predict crime trends and plan for future demands on the criminal justice system. Valid and reliable crime statistics also permit researchers to craft better theories of crime and criminal justice, which in turn help guide the administration of justice. Finally, good crime statistics can be used to evaluate criminal justice policies and programs. For example, we could use crime statistics to see if a mandatory minimum sentencing policy prevents crime.

It is difficult to determine the amount of crime that actually occurs because many crimes do not come to the attention of the criminal justice system. For instance, many victims do not report their victimizations to the police. In addition, some victims may not even realize that they have been victims of crime. Research reveals that, on average, only 40 percent of victimizations are actually reported to authorities (Maguire and Pastore 2006). Because of this underreporting of crime, criminologists often refer to the total number of unreported crimes as the **dark figure of crime** (Biderman and Reiss 1967). Underreporting means that authorities in the criminal justice system often have great difficulty producing accurate crime statistics.

For most places such as cities and states, crime is usually expressed in one of two ways. The first way of expressing crime statistics is as a count. Counts simply report the total number of crimes reported over a given time span. Thus, one city might report that it had three homicides last year. Using raw counts is not without problems. Raw counts do not facilitate easy comparisons of different places, like cities, with different populations. For example, in 2007, New York City reported a total of 496 murders and nonnegligent manslaughters. During that same year, New Orleans reported a total of 209 murders and nonnegligent manslaughters (Federal Bureau of Investigation 2008). At first blush, New Orleans seemed like a safer city in 2007. New Orleans, however, has fewer inhabitants than New York City, so it would seem natural for it to have fewer homicides. A raw count of homicides does not allow us to fairly compare the two.

It is sometimes better to use a **crime rate** instead of a raw count. Rates are usually expressed as the number of events per 1,000 or 100,000 people (or residents) per year. For example, a city with a population of 100,000 people where three people were murdered in one year would report a homicide rate of 3.0 homicides per 100,000 population. Using the New York and New Orleans numbers, the homicide rate in New York City in 2007 was 6.03 per 100,000 population, while the homicide rate for New Orleans in 2007 was 94.73 per 100,000. Not only do rates permit better comparisons of different cities

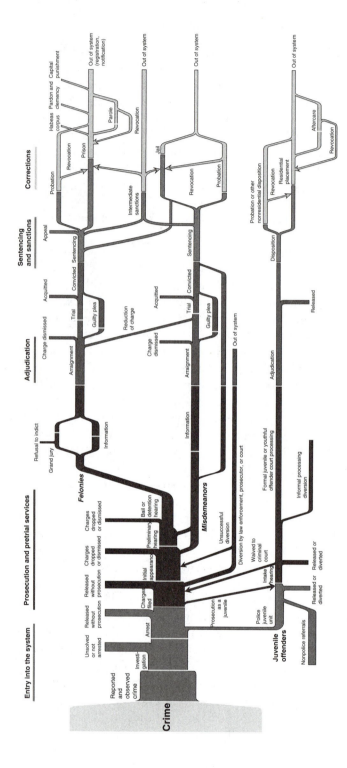

Figure 1.1 What is the sequence of events in the criminal justice system?

NOTE: This chart gives a simplified view of caseflow through the criminal justice system. Procedures vary among jurisdictions. The weights of the lines are not intended to show actual size of caseloads.

SOURCE: U.S. Department of Justice, Office of Justice Programs, Bureau of Justice Statistics. http://www.ojp.usdoj.gov/bjs/largechart.htm

10

or states, they also allow better analysis of crime trends over time. Cities and states grow and shrink over time, too. Rates control for these differences in populations.

Regardless of the measurement, there are three general sources of crime statistics: official (reported) statistics, self-report statistics, and victimization statistics.

Official Statistics

Official statistics are gathered from criminal justice agencies, such as the police, and represent the total number of crimes reported to the police or the number of arrests made by that agency. There are important distinctions among the dark figure of crime, reported crime, and arrests. Recall that only about 40 percent of crime victims report their victimization to the police. Likewise, research indicates that police officers do not arrest all persons they encounter who are suspected of committing a crime (see Smith and Visher 1981). Overall, both reported crimes and arrests are imperfect measures of crime.

The largest and best-known sources of official statistics in the United States are the Federal Bureau of Investigation's (FBI's) Uniform Crime Reports (UCR). The UCR report the numbers of crimes reported to the police and the number of arrests for many of the police agencies in the United States (Maltz 1999). Since 1985, the FBI has also collected crime data from police agencies called the NIBRS (National Incident-Based Reporting System). The NIBRS still collects data on crimes reported to the police, but the NIBRS data better capture incidents where multiple crimes are committed, for example, when a robbery escalates into a rape (Rantala 2000). There are other sources of official statistics as well, as many local and state agencies (such as local police agencies) collect and distribute their own crime statistics.

Official arrest statistics or crimes reported to the police can sometimes provide a reasonable estimate of crime, but one should always be careful when interpreting these official statistics. Police agencies can change their attention to certain events, and thus change their overall number of arrests, regardless of the true crime rate. For example, a police agency may deploy many officers in a red-light district in order to crack down on prostitution. This crackdown may yield a considerable increase in arrests for prostitution, although the true incidence of prostitution has not changed. An uninformed observer might wrongly conclude that the incidence of prostitution is increasing, when in fact the increase in arrests is a result of the police initiative designed to combat prostitution.

Similarly, crimes reported to the police represent just that—crimes where the victims have notified the police of their victimization and the police chose to record them as victimizations. Overall, official statistics provide an estimate of the dark figure of crime. However, if the crime is not reported, if the police do not make an arrest, or if police choose to not record an incident as a crime, official statistics will not provide an accurate estimate of the true crime rate.

BOX 1.1

NIBRS: National Incident-Based Reporting System

NIBRS is designed to replace the FBI's Uniform Crime Report (UCR) system. The UCR recorded information on the incidence of eight serious crimes (called Part I offenses) and arrests for 21 other Part II offenses. NIBRS records information on 46 different offenses and arrests for 11 additional offenses. Because NIBRS is an incident-based data system, it allows police agencies to report multiple offenses committed during a single incident (such as when a bank robbery includes a rape and a murder). This represents an improvement over the UCR's hierarchical reporting system, where only the most serious criminal offense is reported. NIBRS also collects more information about the circumstances of a crime, such as the victim, suspects, their relationships, and weapons involved (Federal Bureau of Investigation 1999).

Self-Report Statistics

Self-report statistics overcome some of the limitations of official statistics. Self-report statistics are gathered from people by asking them to report the number of times they have committed a crime during a set period of time in the past. For example, since 1977, the National Youth Survey has surveyed youths and their parents about a range of attitudes and activities, including illegal activities such as alcohol and drug use. For example, one could ask high-school seniors how many times they have smoked marijuana during the past year. The respondents are usually promised **confidentiality**, which means that the reports cannot be linked to specific individuals.

Self-report statistics avoid some problems associated with official statistics. For example, they are often better at discovering crimes that the victim did not bother reporting to authorities. Further, self-report statistics are good for exploring crimes where there is no victim, called **victimless crimes**, such as illegal drug use or underage drinking. Self-reports are also good for uncovering less serious offenses such as drug use, shoplifting, and the like and for learning about crimes where an arrest is unlikely (Hindelang, Hirschi, and Weis 1979).

Unfortunately, there are problems associated with self-report statistics. First, respondents may exaggerate or underreport their criminal behavior. Respondents may exaggerate their criminal activity in order to reinforce their self-conception as tough characters. Conversely, respondents may underreport because they forgot their criminal activities, because they did not know that what they had done was illegal, or because they are afraid to reveal their past criminal activities. Finally, *who* is surveyed about their criminal activity is important. For example, giving a self-report survey to high-school seniors at their high school is likely to lead one to underestimate the true incidence of crime committed by 17 and 18 year olds. The serious criminals in this age range are more likely to be suspended from school, might be skipping school on that day, or might be locked up in secure juvenile facilities. Thus, self-reports have limitations and do not yield a completely accurate estimate of the true crime rate.

Victimization Studies

The third type of crime statistic comes from **victimization studies**. Victimization studies ask people if they have been victims of crimes during a past time period. One example is the National Crime Victimization Survey (NCVS). The NCVS is a nationally representative survey of U.S. households designed to measure criminal victimization. The survey is conducted annually by the Bureau of the Census for the Department of Justice's Bureau of Justice Statistics. As with self-report studies, victimization studies sometimes encounter problems. For example, respondents may forget victimizations, lie, or fail to tell the interviewers about their victimizations. Sometimes victims will "telescope" a victimization from outside the survey time span. For example, a victimization survey may only be concerned with crimes committed during 2002, but a respondent may report that a 2001 assault occurred during 2002. The dangers of lying, underreporting, and telescoping can all be combated by various methodological techniques. For example, the NCVS uses a technique called *bounding* to mitigate the likelihood that a respondent will telescope.

Overall, these three techniques for measuring crime provide estimates of the dark figure of crime. It is important, however, to keep in mind their limitations when using each one. Each method is subject to problems that may affect the accuracy of the estimate derived.

Critical Thinking Exercise

Which type of statistic would be best suited to study homicide in U.S. cities? What about the sexual abuse of young children? What statistic would be best suited to studying drug use by high-school students? In general, for each of the three types of data (official, self-report, and victimization), what types of crime is each best suited to capture? What types of crime is each poorly suited to capture?

A SYSTEM OF CHECKS AND BALANCES

It has been suggested by some that the criminal justice system in the United States is too punitive when dealing with offenders, while others feel it is not punitive enough. The criminal justice system in the United States attempts to strike a balance between these two concerns.

Individual Liberty Versus Societal Civility

The first important characteristic of criminal justice in the United States is that it represents a balance between a number of opposing forces. First, the system tries to balance the rights of people to do what they want with the requirement that society remains civil, calm, and relatively crime free. Thus the government imposes restrictions on individual behavior through laws and creates the agencies designed to enforce them in an attempt to keep society orderly. This desire for order must be balanced, however, with the public's desire for freedom to do what it wants. If there is too much governmental restriction, people are oppressed. On the other hand, society will veer towards disorder and chaos if there is too much individual freedom. The competing forces of individual liberty must be balanced with the desire for societal order at all levels of criminal justice and all stages of the system.

Crime Control Versus Due Process

Writing in 1968, Herbert Packer noted that the criminal justice system balances the competing philosophies of crime control and due process in its operations. The **crime-control model** advocates the aggressive and quick apprehension, trial, and processing of criminals. Briefly, this crime-control orientation seeks to prevent crime via a number of processes, such as deterrence and incapacitation, and cares less about ensuring that suspects are given specific legal rights. Crime control emphasizes that the system efficiently processes suspects in order to suppress crime. On the other hand, the **due-process model** is more concerned with the process of justice and grants suspects many rights to protect them from overzealous investigation and prosecution. In a due-process model the system should carefully ensure that individual rights are not violated. In other words, a due-process perspective is concerned less with suppressing crime than with ensuring that individuals are not unfairly harmed by their government. In reality, the criminal justice system embodies a balance between these competing philosophies via the creation of policy, although the system constantly swings between these two extremes.

Other Competing Ideologies

Balancing competing ideologies also applies to the philosophies of criminal justice discussed earlier. In effect, the system constantly oscillates among these four competing philosophies and, in many cases, decisions are based upon satisfying two or three of these ideologies. This constant mixture of philosophies means that advocates of one philosophy are never completely happy, for the system never fully implements their version of justice. Instead, the system operates under all four philosophies in most situations. A mix of philosophies is sometimes evident when individual criminal justice employees make decisions. For example, a judge might decide upon a defendant's sentence length based on the amount of time required for rehabilitation, but may also want to punish the offender and send a deterrent message to the community. The criminal justice system cannot be viewed as being committed to any one philosophy; rather, the operation of criminal justice is a simultaneous combination of these different ideologies.

A Loosely Coupled System

Unlike many nations, where there is one national criminal justice system, criminal justice in the United States is composed of many loosely coupled, semiautonomous organizations. For example, instead of one national police force, there are over 20,000 separate police agencies, each acting as a separate, independent agency. Likewise, instead of one court system, there are county, state, and federal courts, and cities and towns have municipal courts. There are thousands of local jails and hundreds of prisons (both state and federal). Likewise, there are thousands of probation and parole agencies, as well as thousands of juvenile courts. Why have Americans created so many organizations to deal with crime and disorder?

This loosely coupled system reflects Americans' distrust of large government and their preference for local control. In some states, certain criminal justice positions are elected, such as sheriffs and judges, while other positions on parole boards are appointed. In this way, citizens exercise local control over their criminal justice system. This loosely coupled system also facilitates a system of checks and balances, where the decisions of one criminal justice agency are reviewed by later criminal justice agencies. For example, prosecutors usually conduct pretrial screenings with arrestees to decide if charges will be filed or the case dropped. In effect, prosecutors review the work of the police officers responsible for an arrest and decide if the suspect should be charged. There is less pressure for prosecutors to rubber-stamp arrests and charge suspects, for prosecutors do not work for their local police agencies.

The separation of these criminal justice components facilitates the review of decisions. Likewise, the prosecutor's decision to charge is not the final decision. Judges have the opportunity to review this decision and, if the case goes to trial, either a judge or jury will evaluate the defendant's guilt. In this way, criminal justice in the United States embodies a system of loosely coupled agencies that check the decisions made by other agencies. Although it may appear cumbersome and inefficient at times to have so many different agencies dispensing justice, the system protects citizens from a single, all-powerful state. It allows local areas to tailor their criminal justice systems to their own local needs and permits the creation of particular balances of competing forces, such as crime control and due process and rehabilitation and retribution, for example.

Discretion

Discretion is an important attribute of the criminal justice system, and in fact, the system could not function without it. Prior to the mid-1950s, however, few people understood or appreciated the nature or importance of discretion. (Walker 1993: 6–8). Discretion involves decisionmaking by people involved in criminal justice—most often but not always employees of criminal justice agencies. These people are usually referred to as criminal justice actors. For example, a police officer decides to stop one motorist but not another. A judge imposes a longer sentence on one convicted criminal than on a criminal with a similar record who has committed the same crime. A parole board releases one prisoner early, but not another. These choices represent discretionary desicion-making by criminal justice actors.

Discretion involves legal and permissible decisions by criminal justice actors, including acting and choosing to not act (Klockars 1985: 93). Discretion does not include decisionmaking where actors break agency rules or the law, such as instances of corruption or misconduct. But within the bounds of permissible decisionmaking there are a wide range of possible actions available for both actors and agencies. Discretion is fundamental to the criminal justice system; it is like the thread that constitutes the cloth of the criminal justice system. The next section treats the criminal justice system as a series of four decision points that involve discretionary decisions.

The Four Cs of the Criminal Justice System (Citizens, Cops, Courts, and Corrections)

The American criminal justice system can be viewed as a conglomeration of quasi-independent organizations, each processing the outputs of the previous agency. The system can also be viewed as a process model, whereby decisions made by one system component influence the following components. This system model can be called "the four Cs of the criminal justice system." The process model highlights the importance of decisionmaking by individuals in the system. Figure 1.1 portrays this model of criminal justice.

Citizens

The first of the system's Cs are people not employed by the system, called citizens. The decisions made by crime victims, complainants, and offenders are crucial for understanding how the system works, for citizens provide the vast majority of inputs for the rest of the system. For example, research indicates that the majority of people arrested by the police are arrested based on the complaint of another citizen. Further, as stated earlier, research indicates that victims do not always call the police to report crimes. This rate of reporting varies depending on the seriousness of the crime, as victims of serious crimes are more likely to report their victimizations. Reporting rates also differ depending on the type of crime. For example, roughly 81 percent of vehicle theft victims report their loss to the police, compared to 17 percent of theft victims where less than $50 was taken (Maguire and Pastore 2006).

Some states have responded to the underreporting of crime by utilizing two different policies. The first policy involves passing laws that require people to report specific crimes to authorities. In many states, physicians, teachers, and social workers are mandated by law to report suspected cases of child abuse.

Some states have also sought to eliminate victims' unwillingness to press charges by requiring that police officers arrest certain types of offenders, even if the victims do not request arrest. This is particularly common in domestic violence cases.

Cops

The second decisionmaking point of the system consists of the police and other law-enforcement agents. Police officers do not patrol the streets arresting everyone suspected of committing a crime; rather, officers selectively enforce the law. In many instances, an officer chooses *not* to arrest, even when there is probable cause. Not fully enforcing all the laws all the time is a good thing; the full enforcement of every law is not possible, and society would probably not tolerate it (see Klockars 1985). Again, the police exercise considerable discretion about what situations to get involved in and how to resolve these situations. The police decision to arrest is influenced considerably by the seriousness of the suspected offense, the wishes of the victim or complainant, and the demeanor of the suspect (Smith and Visher 1981). The letter of the law only plays a part in an officer's arrest decision and, in the majority of cases, the police do not make arrests.

Policies have been implemented in the hopes of controlling how police officers act. As mentioned earlier, some state laws require that police officers arrest suspects who are believed to have committed domestic violence. In this way, policymakers hope to control the unwillingness of some victims to press charges. Such policies also take discretion away from police officers, who will often not arrest in such situations. Individual law-enforcement agencies can also create rules and regulations to control employee behaviors. Indeed, many agencies have rules mandating when officers may use deadly force and engage in vehicle pursuits, for example (Walker 1993).

Courts

The third decisionmaking point is composed of court workers, such as pretrial intake workers, prosecutors, defense attorneys, and judges. This third decision point is unique, for not all of the people who work in this area are employed by a particular court, nor are they necessarily employed by the criminal justice system. For example, defendants may employ their own defense attorneys who are not employed by the government. Thus, courtroom decisions are not made by members of the same organization, but rather by a range of actors who meet in a court "arena." This is known as the **courtroom workgroup**. The workgroup members exercise considerable discretion about a range of decisions, such as whether cases should be plea bargained, sent to trial, or dismissed. The workgroup often negotiates the charges to be brought and the possible sentences. For example, a prosecutor may negotiate a plea agreement with the defense attorney, reduce the charges against a suspect, and recommend a possible sentence to the judge. Likewise, defendants and defense attorneys can also decide to accept a plea bargain or invoke their right to a trial. Finally, judges make important decisions concerning such things as the admissibility of evidence and sentencing.

Decisions made by court workers are also affected by policy. For instance, a judge will set policy regarding the way in which his or her courtroom will operate. Further policies, in the form of laws, mandate a range of activities, such as how soon a trial must be held, how plea bargaining and trials are conducted, and how defendants are sentenced.

Corrections

The final decisionmaking point is composed of criminal justice system employees who work in corrections and includes probation and parole officers, correctional officers, and workers who provide services to offenders, such as social workers. Probation and parole officers are responsible for the supervision of offenders in the community and correctional officers are responsible for maintaining security in a correctional institution, whether it is jail or prison.

The behaviors of correctional workers are also shaped and constrained by policy. For instance, state and federal laws mandate that prisoners have the right to adequate medical care while incarcerated. In other instances, the policies are created by individual correctional agencies and might cover such activities as how often probationers are drug tested or what happens to probationers who fail drug tests. Policies also cover such things as appropriate dress codes for employees and the procedures for dealing with offenders who do not follow the conditions of probation or the rules of the institution.

Each of these decision points is composed of multiple people and actors, all of whom influence the future of the criminal case, the suspect, and the victim. Thus, if a crime victim chooses to not report a crime, it is unlikely that the system will become involved. Likewise, the actors at each of these decision points interact and often negotiate the outcome of that decision point. Such negotiation is common during these discretionary interchanges. Discretion is important for running the system, and understanding discretion is crucial to understanding the system. Despite this, society has long been concerned with controlling and guiding these discretionary decisions in criminal justice (Gottfredson and Gottfredson 1988; Walker 1993). Controlling discretion is an important goal for the system, as it hopes to ensure fair and uniform processes. These attempts at controlling discretion often take the form of policies that are found throughout the system.

RECENT TRENDS IN CRIMINAL JUSTICE

Like all social systems, the criminal justice system has undergone changes over its history. Five changes in the criminal justice system that have occurred since the early 1960s are particularly important. The first recent change in criminal justice began during the early 1960s and has been termed the **due-process revolution**. This revolution originated when a number of court rulings provided protections from the government for those accused of crime. For instance, the U.S. Supreme Court ruled in 1963 that defendants have the right to an attorney if they are charged with felonies (*Gideon v. Wainwright* [1963]). Later court rulings provided additional protections to prisoners and probationers. For example, prisoners are granted certain rights regarding freedom of religion while incarcerated (*Cruz v. Beto* [1972]). Likewise, adults under community supervision were given due-process protections during probation and parole revocation hearings (*Morrissey v. Brewer* [1972]). Taken together, the due-process revolution limited the power of the state over its citizens and hence afforded greater protections to citizens, suspects, and prisoners.

Policy has played a large role in furthering the due-process revolution. In many instances, due-process reforms were mandated by law. In some cases, these laws entailed further policies to ensure that the laws were implemented properly. For example, many police agencies now require that their officers undergo a set number of hours of in-service training each year, so that officers can keep up to date with recent legal changes. In other cases, local agencies will create rules and regulations to ensure that their employees act in accordance with federal or state law. In this manner, policy often begets other policies.

The second recent trend in criminal justice has been the **civil rights movement** and, most importantly, the increased representation of people of color and women as criminal justice employees. Historically, even until the late 1960s, criminal justice employees have almost always been white males. As the civil rights movement gained momentum in the United States during the 1960s, the system began to open employment opportunities to people of color. For example, many city police agencies began actively recruiting blacks as police officers during the mid- and late 1960s. Likewise, prisons and probation and parole departments also recruited and hired people of color in attempts to make the employees of the system more representative of the country's population. The employment of women as system employees followed a similar trend, beginning in the late 1960s. The increased representation of people of color and women as system employees is, however, a relatively recent trend, and it is due in large part to the broader civil rights movement.

This second trend also entailed a range of new policies. Some agencies had implemented minimum educational requirements that inadvertently discriminated against hiring people of color. Likewise, some agencies had minimum height and weight requirements for employees, requirements that deterred the employment of women. New policies had to be created to mend these problems and open the field up to a more diversified range of potential employees. Further, once hired, women had to be provided with specific accomodations, such as their own locker rooms and uniforms, and new policies on **harassment** and maternity leave were created. Again, larger social trends have influenced trends in the system, which in turn has required the creation of new policies.

The third recent trend in criminal justice has been the inclusion of community in many facets of the system. Since the mid- and late 1980s, various aspects of the system have sought to include the views, opinions, inputs, and even assistance of local community members. Such was not always the case. These criminal justice innovations include community policing, changes in community corrections, and the creation of specialized courts, such as drug courts. Even various alternatives to traditional courts, such as mediation and restorative justice, can be included here, for they all change the role that community members and victims play in criminal justice processes. Each of these community-oriented changes has sought to include victims and community residents in order to tailor local criminal justice responses to each locale.

As one might expect, the increasing inclusion of community influences in the system has led to new policies. These new policies have helped create new arrangements and relationships between the system and communities. For instance, many jurisdictions now have arrangements between their local courts and local service providers, such as community centers, homeless shelters, and substance abuse clinics, where defendants in need of services are referred. In some cases, such referrals are part of the defendants' formal disposition, and this entails new policies to formalize such arrangements. Further, new policies have also delineated the boundaries between communities and the system. For example, halfway houses often have policies as to who can be placed there, the conditions the residents must abide by in order to remain, and how rule violations are handled.

The fourth recent trend in criminal justice has been a move towards increasing punitiveness in the system. This trend has been evident since the 1970s and has affected all aspects of the system. For instance, mandatory arrest laws reflect a more punitive attitude towards domestic violence offenders. In addition, some states have abolished plea bargains in an effort to prevent lenient punishment of offenders. Finally, many states have adopted mandatory sentencing policies that keep certain offenders locked up in prison for an extended period of time. These punitive policies have resulted in an increase in the number of offenders in the criminal justice system. This is evident in the dramatic increase in the incarceration rate over the past 25 years. In fact, the United States has the highest incarceration rate of any western country—645 inmates per 100,000 population. Only Russia has a higher incarceration rate worldwide, at 685 inmates per 100,000 population (Albanese 2002). The increase in punitiveness may satisfy retributivists, who feel that punishments must fit the crime and that offenders must pay for their deeds. It may also satisfy those who agree with the incapacitation philosophy of punishment—if offenders are kept away from society, they cannot harm it. It remains to be seen, however, if increased punitiveness has had an effect on deterrence, as many studies show that increased punishment does not necessarily deter crime (see Blumstein, Cohen, and Nagin 1978).

The fifth recent trend has been the effects of September 11th on the criminal justice system. In many ways these effects have only begun to run their course and it is not clear what their final results will be on how the criminal justice system operates. At this point it is clear, however, that the system in many places is responding to the threat of future terrorist attacks.

For police, the expectation is that local law enforcement will play a crucial role in uncovering and preventing future terrorist attacks, in collaboration with federal agencies. For most agencies this involves gathering information from the community, something most police agencies already attend to each day. Federal law enforcement agencies play a role. For example, the FBI coordinates the terrorist prevention activities of some local law enforcement, especially through its Joint Terrorism Task Forces, but the FBI lacks the manpower to field sufficient eyes and ears across the United States. In 2005, The FBI has 2,196 agents devoted to anti-terrorism, while local law enforcement agencies fielded more than 700,000 officers (Maguire and King 2009). Local law enforcement personnel will play a crucial role in information gathering for the foreseeable future. Some agencies have established formal, systematic ways to enlist the help of local citizens in preventing future terrorist attacks. For example, the Washington DC Metropolitan Police Department created a program to educate the public about suspicious behavior that might be associated with a terrorist group and urged the public to call a hotline for gathering these tips (mpdc.dc.gov/mpdc/lib/mpdc/info/comm/TIPPBroch. pdf). Such efforts in the United States mirror recent developments in policing in the United Kingdom (Innes 2006).

The court system has also been influenced by the focus on terrorism since September 11th. At the federal level, federal prosecutors have increased the percent of terrorist cases they chose to prosecute, but as of 2002 they still decline to prosecute approximately half of all terrorist cases brought before them (TRAC Reports 2002). Prior to September 11th, federal prosecutors were most likely to prosecute suspected terrorists for relatively common offenses (such as racketeering and firearms offenses) and not for terrorism (Smith and Orvis 1993). Other thorny legal issues involve the rights of individuals detained overseas on suspicion of terrorism, the legal limits of interrogation techniques, and the proper venue for detainee trials. These issues will be revisited in the years to come, as America responds to future terrorist threats.

Critical Thinking Exercise

Increasing punitiveness has characterized the criminal justice system since the 1970s. Do you think this trend will continue for the foreseeable future? Or do you think a different trend will guide the overall practice of criminal justice?

CONCLUSION

As evidenced above, the criminal justice system is a rather complex mix of philosophies and policies. These philosophies and policies cannot exist, however, without individuals whose job it is to keep the criminal justice system operational.

Individuals create policies based on their own philosophy of how they feel the criminal justice system should operate. The individuals who shape these policies represent a broad spectrum of society—legislators, judges, prosecutors, police, victims—who have different ideas as to how to deal with the crime problem. What is evident is that no philosophy or policy is perfect for every individual, so the system must continually try to improve itself by creating and enacting more policy—a cycle that never ends.

Critical Thinking Exercise

This chapter has outlined four very large historic trends in criminal justice. What trends do you think we will see over the next 20–30 years? How will the system react to these larger social trends, and how will justice be affected?

KEY WORDS

anonymity	due-process model	official statistics
civil rights movement	due-process revolution	Positivist school
Classical school	felony	rehabilitation
confidentiality	general deterrence	retribution
courtroom workgroup	harassment	self-report statistics
crime-control model	incapacitation	specific deterrence
crime rate	informal social control	victimization studies
dark figure of crime	just deserts	victimless crimes
deterrence	mala in se	
deviance	mala prohibita	
discretion	misdemeanor	

SUGGESTED READINGS

Gottfredson, M., and Gottfredson, D. (1988). *Decision-making in criminal justice: Toward the rational exercise of discretion.* New York: Plenum Press.

Johnson, H., and Wolfe, N. (1996). *History of criminal justice,* 2nd ed. Cincinnati, OH: Anderson Publishing.

Klockars, C. (1985). *The idea of the police.* Beverly Hills, CA: Sage.

Walker, S. (1998). *Popular justice: A history of American criminal justice,* 2nd ed. New York: Oxford University Press. ✦

CHAPTER 2

Issues of Law

CHAPTER OUTLINE

Laws are sets of rules that govern the conduct of individuals, groups, businesses, government entities, and the like. Laws are created and enforced by the power of the state, that is, local, state, and federal government bodies. The U.S. Constitution gives the responsibility of law creation to the federal legislature, the U.S. Congress. The Constitution also allows the federal court system to "interpret" the laws created by the federal legislature. In doing so, the federal courts work to ensure that the laws that are created are fair and applied equally to all citizens.

The various state constitutions also give the responsibility of law creation to their respective state legislatures. Just like the federal system, states allow their court systems to interpret the laws in much the same way as the federal courts. Within states, legislative bodies such as county commissions and city councils create laws that apply to their geographic areas.

As stated above, the federal and state legislatures create laws that govern the behavior of a variety of entities. Individuals are subject to laws that prohibit certain types of conduct, such as killing a person or burning down a house. Groups of individuals who assemble are required by law to do so peacefully and not to incite riots. The conduct of businesses is regulated so that these businesses do not engage in fraudulent practices or environmental harm. Government entities are required to follow the law as well, in that they cannot engage in discriminatory practices when they enforce the law. In addition to these prohibitions, the law ensures that violators will be punished. These are just a few examples of the law in effect, but the main point is that the law applies to everyone, even those government bodies that are responsible for its creation. This is known as the "rule of law" and is traced back to the early origins of American law (see Rembar 1989).

HISTORY OF LAW IN THE UNITED STATES

American law is rooted in European, particularly English, law. Historically, English law was largely unwritten and parochial, in that communities relied on local customs and norms to guide conduct. These customs were transmitted from generation to generation and were altered occasionally if necessary. After the Norman Conquest in the eleventh century, William the Conqueror instituted a practice of collecting these customs and norms and recording them so that they could be applied to the country as a whole. This practice of transforming unwritten local customs into written codes of behavior for the entire country established the English tradition of **common law,** or law that was common to all throughout the country. Local judges were responsible for applying the common law, and their decisions were recorded to help guide future judges when making their decisions. This is known as **precedent,** and this practice continues to exist today.

Over time, local English judges refined and recorded many laws, many of which were criminal laws. By the seventeenth century, these judges had created the crimes of murder, robbery, arson, and rape, among others. Judges also created less serious crimes such as libel, perjury, and disturbing the peace (see generally Blackstone 2002).

The criminal law that exists today is taken from the English tradition of common law. The United States was founded by British colonists who brought their legal tradition to American shores. After declaring independence from England in 1776, the new states incorporated the English common law and adopted many of the criminal laws that had been defined. The newly created federal government chose not to incorporate English common law; instead, Congress established its own laws, including criminal laws, that were similar in content to common law, but not directly taken from it. An exception to the incorporation of common law is Louisiana, which bases its law on the Napoleonic Code, a uniform system of laws adopted by Napoleon from ancient Roman law (see Scheb and Scheb 1999).

SOURCES OF LAW IN THE UNITED STATES

Although English common law is the root of most of the law in the United States, various government bodies are responsible for shaping, applying, and interpreting the law. As stated earlier, the responsibility for law creation lies with legislatures, which create **statutory law.** Other government entities, however, are also involved in the creation of the law. The most important entities, state and federal constitutions, are the highest sources of law in the country. Other entities represent all branches of government—legislative, executive, and judicial.

Constitutions

Constitutions are considered the highest sources of law in this country. All other laws that are created must abide by constitutions. Each state and the federal government have their own constitutions, which outline the structure of the governments and how they will operate. These constitutions designate government power, indicating what the government can and cannot do. This is called **constitutional law.** For instance, California's constitution specifies that tax money cannot be used to support religious schools (see Constitution of California, Article 9, Section 8), and the federal constitution specifies that the federal government cannot abridge an individual's freedom of speech (see U.S. Constitution, Amendment 1). State constitutions are the highest form of law in each state, but the U.S. Constitution is the highest form of law in the country; that is, all laws (state and federal) and state constitutions must abide by the U.S. Constitution. Any law or constitution that conflicts with the U.S. Constitution is not allowed to stand.

Legislative

Aside from the actual legislature, the legislative branch creates government bodies that carry out some law-making responsibilities. These bodies are typically referred to as agencies, bureaus, and so forth. These administrative agencies include federal bodies such as the Federal Communications Commission and the Food and Drug Administration (FDA), as well as state bodies such as the

Ohio Public Defender Commission. Adminstrative agencies have the responsibility of enforcing **administrative law**. These agencies create rules and policies that govern their responsibilities. For example, the FDA establishes guidelines for allowing medicines to be available to consumers either by prescription or over the counter. The Ohio Public Defender Commission establishes guidelines for its public defenders to follow when representing poor defendants.

Executive
The executive branch also has some law-creation responsibility. The executive branch is composed of individuals such as mayors, governors, and the president. These individuals have limited law-making ability, and the laws that are created are usually quite narrow and issue specific; however, they are important nonetheless. For example, a mayor may impose a curfew in a particular city, or the president may impose regulations on driving cars through national forests.

Judicial
The judicial branch of government, embodied by the various state and federal courts, engages in law creation. During the early period of common law in England, local judges were primarily responsible for creating and disseminating laws throughout the country. Today, however, judges have been stripped of most of their law-making authority. Whenever a judge makes a decision in a particular case, he or she is engaging in law creation. This type of law, called **case law**, is usually based on laws that were created by some other body. For instance, in the early 1960s, the state of Florida did not allow a poor defendant to have an attorney provided to him or her. In 1963, the U.S. Supreme Court ruled that Florida and other states must provide poor defendants with an attorney in certain criminal cases (*Gideon v. Wainwright* [1963]). As a result, the U.S. Supreme Court engaged in law creation by forcing the states to adopt its mandate.

SUBSTANTIVE LAW

Regardless of which government body creates the law, the law is either substantive or procedural in nature. **Substantive law** is often called the "what" of the law, in effect, the law that defines rights and duties. Substantive law is distinguished from **procedural law,** which describes the procedures that must be followed when carrying out the law. An example of substantive law is law that defines first-degree murder as the deliberate, premeditated killing of another. An example of procedural law is law that states that poor defendants must be given an attorney if charged with certain crimes. Procedural law will be discussed later in this chapter.

Two primary examples of substantive law are civil law and criminal law. Civil law deals with issues pertaining to private maters between two individuals. Civil law encompasses torts (e.g., wrongful injury), contracts and property issues, and domestic relations. Civil law allows individuals who feel wronged by another to take their cases to court for a remedy. For example, if person A is involved in an automobile accident with person B, who is uninsured, person A may sue person B in civil court for the money needed to replace the disabled car. Civil law also governs issues such as divorces, child custody, inheritance, wills, and the like.

Criminal law is another primary example of substantive law. Criminal law concerns issues between the government and individuals who are accused of violating government-created laws.

Unlike civil law, in which an individual is responsible for finding a remedy to his or her problem, criminal law involves the government prosecuting an individual if that individual has committed a crime.

Substantive criminal law is defined by government bodies, and it specifies what individuals can and cannot do and the punishments for wrongdoing. This is called the **principle of legality;** in effect, the government cannot punish individuals for wrongdoing unless a law exists to define the conduct as a crime and to prescribe a punishment for it. Traditionally, individual conduct has been defined as **mala in se**, or inherently bad, and **mala prohibita**, or prohibited but not necessarily bad. Governments have considered acts such as murder and rape as mala in sc and acts such as gambling and speeding as mala prohibita. As a result, behaviors that are considered inherently bad are typically punished more severely than others.

Critical Thinking Exercise

Develop a list of mala prohibita laws and discuss each one. Should they be prohibited? Why? What impact does enforcement of such laws have on the criminal justice system? What value do these laws have for society in general? What negative effect might these laws have on society?

When governments specify which behaviors to deem criminal, the crimes must have two elements: act and intent. The act, called **actus reus,** is the most important element of criminal liability; it represents the physical action involved in conduct. The act must be voluntary, in that it is not the result of coercion or some condition that affects voluntary movement (such as a seizure). For example, for the crime of larceny, the act would be the taking of another's property.

Although a voluntary act is needed to establish actus reus, there are instances in which a failure to act constitutes actus reus. In these cases, an act of omission can result in criminal liability. The act of omission comes into play when individuals are required by law to act, but fail to do so. For example, lifeguards are required by law to aid drowning individuals; failure to do so can result in criminal liability. The same is true of physicians, who are legally bound to tend to patients in their care.

Critical Thinking Exercise

Some states have proposed legislation called "Good Samaritan Laws," which impose criminal liability on individuals who witness crimes but do nothing to stop them. This would create a type of act of omission. For instance, while person X is walking down the street, he sees a mugger attack a woman and steal her purse. If he continues on his way without acting, he would be breaking the law. What are the advantages and disadvantages of having such laws in place? What would be the difficulties in enforcing such laws? Do you feel they are a good idea?

In addition to an act, a crime must also have intent, called **mens rea.** In effect, an individual must intend to commit the act in question; that is, the individual must have a blameworthy state of mind. Establishing intent is rather difficult; in fact, intent is usually inferred from the act. For example, if an individual grabs someone's purse and runs away, we can infer that the individual intended to commit theft. This may seem obvious, but the issue of intent is most important when an individual's *degree* of liability is in question. Take the following example: Person A points a gun at person B in an attempt to scare person B. The gun accidentally discharges, killing person B. Person A can be held liable for the death of person B, even though person A did not intend to kill person B. In effect, even though person A will be held liable for murder, he would not be held liable for the more serious crime of first-degree murder, since he did not intend to commit murder in the first place.

As with actus reus, there are instances when intent need not be present in order for an individual to be held liable for a crime. This is called **strict liability,** in which liability is imposed without intent. Strict liability applies to behaviors that are typically considered mala prohibita (not inherently bad), such as serving alcohol to minors and committing traffic offenses. In these instances, it makes no difference whether an individual intended to engage in the act or not; he or she can still be held liable. A common example of a strict liability crime is statutory rape; if an individual engages in intercourse with a person who is below the age of consent, that individual will be held liable for his or her behavior, even if he or she had no intent to engage in intercourse with a minor.

TYPES OF CRIMES

Throughout this chapter, specific crimes have been used as examples to illustrate various concepts in criminal law. The following discussion expands this, describing the various categories of crimes that exist in criminal law. This discussion will not, however, provide a detailed discussion of all of the crimes on the books; it merely provides an overview and uses a couple of states as examples.

Crimes Against the Person

Personal crimes are generally considered the most serious crimes and are treated as such by the criminal justice system. Homicide, rape, assault, and kidnapping are crimes that come to mind when discussing personal crimes. Although these crimes may seem fairly straightforward, they are not so easily categorized. Each crime carries with it differing degrees of liability. For instance, killing another person could carry a sentence anywhere from probation to the death penalty; the circumstances surrounding the killing determine how an individual is to be handled by the system. The crime of homicide will be used as an example. See Box 2.1 for an illustration.

As seen in Box 2.1, there are varying degrees of liability when it comes to the killing of another. The same is true for other personal crimes as well, but time and space do not permit an examination of them all. Each state defines its crimes and establishes punishments for their violation; these statutes are available for public consumption either at the local library or on the Internet.

Crimes Against Property

Property crimes are not treated as severely by the criminal justice system as personal crimes, but they are considered serious nonetheless. Typical property crimes include larceny/theft, burglary, arson, embezzlement, and trespass. One type of property crime, robbery, is also considered a personal crime, since force or the threat of force is used to steal an individual's belongings. Property crimes typically do not involve harm to individuals, and thus the punishments are less severe. For example, an individual cannot receive the death penalty for engaging in a property crime.

Like personal crimes, individual property crimes have varying degrees of liability. An example of this is seen with the crime of burglary. In Ohio, burglary involves trespass into an occupied structure with the intent to commit a crime. If an offender is carrying a gun or inflicts physical harm on a person within the structure, he or she is committing "aggravated burglary." If the structure is not occupied, he or she is engaged in "breaking and entering." Aggravated burglary is the most serious charge of the three, resulting in a punishment of up to 10 years in prison. Breaking and entering is the least serious charge, resulting in a punishment of up to one year in jail. Although intent is present, the degree of liability differs depending on specific circumstances (see generally Ohio Revised Code, §2911.11, §2911.12, 2005).

Crimes Against Public Order

Public order crimes are categories of offenses that do not necessarily harm other persons or property. These offenses are largely victimless crimes, where there is no readily identifiable victim. Public order crimes are seen as harming society as a whole, and the criminalization of such conduct aims to maintain social order. In comparison to personal and property crimes, public order crimes are committed by far more people, although they are not punished as severely. Examples of public

---

BOX 2.1

Degrees of Liability for the Crime of Homicide

Homicide laws vary from state to state, but each state allows for differing degrees of homicide to account for attendant circumstances. The most serious form of homicide is typically called "first-degree murder" or "aggravated murder," depending on the state. This typically involves the deliberate, planned killing of another person. In Ohio, "aggravated murder" has a number of definitions, one of which is the following: "No person shall purposely, with prior calculation and design, cause the death of another . . ." (Ohio Revised Code, §2903.01 (A), 2005). In California, "first-degree murder" also has a number of definitions, one of which is " . . . the unlawful killing of a human being . . . with malice aforethought" (California Penal Code, §187 (a), 2005). In these examples, the actus reus is "causing the death of" or "unlawful killing of" another person, while the means rea is found in the "prior calculation and design" and "malice aforethought" elements. In these states, aggravated or first-degree murder carries the possibility of a death sentence, although a death sentence is not mandatory. Other punishments for this crime include life imprisonment without the possibility of parole or life imprisonment with the possibility of parole after a certain number of years.

A less serious form of homicide is called "second-degree murder." This form of homicide is not as easily definable as first-degree murder. In second-degree murder, an individual typically has no specific intent to kill another, but engages in extremely harmful conduct that runs the risk of the victim being killed. For example, an individual can be charged with second-degree murder if, during the course of a severe beating, the victim dies. The intent was not to kill the victim; however, the individual engaging in the beating should have known that death was possible, but chose not to stop his or her conduct. In Ohio, second-degree murder is defined as " . . . purposely causing the death of another" and carries a punishment of a minimum of 15 years in prison up to life (Ohio Revised Code, §2903.02 (A), §2929.02 (B), 2005). In California, second-degree murder is largely defined by what it is not; in effect, various types of first-degree murder are defined, while second-degree murder is defined as " . . . all other kinds of murders" that are not listed in the first-degree murder category. This crime is punished by a minimum of 20 to 25 years in prison up to life (California Penal Code, §189, §190, 2005).

Other less serious forms of homicide include voluntary manslaughter and involuntary manslaughter. Voluntary manslaughter is homicide that is provoked or is committed "in the heat of passion." Ohio defines voluntary manslaughter as being committed " . . . under the influence of a sudden passion or in a sudden fit of rage" and sets the punishment as up to 10 years in prison (Ohio Revised Code, §2903.03, §2929.14, 2005). In California, voluntary manslaughter is defined as " . . . unlawful killing . . . upon a sudden quarrel or heat of passion" and is punishable by up to 11 years in prison (California Penal Code, §192, §193).

Involuntary manslaughter is the unintentional killing of another that involves reckless behavior on the part of the perpetrator. Ohio defines involuntary manslaughter as " . . . causing the death of another" as a result of the commission of certain lower-level felonies or misdemeanors and punishes the act with up to

10 years in prison (Ohio Revised Code, §2903.03, §2929.14, 2005). California specifies that involuntary manslaughter occurs during the commission of a lawful or unlawful act "...without due caution and circumspection" and punishes the act with up to 4 years in prison (California Penal Code, §192, §193).

Critical Thinking Exercise

In 1999, Dr. Jack Kevorkian was convicted of second-degree murder in Michigan for assisting an individual with ALS, or Lou Gehrig's disease, in committing suicide. To what extent do you feel Dr. Kevorkian and others should be punished for assisting ailing individuals in taking their own lives? To what extent does an individual's health status (terminally ill, in chronic pain, etc.) play a role in your decision?

---

order offenses are driving under the influence of alcohol, disorderly conduct, vagrancy, and loitering.

Related to public order offenses are public morals offenses. These offenses are those that offend the morality of certain groups in society. Many public morals offenses involve sexual behavior—behavior that is not necessarily bad, but is considered immoral and deviant by some. Prostitution is perhaps the most common example of a morals offense.

Drug Offenses

Laws that criminalize the illegal use of drugs and alcohol could probably be categorized as public order offenses, but they deserve a section of their own. The reason is that the government's reaction to illegal drug use has dramatically altered how the criminal justice system deals with these offenses. The "war on drugs" has led to an increased focus on drug offenses, sometimes to the exclusion of other offenses.

Numerous criminal behaviors are associated with the use of drugs. Possession of illegal drugs, such as marijuana and cocaine, and possession of paraphernalia, such as needles, constitute perhaps the largest number of drug offenses, but laws are in place that focus on all levels of the illegal drug trade, such as trafficking, manufacturing, and selling. Punishment for drug offenses depends on a variety of factors. These include the type of drug being used, the amount of drugs involved, and where a drug transaction takes place (for instance, near a school). Because of increased attention to drug offenses by both state and federal governments, the punishments for drug offenses have increased, ranging from probation to the death penalty.

Critical Thinking Exercise

One response to drug use and abuse has been the enactment of legislation mandating harsh penalties for offenders. Examine the Anti-Terrorism and Effective Death Penalty Act of 1996 (a link can be found on the textbook website at http://www.oup.com/us/labessentials), which mandates the death penalty for drug kingpins. Discuss the pros and cons of this legislation.

White-Collar Offenses

A final category of offenses concerns those that are committed by individuals during the course of their jobs. The term *white collar* refers to the idea that individuals from a higher socioeconomic status are more likely to commit these types of crimes. It should be noted, however, that individuals of a lower socioeconomic status are capable of and do commit white-collar offenses.

The better-known white-collar offenses are committed by individuals who use their job positions as a mechanism to engage in illegal behavior. Lower-level offenses such as employee theft do not receive as much attention as other white-collar offenses, although these lower-level offenses are perhaps more frequent. Tax evasion, price fixing, and insider trading are better known and more widely publicized. See Box 2.2 for an illustration of insider trading and the Martha Stewart case.

Many other crimes are defined in state and federal statutes, but they are simply too numerous to mention here. All states and the federal government publish their statutes or place them online for public access (see the textbook website at http://www.oup.com/us/labessential for links to such legislation). The next section deals with an issue that has already been addressed—liability—and instances in which individuals are not held liable for engaging in criminal behavior.

DEFENSES TO CRIMINAL LIABILITY

Throughout this chapter, the issue of liability has arisen to describe when an individual is held accountable for illegal behavior. The notion of criminal liability rests on the assumption that an individual knowingly commits a crime and has the intention of doing so. There are some situations, however, in which an individual is not held responsible for a criminal act and is not punished for wrongdoing. These situations constitute defenses to criminal liability.

Justification

In some situations, a crime is justified based on an individual's belief that what he or she did was the right thing to do. Perhaps the best-known **justification** is self-defense. Self-defense is used to deter an unwanted attack—force is used if an

---

BOX 2.2

Insider Trading and the Martha Stewart Case

Although Martha Stewart was never charged with insider trading, her lawyer admitted as much during her criminal trial in 2004. In general, fair practices involve engaging in business when information is publicly known, in effect allowing the public the opportunity to compete in an open marketplace. When individuals engage in business practices based on information that is not publicly known, they are engaging in illegal behavior.

In Stewart's case, she purchased stock shares in ImClone, a pharmaceutical research company founded by her friend, Sam Waksal. Stewart's ImClone shares had returned a profit, and she continued her investment in the company. ImClone had high hopes for its cancer drug, Exbitux, and was waiting for FDA approval in order for it to be placed on the market. With FDA approval, ImClone stock would rise, giving its investors a return on their investment. Without FDA approval, ImClone stock would suffer, resulting in losses on the part of investors.

In fair business practice, the FDA informs the company privately of its decision and then makes plans to announce its decision publicly, so that all investors are in the same situation with regard to good or bad news. In ImClone's case, the FDA told Waksal that it would not approve the cancer drug and would make the public announcement shortly. Before the public announcement, Waksal sold his ImClone stock, for he knew that FDA disapproval of his company's cancer drug would result in decreased value of ImClone stock, which in turn would result in Waksal losing money on his investment. Waksal informed Stewart of the FDA's decision and Stewart proceeded to sell her stock as well. Until the public announcement, ImClone shares were still performing well, so selling shares before the FDA's announcement allowed Waksal and Stewart to earn a profit from ImClone shares because, publicly, ImClone stock was still viable. After the public announcement, ImClone stock plummeted, and investors who were not privy to Waksal's and Stewart's information lost money on their investment. Because Waksal and Stewart had access to information "on the inside"—that is, nonpublic information—they were able to avoid losing money once the FDA's decision became public. This is illegal and an example of insider trading. For more information, consult the websites linked to the textbook website (http://www.oup.com/us/labessentials).

---

individual *reasonably* believes it is *necessary* for *protection* against an *impending* attack. The italicized words indicate what must be proven by an individual who claims self-defense. *Reasonable* means that an ordinary person would believe that force is to be used. *Necessary* indicates that force is needed to defend oneself. *Protection* suggests that the only reason that force is to be used is to protect oneself from harm, not to inflict harm needlessly on another person. *Impending* implies that an attack must be imminent and immediate, that there is no time to escape. The amount of force used must also be reasonable; for example, an individual cannot use **deadly force** if an offender merely steals a purse. Individuals who claim self-defense must prove that an ordinary, reasonable person would have acted in the same way if attacked.

Critical Thinking Exercise

The defense of one's home is a prime concern for most citizens. The degree to which individuals can use force, even deadly force, in the defense of their homes or property has received a great deal of attention and debate, both academic and lay. Can a resident use deadly force to protect his or her home? In your opinion is this a reasonable option? Why or why not?

Mental Capacity

An individual can be relieved of criminal liability if his or her **mental capacity** is such that it renders the individual incapable of understanding the wrongness of his or her actions. Insanity is a common example. The term *insanity* is a legal one; it is not a medical diagnosis like schizophrenia or bipolar disorder. The term is defined differently from state to state, so there is not one clear-cut rule that establishes whether someone was insane at the time of the offense.

The first legal definition of insanity was known as the M'Naghten Rule. M'Naghten was an English citizen suffering from delusions of persecution who felt it was necessary to assassinate Sir Robert Peel, the founder of the British police system and the home secretary at the time. M'Naghten did not kill Peel, but instead killed Peel's secretary, whom M'Naghten mistakenly believed was Peel. M'Naghten's lawyers claimed that he was insane at the time of the crime and should not be found guilty. As a result of this case, the M'Naghten rule was established and has become known as the "right versus wrong" rule. Under this rule, individuals must prove that they were in such a state of mind that they could not know what they were doing or that they did not know that what they were doing was wrong (see *M'Naghten's Case* [1843]).

Most states and the federal government adopted the M'Naghten rule, but other states felt that the rule should be expanded to account for issues involving self-control. The substantial capacity test was proposed in 1962, and it states that an individual

> is not responsible for criminal conduct if at the time of such conduct, as a result of a mental disease or defect, a person lacks substantial capacity either to appreciate the wrongfulness of his conduct or to conform his conduct to the requirements of the law. (American Law Institute 1962)

It was thought that the M'Naghten rule was too strict, and this test provided more leeway for individuals who knew right from wrong, but could not control their behavior. Today, some states and the federal government adhere to the

M'Naghten rule in some form, while other states apply the substantial capacity test (for more information about the insanity defense, both its history and new developments, see Reider 1998).

Critical Thinking Exercise

The textbook websites (http://www.oup.com/us/labessentials and http://criminal.findlaw.com/crimes/criminal-overview/common-defenses-to-criminal-charges.html) list a variety of defenses to criminal liability. Examine that information and discuss the reasonableness of the different defenses.

RECENT TRENDS IN SUBSTANTIVE CRIMINAL LAW

Criminal law is always changing; government bodies propose changes to the law on a regular basis, so that laws that are in place today may not be in effect next year. One of the reasons that the law changes regularly is that certain events in society result in public support for new legislation.

War on Terror

Since the terrorist attacks on September 11, 2001, the United States has been involved in a global "war on terror." This "war" is not a conventional war, as seen in World War I or World War II, which involved identified nation-states and official declarations of war by Congress. Instead, the war on terror is an ideological war, an attempt to stem ideology-driven terrorist acts both domestically and abroad. These terrorist acts are not affiliated with specific nation-states; instead, these acts are performed by organizations or groups of individuals who seek to harm the United States or its interests. For the United States, the war on terror is primarily aimed at Islamic fundamentalists, individuals who were responsible for the attacks on September 11. The war on terror is also aimed at other terrorists, both domestic and international, such as the individuals responsible for mailing anthrax to various agencies in the United States.

Regarding substantive criminal law, federal, constitutional, and international law governs the declaration and implementation of wars, but the wars that are covered by these laws usually involve armed combat between nation-states. Since the war on terror involves a struggle against ideology and groups who seek to fight for it, existing laws governing wars may not apply. For example, in 2001, Congress gave President Bush authorization to use military force against organizations and groups that the president felt were responsible for the attacks on September 11. This authorization was not an official declaration of war, which the U.S. Constitution requires Congress to declare. Instead, it was permission for President Bush to conduct military operations against certain terrorist groups, not nation-states. Because of this, President Bush argued that federal and international law regarding the implementation of war, such as treatment of detainees, did not apply in this situation. As a result, individuals who are captured in the global war on terror have not been subject to the same type of treatment as individuals who are captured in a declared war between nation-states. This has led to many disagreements both in the United States and abroad about how to conduct a global war on terror and what laws need to be applied or implemented to facilitate this.

Cybercrime

Because of the ubiquitous use of computers, computer crime (also called cyber-crime) has emerged. Using a computer to engage in illegal behavior constitutes cybercrime. This type of crime is vast, ranging from the unauthorized use of credit card accounts to dissemination of computer viruses to distribution of child pornography. Another form of cybercrime is cyberterrorism, which involves large-scale attacks on political and economic computer systems in an attempt to interfere with operations. These attacks could result in minor disruptions, such as knocking out electricity, or major disruptions, such as disabling air-traffic control systems. The vast majority of political, economic, and social institutions rely on computers to do business, so the range of cybercrime is virtually limitless.

Trying to control, much less detect, cybercrime is difficult. Computer technology is rapidly changing and efforts to keep up with emerging technology are ongoing and expensive. In addition, cybercrime goes beyond the borders of the United States, so working with other countries is necessary to deal with the problem. State and federal government agencies, as well as private companies, are responsible for detection and control of cybercrime. It is impossible to know how much cybercrime actually occurs, but a federal investigation into online economic crimes, such as identity theft and counterfeit software, provides a glimpse. Undertaken by the Department of Justice from June through August of 2004, the investigation uncovered approximately 150,000 victims who had lost a total of $215 million as a result of cybercrime (*Internet Newsletter* 2004). This does not take into account other forms of cybercrime or any investigations undertaken by other federal or state agencies.

Critical Thinking Exercise

One form of cybercrime that has received a great deal of attention and raises a great deal of concern is online child pornography. Search the Web for information on this problem. How pervasive is the problem? What can be done to protect youths? What punishments are there for cyber child pornography?

PROCEDURAL LAW

Thus far, this chapter has provided a general overview of many of the aspects of substantive criminal law. The following section focuses on an equally important component of the law—procedural law. As stated earlier, procedural law describes the procedures that government bodies must follow when carrying out the law. Most of the procedural law in the United States is rooted in the U.S. Constitution, which has articulated policies that federal, state, and local governments must follow.

U.S. Constitution

The federal Constitution is essentially composed of two parts: the body of the Constitution, which outlines the structure and function of the federal government, and the amendments, which involve changes to the original document. The body of the Constitution is largely a blueprint for the federal government. It defines the three branches of government and specifies the role and responsibilities of each. When the Constitution was being drafted in 1787, the Framers were divided over whether the document should contain provisions that protected the rights of citizens from a newly created federal government. This division was the result of some of the Framers not trusting the new government, since they felt that a stronger federal government would infringe on the rights of citizens. These individuals likened the new federal government to England's government, from which the United States had recently achieved independence. Prior to the American Revolution, the English government had infringed on the rights of the American colonists, abridging their freedom of speech and press, not allowing representation in the English government, and engaging in the practice of entering homes without cause to search for seditious material. Those skeptical of the new federal government wanted to ensure that it would not be another England and pushed for the Constitution to include these protections (see Schwartz 1992). As such, the body of the Constitution contains four protections of individual rights: a prohibition against ex post facto laws, a prohibition against bills of attainder, the right to habeas corpus (all found in Article I, Section 9), and the right to a trial by jury (found in Article III, Section 2).

The **ex post facto** provision prohibits retroactive laws; in effect, a law that is passed tomorrow cannot be applied to behavior that one engages in today. The provision against **bills of attainder** is in place to prohibit the imposition of punishment without trial. The right to **habeas corpus** allows an individual to challenge illegal confinement by the government. Finally, the right to a **trial by jury** guarantees that individuals are judged by a jury of one's peers instead of one or two individuals who may not be neutral. These rights were considered important enough to be placed in the body of the Constitution. Despite this, some of the Framers insisted that these provisions did not go far enough and demanded that more rights be included. These rights were created and passed as the Bill of Rights in 1791.

The Bill of Rights is composed of the first 10 amendments to the Constitution, which were passed en masse in 1791. Since then, the Constitution has been amended 17 times, bringing the total number of amendments to 27. The Bill of Rights was passed to allay the fears of those skeptical of the new federal government, and the provisions found in the Bill of Rights encompass a wide range of protections (Schwartz 1992). See Box 2.3 for a list of the Bill of Rights and what they cover. For procedural criminal law purposes, this chapter will focus on four of

---

BOX 2.3

The Bill of Rights and the Fourteenth Amendment

First Amendment: Congress shall make no law respecting an establishment of religion, or prohibiting the free exercise thereof; or abridging the freedom of speech, or of the press; or the right of the people peaceably to assemble, and to petition the government for a redress of grievances.

Second Amendment: A well-regulated militia, being necessary to the security of a free state, the right of the people to keep and bear arms, shall not be infringed.

Third Amendment: No soldier shall, in time of peace be quartered in any house, without the consent of the owner, nor in time of war, but in a manner to be prescribed by law.

Fourth Amendment: The right of the people to be secure in their persons, houses, papers, and effects, against unreasonable searches and seizures, shall not be violated, and no warrants shall issue, but upon probable cause, supported by oath or affirmation, and particularly describing the place to be searched, and the person or things to be seized.

Fifth Amendment: No person shall be held to answer for a capital, or otherwise infamous crime, unless on a presentment or indictment of a grand jury, except in cases arising in the land or naval forces, or in the militia, when in actual service in time of war or public danger; nor shall any person be subject for the same offense to be twice put in jeopardy of life or limb; nor shall be compelled in any criminal case to be a witness against himself; nor be deprived of life, liberty, or property, without due process of law; nor shall private property be taken for public use, without just compensation.

Sixth Amendment: In all criminal prosecutions, the accused shall enjoy the right to a speedy and public trial, by an impartial jury of the state and district wherein the crime shall have been committed, which district shall have been previously ascertained by law, and to be informed of the nature and cause of the accusation; to be confronted with the witnesses against him; to have compulsory process for obtaining witnesses in his favor, and to have the assistance of counsel for his defense.

Seventh Amendment: In suits at common law, where the value in controversy shall exceed twenty dollars, the right of trial by jury shall be preserved, and no fact tried by a jury, shall be otherwise reexamined in any court of the United States, than according to the rules of the common law.

Eighth Amendment: Excessive bail shall not be required, nor excessive fines imposed, nor cruel and unusual punishments inflicted.

Ninth Amendment: The enumeration in the Constitution, of certain rights, shall not be construed to deny or disparage others retained by the people.

Tenth Amendment: The powers not delegated to the United States by the Constitution, nor prohibited by it to the states, are reserved to the states respectively, or to the people.

Fourteenth Amendment (Section 1 only): All persons born or naturalized in the United States, and subject to the jurisdiction thereof, are citizens of the

United States and of the state wherein they reside. No state shall make or enforce any law which shall abridge the privileges or immunities of citizens of the United States; nor shall any state deprive any person of life, liberty, or property, without due process of law; nor deny to any person within its jurisdiction the equal protection of the laws.

SOURCE: United States Constitution (1789).

---

these amendments: the Fourth, Fifth, Sixth, and Eighth. There will also be a focus on the Fourteenth Amendment, passed in 1868, but this will appear later in the chapter.

Fourth Amendment. The Fourth Amendment is in place to protect against unreasonable searches and seizures by government entities. In colonial times, the colonists were growing increasingly weary of an overreaching English government. Colonists began to speak out and criticize the English government's implementation of strict policies, such as expansive taxation, and the English government itself. In response, the English government considered this criticism seditious libel and authorized the use of general warrants to break into homes and businesses, not only to search for evidence of seditious libel, but also to search for individuals who were disobeying English law, such as those who refused to pay taxes. These warrants permitted government officials to ransack homes and businesses without just cause, and this was the reason for the creation of the Fourth Amendment (Zalman and Siegel 1997).

The Fourth Amendment protects individuals from unreasonable searches and seizures by the government, not all searches. If government officials wish to search an individual's home, they must secure permission to do so from a judge. This comes in the form of a warrant. The information contained in the warrant contains the name and address of the individual or home to be searched, as well as a specific description of the person or items to be seized. This information must be justified by a standard known as *probable cause*. This standard is difficult to define, but the U.S. Supreme Court, in *Brinegar v. United States* (1949), provided a definition: probable cause exists when " . . . the facts and circumstances . . . [and] . . . reasonably trustworthy information [are] sufficient in themselves to warrant a man of reasonable caution in the belief that an offense has been or is being committed" (p. 176). In effect, more evidence must exist than not that an individual has committed a crime. Once government officials have provided this information, they must get a warrant approved by a judge before a search may take place.

At times, government officials engage in unreasonable searches and seizures. For whatever reason, a warrant may not be secured if probable cause does not exist. As a result, the U.S. Supreme Court ruled in *Mapp v. Ohio* (1961) that searches and seizures that violate Fourth Amendment provisions are subject to the **exclusionary rule;** that is, illegally seized evidence is excluded from a prosecution. The exclusionary rule helps to ensure that government officials conduct their procedures in a legal manner and provides a penalty when they do not.

Since its inception, the Fourth Amendment has been the subject of numerous court cases that have attempted to modify it to account for changing times and circumstances. The Amendment's provisions now go beyond someone's home and office to include such things as vehicles, drug tests, telephones, and computers—none of which existed at the time of the creation of the Fourth Amendment. In addition, there are circumstances that do not require the use of a warrant or the standard of probable cause. It would take an entire textbook to delve into the various permutations of the Fourth Amendment; as a result, this chapter only hopes to provide a general overview. For more information about the Fourth Amendment, see Hemmens, Worrall, and Thompson (2004).

Fifth Amendment. The Fifth Amendment features an amalgam of provisions that include a broad range of procedural rights. One of the most important provisions is the due-process clause, which forces government officials to abide by fair procedures when an individual is subject to the criminal justice process. The due-process provision encompasses all other procedural rights, as they are simply specific forms of due process.

Perhaps the best-known provision of the Fifth Amendment is the **self-incrimination** clause. This specifies that an individual cannot be compelled to confess involvement (or noninvolvement) in criminal activity. Historically, the English government, dating back to the 1200s, used torture and psychological coercion to elicit confessions from accused individuals, many of whom were innocent. As a result, the self-incrimination clause of the Fifth Amendment was created to prohibit government officials from compelling individuals to confess to something they did or did not do.

Another important provision of the Fifth Amendment is the protection against **double jeopardy.** The double-jeopardy clause prohibits the government from prosecuting someone again after that individual has been acquitted or convicted. In essence, the government does not get "two bites at the apple" if it is not happy with a particular verdict.

A fourth provision of the Fifth Amendment is the right to a **grand jury** proceeding. A grand jury consists of a number of ordinary citizens who review the charges against an individual and decide if the charges warrant a trial. The grand jury requirement was deemed important by the Framers of the Bill of Rights because they felt that a prosecutor, who is a government official, would have too much power in making charging decisions (Zalman and Siegel 1997).

Sixth Amendment. The Sixth Amendment is often called the "trial rights amendment" because of its provisions regarding aspects of the trial process. The first provision is the right to a **speedy trial**, which benefits both the defense and the prosecution. A speedy trial helps the defense by minimizing the amount of time that an accused individual must endure until his or her case is resolved. This is especially true if the accused is jailed prior to trial. A speedy trial assists the prosecutor because it ensures quick justice, provided the accused is guilty.

Critical Thinking Exercise

The idea of a speedy trial often appears to be violated when one reads about a case finally going to trial months or years after the crime was committed and the offender was caught. Look up the speedy trial guidelines for your state. Based on that information, how long can a trial be put off? Do you believe this is reasonable or justified?

The right to a **public trial** ensures that trials are open to the public. English courts were notorious for secret proceedings, and the Framers of the Bill of Rights wanted the public to act as a watchdog over government proceedings to ensure that illegal procedures were not being used against the accused.

An accused individual also has the right to an **impartial trial.** This means that judges and juries are to be unbiased and neutral when making decisions about an accused individual's case. To ensure this, juries are selected through a fairly rigorous process that hopes to draw out any biases that individual jury members may have.

In keeping with the abhorred practices in England, colonists who allegedly committed crimes were taken to England for trial, which hurt the accused because many English citizens were biased against colonists. The Sixth Amendment provides that an accused individual has the right to be prosecuted in the state and county where he or she allegedly committed the crime. In addition, accused individuals have the *right to know what they are being charged with* (in order to establish a defense against those charges), the *right to know who their accusers are* (to ensure that these witnesses are not fabricating the charges), and the *right to call witnesses to testify on their behalf.* Early English practice did not allow accused individuals to know the charges, to question witnesses, or even to put on a defense.

The final provision in the Sixth Amendment is the **right to counsel**. Most accused individuals do not know the intricacies of the law and need skilled attorneys to assist them. In addition, attorneys are able to offset any questionable governmental actions that could possibly harm the accused, such as trying to elicit confessions. Attorneys are present to ensure that due process is followed. Initially, this provision was interpreted to mean that if individuals could afford attorneys they could use them, but the poor were denied representation. This has since changed, and individuals who cannot afford attorneys can be provided them at the government's expense.

Eighth Amendment. The Eighth Amendment is considered the "punishment amendment" because two of its three provisions deal with criminal punishment. The first provision, the right against **excessive bail**, was created to restrain the government from detaining individuals before they were found guilty. During a bail decision, a judge is prohibited from imposing a bail amount that is too high in relation to the accused individual's crime, flight risk, or threat to the community. The right against excessive bail does not guarantee that the bail amount must be affordable to the accused individual, nor does it guarantee the right to bail in general.

The right against **excessive fines** was created to prevent the government from imposing financial penalties that did not accord with an individual's charge. The **cruel and unusual punishment** clause has a varied history, with lawmakers and judges still trying to decide what the clause actually protects. Some U.S. Supreme Court rulings declare that the clause prohibits not only barbarous modes of punishment, like the rack and thumb screws, but also any punishment that is grossly disproportionate to the crime at hand (see *O'Neil v. Vermont* [1892]). Recent U.S. Supreme Court decisions, however, have backed away from the disproportionality argument. In *Harmelin v. Michigan* (1991), Justice Antonin Scalia declared that the cruel and unusual punishment clause says nothing about proportionality and, in effect, only protects against certain forms of punishment that are not regularly used. Despite this, some judges do consider proportionality to be an Eighth Amendment issue and will overturn a punishment if they feel the punishment is too severe for the offense charged.

Incorporation

The previous discussion outlined the primary criminal procedure rights found within the U.S. Constitution and the Bill of Rights. Since these are federal documents, these provisions protect individuals from violations of rights by the federal government. Protection against state and local encroachment on procedural rights was not guaranteed and individuals had to rely on state constitutions to provide these protections. Some state constitutions followed the federal lead and provided extensive procedural rights to their citizens, while others did not. This was problematic, because it resulted in an unfair and unequal application of the laws (Zalman and Siegel 1997).

Fourteenth Amendment. The ratification of the Fourteenth Amendment in 1868 was the catalyst for extending the reach of the U.S. Constitution and the Bill of Rights to the states. The Fourteenth Amendment consists of five sections, but the first section is most relevant here. This section outlines a due-process clause that applies to states. As mentioned earlier, the Fifth Amendment contains a due-process clause as well; however, because it is in the Bill of Rights, it only applies to the federal government. The Fourteenth Amendment's due-process clause specifies that no state shall ". . . deprive any person of life, liberty, and property without due process of law." Since 1868, the U.S. Supreme Court has issued a number of decisions that have used this clause to justify forcing the states to adopt the procedures found in the U.S. Constitution and the Bill of Rights. The U.S. Supreme Court was given this authority in the cases *Marbury v. Madison* (1803) and *Fletcher v. Peck* (1810). In these cases, the practice of **judicial review** was established, in which the U.S. Supreme Court has the power to review federal and state laws to ensure that they comply with the U.S. Constitution.

Using its power of judicial review, the U.S. Supreme Court has incorporated, or made applicable to the states, most of the procedural rights found in the U.S. Constitution and the Bill of Rights. This process of **incorporation** was selective and time consuming, as the Court had to wait for cases to come before it before the Court could issue a ruling. Initially, the Court only incorporated the procedural rights it thought were "fundamental" and "essential" (see *Palko v. Connecticut*

[1937]), but, over time, the Court came to realize that all rights found within the U.S. Constitution and the Bill of Rights were fundamental; if they were not, they would not be there. Today, all states and the federal government abide by the provisions in these documents. In fact, some states have gone beyond what these documents specify, providing more rights to their citizens than is required.

Despite the fact that federal and state governments must recognize these procedural rights, none of these rights is absolute. As stated earlier, there are scenarios involving searches and seizures that do not require a warrant or probable cause, as specified in the Fourth Amendment. The same is true for the other procedural rights articulated above. Over time, the provisions found in the U.S. Constitution and the Bill of Rights have been modified to account for circumstances that simply did not exist when these documents were created. For example, the number of accused individuals who come into contact with the criminal justice system is much more vast than the number in 1791. The system has had to accommodate these numbers without collapsing. As a result, accused individuals are asked to waive many of their rights, including their right to a speedy trial, their right to have an attorney, and their right against self-incrimination. Courts have also scaled back many of these procedural rights. For instance, only individuals who face more than six months' incarceration are given the right to trial by jury. For more information about the extent of procedural rights in this country, see Samaha (2002) and Zalman and Siegel (1997).

RECENT TRENDS IN PROCEDURAL CRIMINAL LAW

As noted above, courts have restricted many of the procedural rights found in the U.S. Constitution and the Bill of Rights. In many cases, this restriction is the result of security issues that place public safety on a higher ground than individual rights. For instance, because of the potential danger of police work, courts have allowed police to engage in searches without a warrant and arrests without probable cause to ensure that police officers are not placed in precarious situations.

One of the primary examples of protecting public safety occurred as a result of the attacks on the World Trade Center and the Pentagon on September 11, 2001. Soon after the attacks, the U.S. Congress passed and President George W. Bush signed into law the USA Patriot Act in October of 2001. Among other things, this piece of legislation increased the federal government's ability to engage in certain procedures it was not allowed to before the attacks. For example, prior to the attacks, individuals living in the United States who were not U.S. citizens—legal, illegal, and resident aliens—enjoyed the same constitutional protections as ordinary citizens. After passage of the Patriot Act, this is no longer the case. According to the act, if federal authorities have reason to believe an alien is engaging in activity that threatens the country, he or she can be detained indefinitely.

The Patriot Act has also allowed federal authorities to engage in more expansive wiretapping and other electronic surveillance. The act allows more expansive surveillance of telephone and Internet service providers as well as voice mail and email communications. Any activity that federal authorities deem is related to even a remote threat to national security is subject to increased surveillance and fewer constitutional protections. This is something that many view as important for the safety of the nation. Others, however, feel the federal government has given itself too much authority to investigate such activity, since it alone defines what a threat to national security is.

CONCLUSION

Both substantive and procedural law are critical to the function of society and all entities that exist within it. This chapter provided a general overview of the numerous aspects of substantive and procedural law. Many authors devote entire textbooks to each of these aspects, but this text is simply unable to do so. What this chapter does contain, however, is the information needed to understand the presence of the law in the society, in particular, the criminal justice system. The criminal justice system exists because of the law; something or someone must be responsible for the enforcement of the law as written. The criminal justice system, moreover, does not exist in a vacuum; it must abide by the law just as individuals, groups, and corporations must.

As this chapter was not able to delve too deeply into the many permutations of the law, the reader is encouraged to consult the many sources of information provided throughout the chapter to gain a more thorough understanding of both substantive and procedural law.

KEY WORDS

actus reus
administrative law
bills of attainder
case law
common law
constitutional law
cruel and unusual
    punishment
deadly force
double jeopardy
ex post facto
excessive bail

excessive fines
exclusionary rule
grand jury
habeas corpus
impartial trial
incorportion
judicial review
justification
mala in se
mala prohibita
mens rea
mental capacity

precedent
principle of legality
procedural law
public trial
right to counsel
self-incrimination
speedy trial
statutory law
strict liability
substantive law
trial by jury

SUGGESTED READINGS

Friedman, L. (1993). *Crime and punishment in American history*. New York: Basic Books.
Samaha, J. (2002). *Criminal procedure*. Belmont, CA: Wadsworth Publishing.
Singer, R., and LaFond, J. (1997). *Criminal law: Examples and explanations*. New York: Aspen Publishers.
Walker, S. (1980). *Popular justice: A history of American criminal justice*. New York: Oxford University Press. ✦

CHAPTER 3

Policing and Law Enforcement

CHAPTER OUTLINE

Introduction
    Law Enforcement
    Order Maintenance
    Service
Historical Background
The American Experience
    Political Era
    Professional Era
    Community Policing Era
    Intelligence-Led Policing
Structure
    Local
    Sheriff
    County Police
    Constables
    Special Police
    State
    Federal
    Tribal
    Private Police
Organization
    Sworn Versus Civilian
    Specialization
    Geography
    Time
Police Work and Career Paths
    The Hiring Process

INTRODUCTION

We commonly speak of the police as the "gatekeepers" of the criminal justice system, because the vast majority of criminal cases brought before the courts result from decisions made by the police. Although the police are thought of as *law enforcers*, arresting criminals is only a small portion of police work. The police also foster **law compliance** and provide an array of services that are not linked to crime. Almost 80 percent of a patrol officer's time is devoted to activities that are focused on things other than law enforcement. However, the law enforcement image dominates the public face of the police.

As the law reflects the collective will of a people, the police are the "muscle" behind that society's law. Those who do not voluntarily obey the law will have it imposed upon them; the police are the primary means by which the law is imposed. In 1970, Egon Bittner described the role of the police "as a mechanism for the distribution of non-negotiably coercive force employed in accordance with the dictates of an intuitive grasp of situational exigencies" (1970: 46). Though other occupations and social institutions have the right to use force in a limited set of circumstances (for instance, to restrain a patient who may hurt himself, or to discipline children), only the police have a general mandate to use force for the common good.

The police may use force to ensure that the law is obeyed and public order preserved. When the police actually use force is the essence of police **discretion** (Brown 1981). It is not possible to write a law, or a rule, that will cover every possible situation the police might encounter. Nor will the police necessarily know with certainty every factual matter that attends every call they answer. The police combine their knowledge with the array of verbal and nonverbal information that attends each unique situation, make an accurate judgment about what's going on (the "situational exigencies"), and decide on the proper response.

Not every police action is a coercive one, of course. The right to use force on behalf of society lies behind many of the other things police do. In broad terms, there are three primary responsibilities of police work: **law enforcement, order maintenance**, and **service**. These aspects were first explored by James Q. Wilson in his 1968 book *Varieties of Police Behavior*.

Law Enforcement

"Enforcing the law" by apprehending criminals after crimes occur is an important part of police work, but it is only one element of the law enforcement mission. The entertainment media portray policing as an exciting career of hunting criminals, thwarting robberies in progress, engaging in high-speed car chases, making dynamic entries, and apprehending desperate criminals. In truth, these events happen infrequently. Far more than with so-called master criminals, the police are likely to deal with crimes committed by people who are drunk, depressed, mentally ill, or simply overwhelmed by life stresses.

Tense confrontations, take-down moves, and an enticing array of high-tech weaponry and science seem to be the tools of the trade. While these are important, by far the greater tools are patience, good communication skills, and knowledge of human psychology. The ability to enforce the law by bringing criminals to justice rests in large part on the willingness of the public to cooperate with the police (Black 1981; Mastrofski, Snipes, and Supina 1996). The foundation for that is laid in the routine interaction between police and citizens in the course of everyday, nonemergency activities.

Crime prevention has been a prime function of police work, ensuring the safety of the community by denying criminals the opportunity to commit crime and by defusing volatile situations before they reach the point of violence (Lab 2004). Visible **patrol**—on foot, in motor vehicles, on bicycles, or on horseback—is seen as a means of preventing crime by **deterrence**. Active patrol raises the possibility that a criminal will be seen and apprehended. The impression that the police are always around and ever vigilant discourages criminals from committing crime: that is the essence of police deterrence. Often, the presence of authority, backed up by powers of arrest, will scatter potential troublemakers or quiet boisterous behavior.

Police foster crime prevention in other, less flashy ways as well. Officers help organize and support community-based self-help activities, like **Neighborhood Watch**, to observe and report suspicious activity in the neighborhood (Garofalo and McLeod 1989; Rosenbaum 1987). Community involvement may range from supplemental **citizen patrols** to initiating court action against landlords of properties where drug sales take place. A wide range of anticrime activities take place at the block level. Citizen patrols, **property marking** projects, **safe havens** for children, looking after each other's property when people are away, and block parties can all be organized under the umbrella of Neighborhood Watch.

Patrol officers, **school resource officers, Police Activity League** volunteers, and others participate in a wide variety of community-building activities, both on and off duty, to keep youngsters safe and to encourage law-abiding activities (Bond 2001; Newman et al. 2000). Gang intelligence helps defuse feuds that otherwise might turn violent, and skilled officers sometimes negotiate truces between rival gangs. Officers host self-defense workshops and conduct property surveys to help reduce individuals' risks of victimization and make numerous referrals to social service agencies across a wide spectrum of problems they encounter.

Order Maintenance

Crime is not the only thing in modern life that can cause concern. All sorts of conflicts can create alarm, concern, fear, or inconvenience. Loud and boisterous groups of teenagers; heated, chest-thumping bar arguments; and noisy arguments over finances between the husband and wife in the next apartment all disturb the peace and tranquility of neighbors. The police are called to these and many other situations. Those who call for police interventions do not necessarily expect the officers to make arrests, as long as they restore order. Though arrests are possible, most incidents are resolved through other means: mediation, referral, or the mere threat of arrest. In some cases, such as a dispute between a landlord and tenant over the payment of the rent, the police may have no legal authority in the matter (rent disputes are a matter of civil law), but they may serve as referees. Their presence and authority act as a safety valve: both parties can back down without losing face.

Service

Service, the third function of the police, takes a wide variety of forms depending upon the location. Directions, assistance to disabled motorists, funeral escorts, administration of various kinds of permits, emergency relays of blood, checking vacant residences or looking in on vulnerable adults, aiding with traffic control at road construction and emergency scenes, and many more services are provided by local police and sheriffs' deputies.

Because of this wide diversity of tasks, police officers are trained to be generalists. Most officers begin their careers doing uniformed patrol work. They will be called upon to answer an almost unimaginable array of different needs. These include assisting in childbirth, breaking up fights, talking down suicidal "jumpers," interviewing abused children, trading gunfire with desperate criminals, intervening in domestic arguments, assisting mentally ill and confused persons, and investigating corrupt police officers.

Police officers frequently describe their work as "long hours of sheer boredom, punctuated by moments of sheer terror." In contrast to Hollywood portrayals, the reality of police work is that exciting events happen infrequently and favorable results can be elusive. Those who expect exciting careers in law enforcement are likely to find that much of their time is devoted to social work, helping people cope with life, occasionally resolving low-level problems, and building interpersonal relationships with the community.

HISTORICAL BACKGROUND

Historically and legally, the police power was vested in the community and wielded through whatever form of local government existed: village council, tribal chief, or feudal lord. Individuals had obligations to the community that were commonly understood. Formal policing forms were created and changed as a result of larger social changes. Full-time, paid police agencies are a relatively new development: the first modern police agency started in England in 1829. American policing developed out of English models.

The oldest forms of policing, the **constable** and the sheriff, date at least to the ninth century. When crime was relatively infrequent, the general populace could be roused by the **hue and cry** ("Stop, thief!") and obliged to pursue the felon to justice. In 1285, amid great social instability and turmoil at the close of the Crusades, England's **Statute of Winchester** required that all able-bodied men maintain weapons and serve in the Watch to protect villages and towns from fire and outlaws. A year-long turn as the unpaid constable, responsible for bringing lawbreakers before the King's Courts, also became compulsory.

During the 1700s, England underwent a period of rapid transformations in agriculture, technology, manufacture, and commerce known as the Industrial Revolution. People migrated to the cities in search of jobs and urban populations expanded dramatically. Crime and disorder became rampant and mob violence was a constant threat. Small, localized private police forces were paid to guard parishes (neighborhoods), toll roads, docks, and warehouses, replacing the unpaid and largely ineffective Watch. Their modern-day descendants are the professional security forces and the special police forces.

Social unrest intensified after the Napoleonic Wars in the early 1800s and the English elite sought ways to suppress or defuse the unemployed, desperate "dangerous classes" that haunted English cities. The military was the only available force capable of dealing with a riot until a reform movement brought Sir Robert Peel to power as prime minister.

In 1829, Peel established the first modern police force, the **Metropolitan London Police.** Organized along military lines and in military-like uniforms to allay fears of a "secret police" (a legacy of the secret network of informers during the French Revolution), the "**Bobbies**" were unarmed. They were primarily intelligence gatherers, getting to know the residents and conditions of a specific area and reporting back to a central administration through a chain of command. When news of trouble was discovered, large numbers of police would flood the area to forestall the violence. Over the years, their peace-keeping duties were established on a reputation for fairness and firmness (see Box 3.1).

BOX 3.1

Sir Robert Peel's Nine Principles of Law Enforcement

1. The basic mission for which the police exist is to prevent crime and disorder as an alternative to their repression by military force and severity of legal punishment.
2. The ability of the police to perform their task is dependent on public approval of their existence, actions, behavior, and on the ability of the police to secure and maintain public respect.
3. The police must secure and maintain the respect and approval of the public as well as the cooperation of the public in the task of observance of laws.
4. To recognize always that the extent to which the cooperation of the public can be secured diminishes, proportionately, the necessity for the use of physical force and compulsion for achieving police objectives.
5. To seek and to preserve public favor, not by catering to public opinion, but by constantly demonstrating absolutely impartial service to law, in complete independence of policy, and without regard to the justice or injustice of the substance of individual laws; by ready offering of individual service and friendship to all members of the public without regard to their wealth or social standing; by ready offering of sacrifice in protecting and preserving life.
6. To use physical force only when the exercise of persuasion, advice and warning is found to be insufficient to obtain public cooperation to an extent necessary to secure observance of law or to restore order; and to use only the minimum degree of physical force which is necessary on any particular occasion for achieving a police objective.
7. To maintain at all times a relationship with the public that gives reality to the historic tradition that the police are the public and that the public are the police; the police being the only members of the public who are paid to give full-time attention to duties which are incumbent on every citizen, in the interests of community welfare and existence.
8. To recognize always the need for strict adherence to police executive functions, and to refrain from even seeming to usurp the powers of the judiciary or avenging individuals or the state, and of authoritatively judging guilt and punishing the guilty.
9. To recognize always that the test of police efficiency is the absence of crime and disorder, and not the visible evidence of police action in dealing with them. (Fyfe et al. 1997)

THE AMERICAN EXPERIENCE

English colonists brought to America the common law and the institutions of constables, county sheriffs, and the Watch. Sheriffs' duties centered on the maintenance of roads and bridges, fire prevention and detection, and the service of writs for civil court matters; "crime fighting" was a minor duty. On the American frontiers of the colonial and "wild West" periods, where formal institutions of government were weak, Committees of Vigilance defended isolated communities from raiders, horse thieves, and other predators. Though **vigilantes** also had a dark side in some locations, the vigilance committees were generally socially constructive, reflecting the older community self-defense modes (Brown 1969).

American urbanization lagged behind England's, but by the 1840s, conditions in American cities were much like those in England. The idea of a police force was adopted, but it took a radically different American form. For instance, Boston had a small "police force" under the City Marshal in 1832, but its duties were more like those of today's boards of health than modern police departments (Lane 1967 [1975]). Where the English police were governed by the Home Office (the equivalent of a cabinet-level department in America), each American city, town, and county exercised control over its own police agency, with its own set of standards.

Scholars speak of three eras of American policing: the **Political Era** of the nineteenth century, the **Professional Era** of the first half of the twentieth century, and the **Community Policing Era** of the late twentieth and early twenty-first centuries (Kelling and Moore 1988).

Political Era

American ward ("machine") politics reflected contests for power between ethnic groups and was built on the **patronage** system (awarding city jobs in return for political support). Political ward bosses had far more clout than supervisors in the chain of command. The police of the era were often unskilled and corrupt, with no job security unless their patron remained in office, so they were more loyal to the person who provided their livelihood than to any abstract notion of "rule of law."

The police were also the instrument of entrenched capitalist interests in the early days of the labor movement. Police were used as strikebreakers and clashes with striking laborers were often violent. The Pennsylvania State Constabulary, the first modern state police agency, was created in 1905 to deal with striking miners.

Professional Era

The good-government Progressive movement of the late nineteenth century sought to reform patronage politics (see Digital History 2007). The Pendleton Act of 1883 established the federal civil service, under which public jobs were held on the basis of merit regardless of political view (U.S. Department of State 2005). States quickly created their own civil service laws, though machine politics and patronage survived in some cities into the latter half of the twentieth century. When the Progressive movement ceased to be part of the American political scene, a vanguard of police leaders continued to promote professionalism within the police service.

Police leaders advocated professionalism based upon education, training, and scientific crime detection methods. August Vollmer, the chief of police in Berkeley, California, instituted many innovations, including the first crime lab. His protégé, O.W. Wilson, was police chief in several cities and, as commissioner of the Chicago

Police Department, he established the fundamental principles of police administration in the early 1960s.

Professionalism was stunted by the **Boston Police Strike of 1919.** When one of the nation's most professional departments went on strike for higher wages (Boston officers were paid less than streetcar drivers), riots broke out. The union movement, with its socialist origins, was linked to the "Red Scare" of the Bolshevik Revolution that was being fought in Russia at that time. Governor Calvin Coolidge declared that "there is no right to strike against the public safety by anybody, anytime, anywhere," and called out the Massachusetts state militia to police the city. The striking officers were fired, and the movement for police unionism collapsed until the 1960s. Police remained low paid, largely uneducated, and ill-trained. As a result, bootlegger money in the Prohibition era was used to corrupt the local police in many areas, allowing the illegal import and sale of alcohol. Promotions and assignments often were based upon seniority and favoritism rather than merit. The 1931 **Wickersham Commission** reported on the brutality of police methods. **Police brutality** would resurface as one of the central themes of the most recent period of social unrest, the 1960s.

The development of federal law enforcement in the twentieth century was most visible in the rise of the Federal Bureau of Investigation under its most famous director, J. Edgar Hoover. A canny use of publicity helped forge the "law enforcement" image of the police, especially against the gangland murderers of the Prohibition era (such as Al Capone) and the bank robbers of the Depression (Bonnie and Clyde, Pretty Boy Floyd, John Dillinger, Ma Barker's gang, and others).

Critics blame three things for the failure of professional-model policing. One of these is the isolation of the squad car, which discouraged police interaction with the public. Another is the overreach and overdependence upon 9-1-1 systems, which relinquished control of the police mission to those who were not as competent to direct it. Finally, there was increased emphasis on felony-level crime because it was seen as the only "real" police work, with reliance on the UCR crime rate as the only true measure of police effectiveness. After the problems of the 1960s, dissatisfactions with the professional model led to calls for community policing, under which police focus on improving citizen satisfaction with police services, reducing fear of crime, improving quality-of-life problems, and enhancing community-building efforts.

Community Policing Era

Four major social trends converged during the 1960s and early 1970s and the police played important roles in many of them. Social individualism was asserted in many ways, seen in challenges to mandatory school prayer; the free speech movement; the rock and roll, folk-song protest, "free love" mentality of the hippies; and the emergence of the women's and gay rights movements. This individualism challenged reigning social mores. Most police were socially and politically conservative, viewing these developments with distaste and alarm, and often used extralegal tactics to suppress them.

At the same time the police were being criticized for a rising crime rate, a series of landmark cases ruled upon during the 1960s reasserted the rights of accused individuals and curtailed the powers of the police. The *Mapp v. Ohio* Fourth Amendment search-and-seizure case extended the **exclusionary rule** to state courts in 1961. The Supreme Court extended to all police agencies the rule that "evidence illegally gathered must be excluded from trial." *Miranda v. Arizona* in 1966 required the police to inform criminal suspects in custodial interrogation of their Fifth Amendment rights against self-incrimination.

The civil rights movement for racial equality came to public attention in the late 1950s and 1960s. Originally marked by nonviolent protests (in the face of violence by white mobs and the police), the more violent protests and rhetoric and the urban riots of 1965–1968 dominated the public consciousness. News footage documented police violence against peaceful protestors to break up demonstrations. Police inaction and occasional collusion in crimes committed against blacks and civil rights workers was publicly known or suspected. Police actions precipitated many of the urban riots in the mid-1960s: in the Watts district of Los Angeles in August 1965; in July 1965 in Newark, New Jersey; in July 1965 in Detroit. Federal law enforcement was often in opposition to local police during this era. For example, U.S. Marshals protected African-American children who were integrating local schools and the FBI investigated crimes against the black community.

The antiwar movement protesting U.S. military involvement in Vietnam began with draft-eligible college students, who were initially marginalized as cowards, traitors, and communist sympathizers. After the Tet Offensive in January 1968, however, opposition to the war grew rapidly. The actions of the Chicago Police against demonstrators at the August 1968 Democratic National Convention were heavily covered by the media and showcased police brutality to a nationwide television audience.

Police ineffectiveness at curbing crime, insensitivity to civil rights, and isolation from the community produced a crisis of public confidence in the police. Presidential commissions examined the causes of the urban riots and the widespread criticism of the police. The 1967 report of the **President's Commission on Law Enforcement and the Administration of Justice** found the police were poorly educated, poorly trained, poorly equipped, and poorly led. The federal government embarked on an improvement program under the 1968 Omnibus Crime Control and Safe Streets Act. Through the Law Enforcement Assistance Administration, the government spent millions of dollars to improve police equipment and training. The Law Enforcement Education Program financed college education for both serving officers and prospective officers.

The 1967 President's Commission report contained a recommendation that there be three levels of police employment. *Community service officers* would be in uniform but unarmed and would be responsible for many of the "routine" activities now done by patrol officers: taking "cold" reports of crime, which constitute the bulk of the crime reported to the police; performing the community service functions; and carrying out some other limited duties. *Police officers* would be freed up to respond to in-progress calls for crime and disorder and would handle basic criminal investigations in which leads could be followed. *Police agents* would be investigative specialists and handle complex cases, much like detectives do now. It was assumed that employees would move from one level to the other with experience and demonstrated skill. Those recommendations were generally ignored at the time because of strong union pressure and a lack of clear paths to making the changes.

During the 1970s, some police agencies undertook research into their operations, hoping that scientific validation would improve their resources, but the early results were a shock. The **Kansas City Preventive Patrol Experiment** suggested that routine police patrol had almost no impact on crime, fear of crime, citizen awareness of the police, or citizen confidence. Rapid response was found to have little impact on crime except for the rare instances when a crime was reported in progress. Contrary to the image projected in television shows and movies, a multicity study of detective work revealed that most crimes were solved by, or on the basis of work done by, uniformed patrol officers. Detectives mostly did the paperwork for court.

New approaches to policing emerged in the late 1970s and early 1980s. Herman Goldstein criticized the police for being concerned with the means of policing over ends that policing accomplishes and proposed that the police focus instead on problem-oriented policing approaches. Building upon the experiences of the **Flint (Michigan) Neighborhood Foot Patrol Program,** others began asserting the need for community-oriented policing that emphasized greater contact between police and citizens than was possible in motorized patrol.

At the current time, the community-policing model contends with a resurgent professional model that includes zero-tolerance policing and CompStat models of administration (discussed in the following pages). Ironically, each of the models looks to the so-called **Broken Windows** theory for legitimacy and to problem solving for tactics.

"Broken Windows: The Police and Neighborhood Safety" was the title of an article by Wilson and Kelling published in 1982. Its central metaphor was the broken window that goes unrepaired, signaling that "no one cares" about an abandoned property and inviting further vandalism. Extending the metaphor to disorder such as public drug sales, drunkenness, and prostitution, the authors argued that the police should be more attentive to conditions that signal that an area is ripe for criminal plunder. The article advocated "order-maintenance policing," a focus on the "small things" that the police had traditionally overlooked because they were not serious felony crimes. "Broken Windows" became the foundation for two distinct but complementary changes in police practice—problem-oriented and community-oriented policing.

Problem-oriented policing (POP) emphasizes analysis of crimes and situations, looking for patterns that may cross categorical lines. It seeks specific causes that may give rise to multiple events and fashions solutions to the causes, not the symptoms. Unlike order-maintenance policing, POP extends beyond police service, integrating appropriate roles from other criminal justice, social service, and private agencies, as indicated by the problem analysis.

Community-oriented policing (COP) distinguishes itself from the older professional model in several ways. First, it recognizes that the police have responsibilities for a wide variety of noncrime conditions, some of which may be criminogenic (crime-producing) and some merely annoying. Abandoned buildings, trash-strewn lots, and barking dogs are not considered "real police work," but they remain matters of great concern to neighbors because they diminish the quality of life for community residents. The Broken Windows rationale linked quality-of-life issues to the potential for criminal incidents, making them legitimate police concerns. The police have been a powerful catalyst, organizing communities to act on their own behalf and effectively mobilizing other resources such as health and housing inspectors, public works, nonprofit agencies, and many more to help abate problem conditions in communities.

Second, community policing includes community representatives in the decision-making processes of the police department. Formal advisory boards at the agency and precinct levels help to establish priorities for action. Police participation in neighborhood meetings provides two-way communication of information and concerns.

The 1982 Flint (Michigan) Neighborhood Foot Patrol Program demonstrated a marked improvement in citizen satisfaction with police who patrolled their neighborhoods on foot, even though the actual crime rate changed little. Similar results were found in foot patrol and fear-reduction projects in Houston, Texas, and Newark, New Jersey, in the same time period. With the success of early problem-solving initiatives in Newport News, Virginia, those efforts initiatives coalesced into a community-policing movement that looked for more than simple law enforcement.

The ultimate goal of community policing is a safer community. That goal is also sought by professional-model policing, but community-policing proponents seek to build and maintain a community capacity to self-regulate the conduct of residents and visitors without resorting to the enforcement arm of the police except in extreme, and hopefully rare, cases.

As a philosophical umbrella, COP stresses routine nonemergency interaction between police officers and the communities they serve. By breaking down previous barriers of mistrust, this approach provides a sound foundation for mutual problem-solving efforts, helps develop critical information about individuals and conditions in the neighborhoods, and ultimately leads to greater citizen participation in law compliance and crime prevention. In practice, community-policing initiatives have ranged from half-hearted failures to innovative and highly effective programs. COP has been a new label for old programs such as crime prevention, community relations, and even enhanced patrol. It has also been a vehicle for an entirely new approach to policing—including the community as an active partner in public safety. The wide range and mixed effectiveness of local COP initiatives leads critics to questions whether the claims of community policing are merely rhetoric or a new reality.

Community policing gained a political push during the Clinton presidency. The Office of Community Oriented Policing Services more familiarly known as "the

COPS Office") was charged with putting "100,000 cops on the street," to fulfill one of the president's campaign promises. In order to be eligible for funds for new hires, cities and towns had to demonstrate a commitment to community policing (current or future) and to sustaining the positions beyond the three-year period of federal support. Grants for upgrading equipment and programs were also available, if the purchases freed up officer time for street patrol or investigations. A complementary program known as Troops to Cops attempted to reintegrate soldiers demobilizing from the Gulf War by hiring them as police officers.

Whether the program actually increased the number of police officers on the street, and for how long, has been a topic of political contention. The COPS grants came at the end of the 20-year career cycle of the large numbers of police hired in response to the civil unrest of the 1960s and early 1970s. Critics charge that COPS grants helped cities stabilize their numbers from attrition but did not substantially increase the number of officers on patrol.

In 2009, the office of Justice Programs began a new round of hiring and retention grants as part of President Obama's economic stimulus bill. Those initiatives are more overtly tied to the creation and preservation of jobs in the face of severe economic decline, but they also demand the improvement of criminal justice system functions as a result of the hiring.

Resurgent professionalism emerged as the police culture resisted some of the changes demanded by community policing. Many officers, supervisors, and agencies still consider law enforcement to be their primary mission—deterring criminals through aggressive patrol and arresting those who are not deterred. Some reject community-policing precepts outright as "not police work"; others may recognize the inherent value of the activities, but conclude that they are too labor intensive and time consuming in the face of overwhelming demands for police service and shrinking resources.

Professionally oriented police take their inspiration from New York City's dramatic crime decrease in the mid-1990s under Commissioner William Bratton. The NYPD mounted an aggressive campaign against low-level law violations that had previously been ignored—sidewalk drug sales, loitering, turnstile-jumping in the subways, loud music, public drinking, and so forth. Police culture christened this approach **zero tolerance** after an earlier U.S. Customs drug interdiction program, under the catchphrase "If you take care of the little things [disorder], the big things [crime] will take care of themselves."

At a practical level, the zero-tolerance version of order-maintenance policing translates into "arrest as many people as possible for as many things as possible." It is not always done that way, of course, but it allows the police to focus on the arrest—law enforcement—as the primary crime-fighting tool, to the exclusion of the "softer" community-building duties of community policing. As originally conceived, however, order-maintenance policing has a much broader mandate than just "arrest 'em all and let the courts sort it out." The original Broken Windows prescription looked at arrest as a last resort. Setting and enforcing local rules of civility and conduct were a more important elemant of true order-maintenance policing. A zero-tolerance campaign may help restore order in hard-pressed areas, but it is not necessarily a long-term strategy that will restore community competence.

CompStat was the other major factor of the NYPD experience. Briefly put, **CompStat** was the use of weekly statistics as a basis for police operations, rather than simply responding to 9-1-1 calls. Police administrators were held to account for the conditions in their precincts, and that accountability in turn drove the targeted police actions on the street. The name "CompStat" stood for "Comparative Statistics" and was promoted as a rational basis for police decision making and resource allocation (Henry 2002; Silverman 1999).

Not everyone believes that aggressive law enforcement was solely responsible for the drop in crime in New York. More cautious scholars note that many other cities experienced a downturn in crime during the same period without anything like New York City's dramatic focus on CompStat and aggressive street policing. Others note that CompStat fueled a police crackdown, directing increased resources at problems that previously had been ignored. Such crackdowns usually produce dramatic reductions in crime or other activities, but the reductions are seldom long term. There are additional concerns that aggressive police actions serve to alienate the community rather than enlist it as a partner and that an enforcement based faith in deterrence forfeits the benefits of other crime-prevention approaches.

Intelligence-Led Policing

Drawing upon the example of "intelligence-based medicine," the police of the modern era are basing decisions more and more upon crime analysis and other data systems. With roots in the Kansas City Preventive Patrol Experiment, the Minneapolis Domestic Violence Experiment, and the other evaluative projects of the 1970s and 1980s, crime analysis has become more than the mere production of year-end statistics. New York's CompStat process was the first contemporary use of integrated statistics in real time. Advances in computer technologies now make it possible to do far more. Mapping tools and analytic software manage not only crime data, but also trend data from other functions that might affect police operations: land use, economic development, demographic trends.

The expansion of criminal enterprises in a global economy has created demands for better information about conditions beyond local boundaries. The war on terror has led to the creation of fusion centers to collect, assess, and coordinate information about possible terrorist activities. The centers are also tracking the connections among other criminal enterprises as well: guns, drugs, gangs, human trafficking, child pornography, and many others. Police professional associations also update their members across jurisdictional lines, on topics such as tactics, new threats, new technologies, and legal developments in the various federal districts.

There is now a Society of Police Futurists, an offshoot of the World Futures Society. A memorandum of understanding between the FBI and Police Futurists has created a Futures Working Group, coordinated through the Behavioral Science Unit of the FBI Academy. The group assesses current trends on select topics, assessing the ways in which individual trends, or the intersection of several trends, might create new demands upon the police. The goal is to recognize emerging futures and do advance preparation for multiple possibilities before they occur.

STRUCTURE

Police agencies have different mandates depending on their level of political authority, region of the country, and specific charter of the agency. Government police agencies are authorized at the local, tribal, county, state, and federal levels. In addition, various special police forces may be authorized. Approximately 18,000 separate police and law enforcement agencies exist in the United States today (LEMAS Data Sets 2006), employing almost 837,000 officers and agents (http://www.ojp.usdoj.gov/bjs/lawenf.htm).

Local

The blue uniforms and patrol cars of the nation's municipal police forces are the image most associated with the police. Their legal jurisdiction is usually limited to the borders of the town or city that hires them, though there are exceptions. Fresh pursuit of a suspect, **mutual aid** compacts among municipalities, and being sworn in as special officers or deputies for other agencies all may extend police officers' local authority.

Most municipal police agencies are small. Uniformed generalist patrol work is a universal entry point, and many officers spend most of their careers doing patrol work. In larger departments, increased specialization in the form of detectives, juvenile officers, SWAT (Special Weapons and Tactics) team members, and the like is possible in later career steps, as are promotions to supervisory positions.

Sheriff

The county **sheriff** is one of the oldest police offices and in many states is authorized by the state constitution. Unique among law enforcement personnel, sheriffs serve all three branches of criminal justice: policing, courts (sheriffs provide security to courtrooms and serve civil and criminal writs), and corrections (sheriffs run most county jails). Deputy sheriffs often start their careers in jails as correctional officers and work their way up to uniformed patrol and investigations.

Sheriffs are elected officials in 48 of the 50 states, but the duties of sheriffs' departments vary regionally. In the South and West, they are the primary law enforcement services for many rural and unincorporated areas. In the urban centers of the Northeast, sheriffs tend to be court officers, but provide only limited law enforcement because most of their jurisdictions have full-time municipal police.

County Police

In some densely populated urban areas, county police departments have taken over the law enforcement duties of the sheriff. Organized like large municipal departments, county departments are responsible to the county executive or county council rather than to an elected sheriff. County police may have concurrent jurisdiction with municipal police agencies located within the county. In such instances, like the sheriff's offices and state police, the county police tend to concentrate on areas without other police resources, cooperating with the municipal departments when the need arises.

Constables

In many parts of the country, the old office of constable has been abolished or restricted to minor court and service duties. In Texas, the office of constable is comparable in many ways to the sheriff or the county police, generally serving court writs but also providing patrol services in some areas.

Special Police

State laws authorize police forces for special limited purposes, such as railroads (which run through multiple jurisdictions), college campuses, school districts, mass-transit systems, parks and woodlands, and the like. The best known is the Port Authority of New York and New Jersey Police, which lost many officers in the September 11, 2001, attack on the World Trade Center.

A variation on the "special police" concept are the part-time officers (variously called "reserves," "special officers," or "auxiliary officers," among other titles) who work for municipal, county, and sheriffs' departments in addition to their regular jobs. They may work on either an hourly paid basis or as volunteers, depending upon the agency and the state's authorizing statutes. With proper training, they may perform full police duties, especially in rural areas. Otherwise, they supplement regular police in support roles: directing traffic, providing crowd control at major events like concerts and fairs, and assisting in a variety of roles. Many sheriffs' departments have "sheriffs' posses" who can be called upon for additional staffing of special events and search-and-rescue operations. Their powers usually are less than those of full-time officers, but they provide valuable resources and expertise.

State

State police functions take one of two forms. State police have standard law enforcement duties and general jurisdiction throughout the state. State patrols or highway patrols primarily enforce traffic laws on state highways; they have police powers and training, but no general police jurisdiction. States with highway patrols may also have an independent bureau of criminal investigation that provides criminal investigation and crime lab services across the state. Other elements of state government may employ investigators and officers with special police powers, such as the welfare, motor vehicle, revenue, alcoholic beverage control, and natural resources departments. Some jurisdictions grant police powers to corrections employees, especially probation and parole officers.

Federal

Federal agencies have specific powers and jurisdiction under federal law and do not enforce state or local laws. There are more than 80 federal law enforcement agencies, including the Border Patrol, Customs Service, Federal Protective Services, U.S. Mint Police, and smaller police forces for various parts of the federal government (the Capitol, Supreme Court, Environmental Protection Agency, etc.). Some crimes, such as bank robbery, are found in both state and federal statutes, leading to concurrent or overlapping jurisdiction. In many cases, federal and state jurisdictions overlap as drugs, firearms, explosives, and bank robberies may all be part of an interstate or even international criminal enterprise. In such cases, federal and state agencies coordinate their investigations through **Multi-Jurisdictional Task Forces**, usually under the direction of the regional United States District Attorney.

Many smaller agencies were incorporated into the new Department of Homeland Security (DHS) in the wake of the September 11 attacks against American targets. In order to coordinate the nation's defenses and deal more effectively with the threat of international terrorism, agencies with relevant missions were brought under the direction of a single agency. Among the components of the new DHS are the Secret Service; the Border Patrol, renamed Customs and Border Protection; the Immigration and Naturalization Service, renamed Immigration and Customs Enforcement, or ICE; the U.S. Coast Guard; the Federal Law Enforcement Training Centers, or FLETC, which train the agents for 80 of the federal enforcement agencies; and the Transportation Safety Administration. Other components relating to nuclear detection, threat assessment, intelligence, animal research, and similar functions were brought under the DHS umbrella selectively from their former homes in other federal agencies.

Created in 1908, the FBI has a mandate to investigate approximately 200 federal crimes, including bank robbery and kidnapping, unless Congress specifically designates jurisdiction to another agency. Criminal acts and conspiracies that cross state lines usually fall to the FBI, the enforcement arm of the Justice Department. The FBI crime lab provides forensic support for investigators throughout the nation, and the National Academy provides advanced training for state and local officers. Recognizing the emerging needs created by globalization, the FBI has established offices in foreign countries and has been involved in the training of police forces in emerging nations and the countries of the former Soviet bloc. In 2005, the Bureau began training all new agents to be intelligence-gathering officers, both in antiterror investigations and in the investigation of transnational enterprise crime.

The Drug Enforcement Administration (DEA) was established in 1973, combining several existing antidrug offices under the Justice Department. The DEA has primary responsibility for coordinating national drug enforcement efforts and is the sole agency authorized to pursue overseas drug investigations.

The Alcohol, Tobacco, Firearms and Explosives Bureau (still referred to as the ATF or BATF) is an enforcement arm of the Treasury Department. Created in 1972 when it was split from the Internal Revenue Service, ATF has powers based in the tax laws and other federal laws and regulations relating to alcohol, tobacco products, firearms, explosives, and arson. Another Treasury function, the Secret Service, was created in 1865 to investigate money counterfeiting. Protection of the president of the United States was added after the 1901 assassination of President McKinley. Fraud in commerce and fictitious securities documents also lie within its investigative mandate.

The U.S. Marshals Service is the oldest federal law enforcement agency, created by the Judiciary Act of 1789. Marshals protect the federal judiciary, transport federal prisoners, and protect endangered federal witnesses (the Witness Protection Program). In addition, marshals manage assets seized from criminal enterprises and may even run businesses until their sale under the asset forfeiture laws.

Tribal

The U.S. Constitution recognizes Indian tribes as sovereign entities, and tribal lands may have their own police forces. The Navajo nation is representative of the more developed agencies. The federal Bureau of Indian Affairs also has a separate police force for tribal lands, whose territorial dimensions may cross municipal, county, and even state lines. Like their municipal and state counterparts, tribal police have jurisdiction over anyone on tribal land, whether Native American or not. Tribal jurisdiction over its own members may include traditional methods of dispute resolution (community circles, banishment, property exchanges) as well as the contemporary criminal and civil courts.

Private Police

Over the last several decades, the United States has seen a growth in special **private police** forces. They are not "police" in the same sense as state or municipal officers because they do not have the authorization of law or general police powers that come with a sworn position. Nevertheless, they are uniformed and equipped in much the same way as their municipal counterparts, and many have completed preservice police training. A specialized component, with special training, provides personal protection for corporate executives at home and abroad, much as the Secret Service Dignitary Protection Agency does for public figures.

The private police forces are an augmented face of private security, and their powers derive from the property rights of the corporate and incorporated entities that employ their services. They are often **first responders** for alarms (intrusion, fire, and health emergencies), exercise a qualified set of access control powers to limit visitors to the properties under contract, and sometimes handle disputes in much the same way that police patrol officers would. Professional organizations make a point of coordinating and interacting well with local police agencies, though there are fly-by-night, disreputable agencies as well.

Private police provide more systematic patrol presence for those who can afford their services. In addition, they relieve the pressure on local agencies to answer alarm calls, the vast majority of which are false alarms (accidental activations or equipment malfunctions). The modern equivalents of the ancient night watchman and the store detective, their level of training, and range of duties are considerably greater than those of their predecessors, reflecting the more complex requirements of asset protection and personal security in the modern age.

The former sharp distinctions between public and private policing have blurred in recent years. The new electronic commerce has created new challenges and opportunities. The need for the physical security of locked doors has not disappeared, but it has been augmented by demands for protection of the electronic infrastructure (data), intellectual property (trade secrets), and goods in transit. Corporations now address the issues of asset protection, including electronic surveillance, personnel background checks, process integrity, data protection and verification, and the personal protection of corporate personnel.

In addition, private security forces now often work under contract for public police agencies, providing security at crime scenes, guarding prisoners in hospitals, and even conducting background checks on potential new employees. Their relationship to the formal police authority is similar to that of private security contractors in military zones overseas, such as Blackwater International (now Xe), DynCorp, and Triple Canopy in the Iraq and Afghan theaters.

ORGANIZATION

Sworn officers in American police and law enforcement agencies are organized in a hierarchical form, with a **chain of command** conveying information from the line to the administrative decision makers and conveying orders and information back down. In larger departments, patrol officers report to shift supervisors (sergeants), who report to shift commanders (lieutenants), who report to precinct commanders (captains). Precinct and unit commanders report to divisional heads (deputy chiefs). Police work is organized by task requirements (sworn or civilian) as well as by geography and by time.

Sworn Versus Civilian

For many years, almost every position in a police department was held by a uniformed police officer or a plainclothes detective. Women held only secretarial jobs and "matron" positions in jails. Support positions could be places to which officers were assigned as a punitive measure or "plum jobs" that offered a daytime Monday–Friday refuge from rotating shift work.

In modern times, many departments employ civilians (also called nonsworn or contract employees) to perform tasks that do not require the extensive training and experience of a sworn officer. Records, dispatching, fleet maintenance, personnel and budget, and even crime-scene investigations may be staffed by nonsworn personnel. They are trained only for their special function, do not have police powers or carry weapons, and generally are paid much less than sworn officers. Some agencies practice "outsourcing," contracting with private security agencies to perform many services formerly done by uniformed police officers:

guard crime scenes, transport prisoners, and guard prisoners while they are in medical facilities.

Specialization

Patrol officers have general duties attending to a wide variety of calls and situations. In order for police departments to function efficiently, however, a number of specialist positions must be filled. Best known are the detectives or investigators, who do not answer calls. Their time is spent interviewing witnesses and following up on leads in unsolved crime cases. Detectives may specialize in a certain type of crime (homicide, burglary, robbery, sex crimes, etc.) or conduct all kinds of criminal investigation. Crime analysis, gang intelligence and intervention, school resource officers, training coordinator, **HAZMAT** (hazardous material), and high-risk warrant service, among others, are task-specific functions for sworn officers. Supervision is also a specialty job: as a rule, once promoted to sergeant or above, police officers do not handle calls unless circumstances force them to take police actions. Their primary responsibilities are to observe and assist patrol officers or investigators and to coordinate efforts. The farther up the hierarchy one rises, the more the duties are managerial and administrative in nature, except in small agencies where everyone is a generalist.

Geography

In the smallest local departments, officers are responsible for covering the entire town or village. Elsewhere, patrol officers patrol specific parts of town called **beats**. Officers are responsible for answering all calls within that beat, as well as for preventing crimes and resolving problems.

Larger agencies are organized into **precincts** containing several beats. There are, for instance, 76 precincts in New York City, six in Austin, Texas, and four in Minneapolis, Minnesota. It is easier to manage smaller areas within a large city, enabling the precinct commander to be more responsive to citizen concerns.

Sheriffs' departments may also be divided into different districts or may operate out of a central office. In addition, sheriffs' offices may assign deputies to local municipalities, known as contract cities, for a specified number of hours according to a contract negotiated between the city and the sheriff. Contracts guarantee basic police services while relieving smaller cities of part of the expense of maintaining their own departments.

The phrase **beat integrity** refers to a policy of keeping officers assigned to one specific beat consistently in order to develop knowledge about the players and build relationships with the community. This represents a significant change from the pre-1960s policies that moved officers frequently to different areas of the city in an effort to thwart corruption. However, officers may cross beat boundaries to assist other officers if necessary.

State police agencies must cover entire states and organize into **troops** for reasons that police departments organize into precincts. In rural areas, troopers may operate out of their homes (such as the Connecticut Resident Trooper program), but are responsible to a troop-level administration.

Federal agencies responsible for national coverage organize into administrative regions and generally maintain offices in major cities. Federal agencies also work cooperatively with local and state agencies through **regional task forces** for various purposes, recognizing that crime does not confine itself to jurisdictional boundaries. Short-term task forces may devote their efforts to tracking down a serial rapist or a prolific bank robber. Long-term resources are devoted to organized crime such as racketeering, insurance fraud, illegal drug importation and distribution, and smuggling.

Time

Because crime and public emergencies occur around the clock, dispatch services and police coverage must be 24 hours a day seven days a week. Police agencies tend to staff their shifts differently according to the volume of activity expected for various parts of the day. There are many different shift schedules ranging from the standard 40-hour workweek of five eight-hour days to the popular 4–10 and 3–12 shifts (four 10-hour or three 12-hour days). The two basic models are **rotating shifts** in which officers periodically change from days to evenings to nights and **steady shifts** in which work hours are determined by a seniority system or a bid lottery.

Overlapping shifts and "**power shifts**" provide extra police presence during the active evening hours and on weekends. More officers are available to handle the call load and provide backup in dangerous situations. Depending upon the nature of union contracts or other work rules, the power shifts may be staffed by officers who volunteer to work the evening hours on a regular basis, without rotating to day and midnight assignments.

Smaller agencies may provide nighttime coverage by an "on-call" arrangement. Officers work their shifts and return home to sleep, but can be called out again for an accident or some criminal incident. Another agency such as the sheriff's office or state police also may provide after-hours coverage.

Investigators and crime-scene technicians generally work day and evening shifts, with either minimum staffing or on-call status for the overnight hours. Other support positions such as records, planning and research, personnel, and purchase and supply usually do not work around the clock or on weekends. They tend to be Monday–Friday offices because their work entails interaction with other public- and private-sector offices on the standard work schedule.

POLICE WORK AND CAREER PATHS

Municipal policing remains a single-point-of-entry career. Officers working in municipal departments begin in patrol, doing shift work and answering a wide variety of calls. The diversity of patrol activities provides a learning base of experience. After that, three basic career paths are possible: officers may remain in patrol for their entire careers; they may move from patrol into some specialty role, most typically as investigators or detectives; or they may follow a mixed career of supervisory promotions and specialty assignments that lead to administrative posts.

Sheriffs' departments may have single- or dual-entry tracks. **Single-entry tracks** mean that deputies begin their careers working in the jails, unarmed, supervising prisoners. When a patrol position becomes available, jail deputies have the first opportunity for the slot, subject to seniority and testing rules. The emerging professional movement in corrections has led some sheriffs to create **dual-entry tracks.** Deputies hired for corrections functions are hired with an understanding that they will be working only in jails, and those seeking law enforcement positions apply directly for patrol positions. Jail deputies may apply for patrol slots later if they wish, but they do so on a level playing field, with no seniority advantages or "inside track" compared to outsiders.

Federal agencies have different requirements, depending upon their needs and mandates. Some have uniformed branches as well as investigators; others tend to be exclusively investigative in nature. The FBI is one of the investigative agencies, and because of the sensitive nature of tis work, generally does not hire persons right out of college. The Bureau looks for candidates who have established a solid work record and credit history, among other qualifications, so many aspiring FBI agents work in uniformed police service until they meet the eligibility requirements. By contrast, the Border Patrol has expanded rapidly to meet the demands to secure the nation's borders; many college students have stepped directly into Border Patrol slots upon graduation.

The Hiring Process

The older police career model, which still endures in many areas, began with candidates being hired by an agency. At that point, the town or city sent them to a **police academy** for training and state certification as a police officer. As police training and education requirements expanded, other options developed. Today, persons seeking a police career may pay for their own **preservice training** before being hired, which may give them a competitive edge in the job market.

In some states, candidates can pay to go to a regular police academy. In others, alternative police certification processes are integrated into academic programs at two-year, community, and vocational colleges. Students graduate with an associate's degree and state certification as a police officer, although they have no police powers until an agency hires them. Preservice certification represents a savings for the municipality, which can put the officer to work immediately and the municipality does not have to pay for training.

Police recruits must pass a battery of tests to be hired, even with preservice certification. Written, psychological, and physical tests, as well as **background checks** for character and conduct, are standard in most areas. Some agencies require polygraph exams; still others put candidates through assessment centers to test their skills and instinctive reactions in various situations.

No preservice training options exist for those seeking federal law enforcement jobs. The FBI and DEA maintain their own specialized academies in Quantico, Virginia. All other federal agencies train their agents and officers at the FLETC in Georgia or Arizona.

There are two primary models for police training academies. **Stress-based academies** are run similar to military boot camps: they are residential and isolated from other groups; they tend to concentrate heavily on physical fitness as both a goal and a form of punishment for minor infractions or errors; they incorporate military trappings such as marching in formation; and they interweave classroom instruction with practical, hands-on exercises. **Campus-based academies** are run in two-year and technical college campuses, and the police academy curriculum is often part of an accredited associate's degree. Classroom instruction is augmented by practical exercises similar to those in stress academies, including mandatory state certification in firearms use and defensive/pursuit driving. Because of the setting, where trainees intermingle with students from numerous other academic disciplines, the boot-camp trappings are generally absent. Each model has strong proponents, primarily based in philosophical preferences rather than scientific evaluation of the effectiveness of the model.

Field Training

Most departments have a full-time **Field Training Officer (FTO)** program that provides the bridge between academy learning and autonomous authority in the field. Officers-in-training ride with experienced officers who have a mandate to expose the rookies to as many situations as possible, evaluating and critiquing the trainees' responses as part of the field learning process. Once the FTO program is complete, rookies may work independently, but most undergo an additional period as probationary employees. If their performance is poor, they can be released without any further action. If they successfully pass their probationary period, they become full-fledged members of the agency, accorded all civil service and bargaining unit protections where applicable.

Promotion

The requirements for being promoted to supervisory rank or to specialty positions vary widely. At the low end, seniority is still found in some departments. The person who has been in the department the longest gets the next open position, regardless of training, education, or general fitness for the job. At the other end of the spectrum are batteries of written tests, oral interviews, and assessment center tests. A few departments also incorporate a "promotability score" based upon past performance and supervisors' assessments of the individual's skills that will be necessary for the new job.

Specialties. Criminal investigation often requires a long-term commitment to cases, interviewing people, following up leads, assessing physical evidence, and preparing affidavits for warrants and cases for court. It is difficult to conduct investigations if one is always being called off to answer another call for service, so most police agencies have an investigative specialist position, usually called **detective.** In some agencies, detective is a rank and is considered a promotion above patrol officer. In others, it is considered an assignment and holds the same rank within the organization as a patrol officer.

Because of its high profile and clarity of focus, criminal investigation, or detective work, is a prized assignment for many police officers. In smaller organizations, detectives are investigative generalists. In larger agencies, detectives are specialized, devoting their time to a single category of crime. They may work in several different investigative units over the course of their careers.

Undercover assignments are a special type of investigation, where the officers pretend to be criminals or "fringe players" in order to gather intelligence on criminal networks or to buy drugs and stolen merchandise. Undercover officers differ from plainclothes officers, whose police status is known or acknowledged; an undercover officer's police identity is secret. Occasionally undercover police run **sting operations** where officers pose as criminal fences or drug dealers; **john details** are a variation used against street prostitution and cruising activities. Police officers (usually women, though similar operations are conducted in gay male cruising areas) pose as prostitutes, in order to arrest "johns" who solicit them for sex.

Internal Affairs, sometimes called the Office of Professional Responsibility or a similar title, is the most specialized investigative function. It has the responsibility for investigating allegations of crime and misconduct by other police officers in the organization. Juvenile investigations is both an investigative unit specializing in juvenile crime and a support unit that works with social service agencies to get juvenile offenders back on the straight and narrow.

Other specialties exist. Only a few cities have full-time SWAT squads, but many have trained personnel who can be mobilized into a team at need; smaller cities and towns often participate in regional SWAT teams. Hostage negotiations and barricaded persons situations are typical situations for SWAT. HAZMAT is a similar specialty, requiring additional training and equipment for dealing with incidents like toxic waste or chemical spills, volatile chemicals in clandestine drug labs, or accidents in legitimate business and manufacturing sites. Agencies near large bodies of water often have marine units for monitoring water traffic and for rescue; many densely populated urban areas have police helicopter units for surveillance, search, and rapid deployment across wide-flung areas.

Training is a vital element of any agency for preparing new recruits, updating veterans on changes in law and procedure, and introducing new techniques and technologies to all members of the agency. School resource officers are similar to juvenile officers, but work exclusively in the schools, providing a combination of security, investigation, and public relations. They may deal exclusively with students or may have responsibilities for both student and staff conduct. Drug Abuse Resistance Education is a special form of school liaison, a national antidrug curriculum taught by uniformed police officers. In some departments, crimescene technicians are sworn officers; in others they are civilians.

Police officers are often supervisors for civilianized support units, such as Dispatch or Records. In addition to knowledge of the various police jobs that the unit supports, they have the legal authority to handle difficult questions and requests and can provide technical knowledge of the criminal and procedural laws when needed.

ENDURING ELEMENTS AND ISSUES

Across the multiple types and approaches to policing, there are certain themes common to the American police. Many of them center on what scholars call the **police subculture,** the views of the world shared by many police officers. Police discretion, the **use of force,** corruption, their handling of special constituencies, and their relations with the community, particularly minority citizens, are all intertwined with this hard-to-define concept.

Police Subculture

The idea of a police subculture at odds with mainstream society stemmed from the politically charged era of the 1960s. Two schools of thought emerged to explain the adversarial relationships of the day. Police opponents viewed the overwhelmingly Caucasian, almost entirely male police as racist, ignorant, authoritarian, and thuggish, completely out of touch with a changing society. In this viewpoint, police work attracted mean-spirited bullies.

The other school of thought held that people were drawn to police work out of a sense of altruism, but the nature of police work transformed them. The major scholars of the police of the 1960s drew a picture of police whose "working personality" was marked by concepts of danger, authority, and cynicism (Skolnick 1966; Niederhoffer 1967). The nature of their work meant dealing with people at their worst, handling problems of abuse and death on a regular basis, being personally reviled, and having their motives questioned. These combined to harden police officers, bringing about a defense mechanism. Those scholars also noted that the police were given to the use of stereotypes as a "perceptual shorthand" to discern and minimize danger.

The wider admission of women and minorities to policing has had some impact on police culture, but certain common themes are still recognized. Police officers work within a moral framework as much as a legal one, assessing situations on the basis of the persons they interact with. A feeling of "us against them" predominates in many areas, though community policing has broken down that attitude in many others. Crank (1998) summarized many of the themes of police culture. One theme is the necessity and righteousness of force. Another is reliance upon an undefined "commonsense" and personal bravery in the face of sudden and potential danger. A third is a moral division of the world into "good" and "bad" people, with the police as a "thin blue line" between civilization and chaos. Others include solidarity in the face of opposition, individualism and personal autonomy, unpredictability, and survival.

Because most officers are socially and politically conservative, the police culture adapts slowly and sometimes grudgingly to changes in the social and legal environment. Guyot (1979) likened the process of creating change in police organizations to "bending granite." This resistance often puts the police at odds with large segments of the public, as it did in the 1960s, and gives rise to a series of concerns about police behavior. Common to all of the concerns is the manner in which police exercise their discretion.

Police Corruption

Corruption is the use of the police position for personal gain. While it is common to refer to police powers as those of arrest and the right to use force, police discretion also gives the police the power *not* to arrest, and indeed not to take action at all. In the nineteenth and early twentieth centuries, with police salaries as low as the hiring standards, police were susceptible to bribes to "look the other way," "lose" evidence, or focus their enforcement efforts on business competitors. During Prohibition, bootleggers bribed police in cities on a widespread basis. In modern times, higher standards and better salaries have improved the police as a whole, but pockets of corruption are revealed periodically.

More problematic than the bribing of police by organized crime are cases when the police themselves become criminals. The classic case in modern times was "The Pad" in New York City, revealed by Frank Serpico to the Knapp Commission in the early 1970s. Systematic police corruption shook down merchants for protection money like the racketeers of earlier periods. Police shaking down drug dealers, confiscating their drugs, and selling the drugs themselves has been a problem in several cities, as uncovered by the Mollen Commission's investigation of New York P.D. corruption in the 1980s and the Los Angeles Rampart Division CRASH scandal of the late 1990s.

Harassment

The clear-cut moral division of the world focuses police attention on those they deem "bad." Anyone whose appearance or behavior signals "trouble" is likely to be subjected to scrutiny, usually in a field interrogation contact to determine who they are and what they are up to. Constant police pressure on violent street gangs and drug dealers is considered a good thing, serving law-abiding citizens by reducing the opportunity for criminals to act out. When the net is widened to include law-abiding citizens whose demeanor is without reproach and who bear only a superficial resemblance to the criminals, the police affront the autonomy and personal dignity of citizens. If that happens on a regular basis, the perception grows that the police are merely harassing people they do not like.

Racial profiling is the most recent development, arising from police efforts to intercept bulk drugs before they can be marketed in the cities. Cases in New Jersey and Maryland documented that state police stopped and searched minority motorists' cars in numbers far greater than their proportion of highway users. The underlying assumption equating race with criminality—the belief that African Americans and Hispanics are more involved with drug trafficking than whites—was not borne out by the search results. Drugs were found at equal rates in minority and white motorists' cars. Other jurisdictions have found similar patterns of racial disparities in stops, though in less dramatic numbers. The fundamental objection is to the use of race rather than behavior as a reason for initiating a police inquiry. Other objections arise from the manner in which minority motorists are treated during contact.

Improper Use of Force and Police Brutality

The power to use "nonnegotiably coercive force" in defense of the law and social order is vital to the police role. Across the vast landscape of police–citizen interactions, police use force properly, if at all—most incidents are resolved without force. Like any other power, however, it can be subject to abuse. There are two primary categories of abuse. Wrongful use involves using force for the wrong reason, such as to retaliate against a person for ÒdisrespectÓ to the officer. Disproportionate use occurs when the level of force far exceeds the level of resistance or aggression of the subject. The police are also required to protect the life and safety of those they use force against once the situation is brought under control.

Legitimate force may be used to bring resisting subjects into compliance. This usually means submitting to arrest, although people may also be forced out of areas where they are trespassing. Police are trained and equipped to employ force in accordance with the **force continuum**, which links the level of police force to the aggressiveness and resistance of the citizen.

The force continuum begins with the authoritative presence of the officer, moves through commanding voice and directions to the first actual application of physical force, a guiding push or firm grip to steer a person away from a particular point. Physical resistance from a citizen is required for higher levels of force, including pain compliance holds (wristlocks and other pressure-point techniques), devices like pepper spray and electrical shocks from stun guns, and the use of impact weapons like nightsticks. Deadly force is the final step, reserved for a narrowly defined set of circumstances.

Federal funding has promoted the development of less lethal weaponry to assist the police in their mission while minimizing the risk of harm to officers, suspects, and bystanders. Incapacitating chemical agents like pepper spray, beanbag rounds that knock a person down but do not penetrate the skin, capture-nets fired from shotguns, sticky-foam, disorienting lights and stun grenades, and other weapons still in the development stage all seek to provide safer alternatives to gunfire.

Police have the power to use deadly force only to save their own lives or those of a third party. A common-law "fleeing felon" rule allowed lethal force to apprehend any accused felon. In 1985, the U.S. Supreme Court in *Tennessee v. Garner* restricted the use of lethal force to situations of imminent and articulable danger. While police sidearms are the most obvious instruments of lethal force, blunt objects such as a baton or nightstick are also capable of inflicting deadly harm if used improperly, or against the wrong target, such as a blow to the head.

Periodically, the issue is brought to the public's attention by a high-profile case. The celebrated case of the beating of Rodney King by Los Angeles police officers was partially captured on videotape. Part of the incident involved legitimate use of force to take a resisting suspect into custody. At some point, many feel the event turned into an episode of street justice, the extralegal use of physical force as a punishment for "contempt of cop." The police community is split over whether some of the force was illegitimate, or all was legitimate, and over whether there were alternative tactics that could have been used.

The Abner Louima case in New York City shocked the nation, as an out-of-control police officer sexually assaulted a prisoner with a stick because he thought the man had punched him in a street scuffle. The Louima case was a clear-cut case of brutality, personal abuse of authority to avenge a perceived personal affront. The Amadou Diallo case is more problematic. Diallo was confronted in the early morning by four armed plainclothes officers searching for a rape suspect. Diallo, an immigrant with poor English skills, reached for his wallet, which appeared to the officers as an attempt to draw a weapon. The officers fired a total of 41 shots, killing Diallo. The issue of imminent possible danger and the need to make a split-second decision in defense of themselves and their partners is a major factor that distinguishes the Louima and Diallo cases. The issue of racial prejudice is an element in both cases, like the Rodney King incident and many fatal shootings, because they involved black suspects and white officers.

The Blue Wall of Silence

The cultural theme of feeling unappreciated and under fire combines with themes of danger and solidarity to create the **blue wall of silence.** Some police officers who know of wrongdoing by other police will not take action against them or provide information against them to investigators because of two things. First, police mistrust their superiors and fear being given disproportionately harsh punishment to set an example or to alleviate political pressure on their administrators. Second, they fear alienating their brother and sister officers, upon whom they depend for backup assistance in dangerous situations. Unions also fear that employee rights will be abrogated under political pressure, so they intervene as advocates and lawyers for officers accused of wrongdoing. To the public, it appears that "the police protect their own," even against legitmate grievances and complaints of the community. The blue wall is no longer as strong as it was once thought to be, as professional and community-oriented officers realize that the police must clean their own house for legitimacy and that a rogue officer is as much a danger to them as are criminals. Nevertheless, it is entrenched in some agencies still, and the issues that give rise to it remain salient.

Policing the Police

The periodic scandals that arise from police misconduct are followed by public cries for police reform. In the past, most reforms were promises of better internal management by the police agency. In effect, clear rules would be written, better training would be devised, and supervision would be stricter. Police agencies asserted that the illegal behavior featured in the headlines was solely confined to "bad apples" who were not representative of the majority of police officers, who were honest, fair, and devoted to the public good.

More recently, the cyclical nature of police scandals has led people to question the ability of the police themselves. Because criminal convictions of police officers are difficult to obtain, aggrieved citizens and advocacy groups have pursued lawsuits against police agencies for denial of civil rights. In addition, the federal Justice Department has moved against some police departments, using lawsuits to craft **consent decrees** that articulate specific changes the departments must make. Typically, those changes are monitored by outside entities that report to the federal court; the issue of racial profiling by the New Jersey State Police resulted in one such consent decree.

Federal intervention depends upon the willingness of the current administration to intervene. Lawsuits can also take years to settle. At the local level, residents concerned with police misconduct have begun to call for **civilian review** of police. Allegations of police misconduct are heard by boards composed entirely of residents or a mixture of residents and police officials. Conduct is judged based upon community expectations rather than just police practice. In the best models, police experts identify the acceptable standards and types of training that support police policy. The judgments made are then based on whether or not the officers' conduct was in accordance with law, with policy, and with community expectations of conduct. If discipline is recommended, typically the police chief is responsible for its administration.

Special Constituencies

Police often face issues regarding communities with special needs. The mentally ill are much more prominent on the streets of the nation in the wake of the deinstitutionalization movement in the 1950s that closed asylums and hospitals. Their behavior may be frightening to citizens and some are potentially dangerous. Immigrant communities bring new languages, different social customs and expectations, and often antagonism towards the police based upon their experiences with extremely corrupt and brutal police in their homelands. Police often lack the language skills and social understanding to make contact with the communities, thus hindering service. In both cases, individuals are also vulnerable targets for criminals who take advantage of their inability or reluctance to communicate with the police. In addition, community policing attempts to establish positive relations with immigrants are often in conflict with the federal laws and enforcement mandates to deport those illegally in the country. Some local agencies do not cooperate with the ICE because cooperation would inhibit their ability to protect the legitimate immigrant community. Other agencies complain that when they do apprehend illegal immigrants, the understaffed ICE cannot take them into custody and the police are forced to release them. The elderly are also emerging as a new concern for police, who have to deal with issues such as Alzheimer's disease, dementia, isolation, and loneliness.

FUTURE ISSUES

At the time of this writing, the aftermath of the attacks on the World Trade Center and the Pentagon on September 11, 2001, holds the potential for dramatic changes in the nation's police. The creation of the DHS at the cabinet level combined many smaller federal enforcement functions under a single office. Racial profiling, particularly of Arabs, has received new social support despite the continuing problems of African-American and Hispanic profiling domestically. Immigration rules are being tightened and enforcement increased, but the same problems remain for police who must deal with local immigrant communities. Civil liberties are threatened in exchange for what is believed to be greater security against terror.

Technology also poses many new challenges for the police. Computer fraud and identity theft are new forms of theft for which most police agencies are not prepared. They lack the necessary state-of-the-art equipment, and only a handful of officers have the necessary skills to track cyberspace looters, hackers, and other electronic predators. The very notion of jurisdiction changes in cyberspace, and American laws may conflict with laws of the European Union, China, and others.

Invasive technologies may soon be widely available, threatening traditional expectations of privacy. The case of *Kyllo v. United States* (2001) required the police to observe privacy as it existed in 1789 when the Constitution was adopted, banning police use of any new technologies that revealed intimate details of a house (such as thermal imagers, which were used in the *Kyllo* case). That technology may soon be widely available to the public and to the criminal element, however, requiring both new investigative skills and new countermeasures to protect police resources. Implanted chips, cloning, live human–computer interface, augmented reality systems, and many other issues will raise long-term and potentially profound changes that the police will have to face.

Social expectations are also changing. The nation's punitive drug laws are again coming under attack as too harsh, wrongly applied, and the wrong approach to the problems of drug abuse. The nature of privacy in public spaces is being redefined by closed-circuit TV and other technologies. The line dividing federal and state rights is being redefined in the states' favor by the Supreme Court at the same time that many state crimes are being "federalized" in hopes of securing harsher penalties. The impact of globalization upon the economy, laws, and social expectations of the nation—indeed, in a longer view, even upon the concept of the nation-state and sovereignty—has not fully been realized. Globalization is a long-term force with short-term ripples. The "war on terror" may be a short-term problem, but it has long-term implications for civil rights and civil liberties. Technology has implications for both and presents an even more uncertain future as the definition of what it is to be human is determined. All of these present the possibility of another period of radical change for the police, adjusting to new factors in the human and social condition.

CONCLUSION

The police are a constantly evolving network of agencies and individuals empowered to use force, but expected to use knowledge, insight, and understanding to solve a wide variety of problems that afflict American society. Because of their power to arrest, the police are the gatekeepers of the rest of the criminal justice system, but the greater impact of police work lies in situations that are resolved without arrest. Changes in police work are driven by changes in law, evolutionary changes in social attitudes, and technology. New challenges such as the impact of globalization and the intersection of American law with foreign law will be added to the ongoing challenges of proper selection, training, inculcation of values, and guidance.

Critical Thinking Exercises

1. What are some of the positive and negative consequences of having American law enforcement fragmented among so many different jurisdictions?
2. What advantages would there be to having a national police force with centralized command, universal training standards, and common equipment, salaries, and benefits?
3. Is the cause of justice served by having private police to protect the wealthy? What conflicts are possible when private police and public police jurisdictions overlap?
4. What are the relative merits of the stress academy model of training and the campus academy model? How might each be changed to provide even better preparation for street duty?
5. What can be done to mend relations that are damaged by a good-faith mistake such as the Diallo shooting? If a member of your family, a close friend, or even someone you knew casually were shot and killed by police officers under comparable circumstances, what would you expect to happen?
6. Should citizens have the power to judge the actions of a police officer via civilian review boards or other mechanisms? Or is it necessary to have been a police officer in order to determine that a police officer's decision in any matter was correct or incorrect? Is it necessary to be a doctor in order to judge medical malpractice?
7. How do you think the recent national attention to terrorism will affect law enforcement practices in the United States? How will it affect the daily activities of local police agencies and officers?

KEY WORDS

background checks	Boston Police Strike of	civilian review
beats	1919	citizen patrols
beat integrity	Broken Windows	community-oriented
blue wall of silence	campus-based academies	policing
"Bobbies"	chain of command	Community Policing Era

CompStat
consent decrees
constable
corruption
crime prevention
detective
discretion
dual-entry tracks
exclusionary rule
Field Training
   Officer (FTO)
first responders
Flint (Michigan)
   Neighborhood Foot
   Patrol Program
force continuum
HAZMAT
hue and cry
Internal Affairs
john details
Kansas City Preventive
   Patrol Experiment
law compliance
law enforcement
Law Enforcement
   Assistance
   Administration

Law Enforcement
   Education Program
Metropolitan London
   Police
Multi-Jurisdictional Task
   Forces
mutual aid
Neighborhood
   Watch
order maintenance
patrol
patronage
police academy
Police Activity League
police brutality
police subculture
Political Era
power shifts
precincts
preservice training
President's Commission
   on Law Enforcement
   and the Adminis-
   tration of Justice
private police
problem-oriented
   policing

Professional Era
property marking
racial profiling
regional task forces
rotating shifts
safe havens
school resource officers
service
sheriff
single-entry tracks
Statute of Winchester
steady shifts
sting operations
stress-based
   academies
troops
use of force
vigilantes
Watch
Wickersham
   Commission
zero tolerance

SUGGESTED READINGS

Police Culture

Crank, J.P., and Caldero, M.A. (2000). *Police ethics: The corruption of noble cause.* Cincinnati: Anderson.

Muir, W.K., Jr. (1977). *Police: Streetcorner politicians.* Chicago: University of Chicago Press.

Community-Oriented and Problem-Oriented Policing

Goldstein, H. (1979). "Improving policing: A problem-oriented approach." *Crime and Delinquency* 25:236–258.

Greene, J.R., and Mastrofski, S.D., (Eds.). (1988). *Community policing: Rhetoric or reality.* New York: Praeger.

Sparrow, M., Moore, M.H., and Kennedy, D. (1990). *Beyond 911: A new era for policing.* New York: Basic Books.

Trojanowicz, R., and Bucqueroux, B. (1990). *Community policing: A contemporary perspective.* Cincinnati: Anderson.

Modern Reform: Initial Studies

Klockars, C. (1985). *The idea of police.* Beverly Hills, CA: Sage.

Reiss, A.J., Jr. (1971). *The police and the public.* New Haven, CT: Yale University Press.✦

CHAPTER 4

The Court System

CHAPTER OUTLINE

The court system is often referred to as the link between police and the correctional system, although this is something of a misnomer. While it may be true that the court system is, in effect, the second primary aspect of the criminal justice system, its role spans the entire system. In many cases, the court system is involved in criminal cases before police make an arrest and after a person has been subject to some form of correctional sanction. Generally, the court system has two basic functions: to adjudicate defendants charged with crimes and to ensure the entire criminal justice system is engaging in fair procedures as the law is enforced. This is a large undertaking, which is why the court system is viewed as a complex, and often misunderstood, component of the criminal justice system.

BASIC TENETS OF THE COURT SYSTEM

Federal and state governments have their own laws and court systems. Although these systems may vary from state to state and between states and the federal government, all court systems have the same basic guidelines regarding the administration of laws in their respective jurisdictions.

First, the United States has what is called a **dual court system**, which simply means that the federal government has its own court system and the states have their own court systems. This may seem obvious but, when it comes to the enforcement of the law, having 51 different court systems can become quite complex. The federal court system is responsible for violations of federal law and state court systems are responsible for violations of the laws in their respective states. It becomes complicated, however, when state and federal laws conflict with one another and the court system must get involved. An example of this is seen with the use of medical marijuana. Since 1996, eleven states have passed laws allowing for the medical use of marijuana for various illnesses. Federal law, however, prohibits the use of medical marijuana. Thus, an individual in California, which authorizes the use of medical marijuana, could be held liable in federal court for use of the drug, even though it is allowed under state law. Because of this conflict between laws, the court system has to get involved to resolve the issue. Numerous individuals have challenged the federal law prohibiting the use of the drug for medical purposes, and perhaps as many have challenged state laws allowing for its use. As a result, state and federal courts have both become involved in these cases, illustrating the complex nature of a dual court system.

Another issue involving both federal and state court systems is jurisdiction. The term **jurisdiction** in the court system does not refer to a specific geographic area, but to the authority of courts to hear certain types of cases. For instance, the federal court system only has jurisdiction to rule on cases involving federal law; it does not have the ability to rule on cases involving state law, unless the state law conflicts with federal law or the U.S. Constitution. Appellate courts do not have the jurisdiction to conduct trials; this is the jurisdiction of lower state and federal trial courts. Finally, juvenile courts do not have jurisdiction to hear issues involving divorce or custody issues. In effect, each court, whether at the state or federal level, is limited in the types of cases it is allowed to rule upon. A defendant cannot simply go to any court he or she wishes in order to be heard; he or she must go to the court that specializes in the particular issue at hand.

Another tenet of state and federal court systems is the adversarial system of justice. An **adversarial system** relies on two opposing parties; in criminal cases, this involves a defendant versus the state (in the form of a prosecutor). In addition, this system involves a neutral body, in the form of the judge or jury, that decides the outcome of the case. Generally, it is the responsibility of the state to prove its case against the defendant. This reflects the presumption of innocence; in effect, a defendant is presumed innocent until proven guilty by the state. On the other hand, a defendant must challenge a state's case and question the evidence that the state brings forward. It should be known that a defendant is not responsible for proving his or her innocence at trial; the state must prove guilt.

When adjudicating cases, the court system often must balance the needs of the state versus the rights of the defendant. This is sometimes referred to as the crime-control versus due-process model of justice. Packer (1968) developed models to illustrate how the criminal justice system must try to accomplish its goals while ensuring the fair and equal application of the law. The **crime-control model**, as its name implies, focuses on the reduction of criminal behavior. It stresses the swiftness and certainty of case outcomes, suggesting that any delay in the adjudication of criminal cases undermines the ability of the system to reduce crime. The crime-control model posits that many defendants who are arrested are factually guilty, so the court system should waste no time in convicting and sentencing them. On the other hand, the **due-process model** emphasizes the protection of rights of defendants. This model is concerned about the violation of rights in the name of crime control and works to ensure that the criminal justice system does not violate the law in order to enforce the law. It views swiftness in the administration of justice as a concern, as it increases the likelihood of mistakes being made and innocent people being punished. The criminal justice system has tried to strike a balance between these two competing models although, at times, one or the other predominates. The court system is the primary component of the system that is charged with ensuring that the law is enforced in a fair and equal manner.

Critical Thinking Exercise

How well has the court system balanced the crime-control and due-process models? Which model do you believe is dominant in criminal courts? Is this appropriate? Should it be changed? How? Why?

HISTORY OF THE COURTS

Chapter 2 discussed the origins of criminal law in this country, and the court system has largely been responsible for ensuring that the law is enforced fairly and equally. However, the term *court system* is a very general one and encompasses a number of courts at both the federal and state levels. As such, it is important to understand the history of both the federal and state court systems in order to appreciate the role of the courts today.

History of Federal Courts

As the U.S. Constitution was being drafted, many of the drafters felt it was necessary to create a national court system. During the Constitutional Convention in 1787, two competing plans were proposed to establish the federal court system. The New Jersey Plan called for the establishment of one federal court: a Supreme Court. This plan called for the state court systems to play an active role in adjudicating federal matters. In effect, proponents of the New Jersey Plan were skeptical of a strong, centralized federal judiciary and wanted the states to maintain some control over federal court matters. Under this plan, state courts would conduct trials and other lower-level federal court proceedings, and the process of appeal would take the case to the one federal Supreme Court.

An alternative, the Virginia Plan, proposed a broader and more centralized federal court system with the establishment of a Supreme Court and various lower federal courts. This plan argued that states should not be involved in federal court matters and that the federal government should have a judiciary system just as states do. A compromise between these two competing plans was reached, and the result is found in Article III of the U.S. Constitution: "The judicial power of the United States, shall be vested in one supreme court, and in such inferior courts as the Congress may from time to time ordain and establish." In essence, this created the one Supreme Court that both plans advocated, but allowed Congress to create lower federal courts when necessary. At first, this compromise seemed to benefit the proponents of the New Jersey Plan, as no vast federal court system was created. However, over time, the compromise greatly favored the proponents of the Virginia Plan, who eventually saw the creation of a centralized federal court system.

Since the U.S. Constitution allowed Congress to establish lower federal courts, it was only a matter of time before these courts were created. One of the first concerns of the first Congress was the creation of the lower federal court system. In the Judiciary Act of 1789, the lower federal court system was finally established. This act further defined the role and makeup of the Supreme Court and established two levels of lower federal courts: trial courts and appellate courts.

U.S. Supreme Court. The Judiciary Act of 1789 stated that the Supreme Court was to consist of one chief justice and five associate justices. In its first decade of existence, the Court floundered, not really knowing or understanding its role in a federal system of government. According to Carp and Stidham (1990), the Court did not rule on a case in its first three years of existence and decided only around 50 cases during its first decade. This situation was greatly altered, however, with the appointment of John Marshall as the third chief justice in 1801. Marshall is credited with giving the Supreme Court its vision and establishing rules and guidelines that governed the Court's procedures. One of these guidelines was the issuance of a single opinion of the Court. Until this point, each individual justice issued his own ruling with his own rationale; this made it quite difficult for those responsible for enforcing the rulings to know what to do. Marshall created the practice of allowing one opinion of the Court (now called the *ruling of the Court* or the *majority opinion*) in order for the Court to present an air of unification around a particular ruling. During Marshall's tenure, the Court was involved in a number of rulings that are considered some of the most important decisions in judicial history (see Box 4.1).

The U.S. Supreme Court is considered the final arbiter for issues involving federal law and the U.S. Constitution. Once the U.S. Supreme Court has made a decision in a case, that decision is final and cannot be reviewed by any other court. Although the Court has primarily appellate jurisdiction, it does have original jurisdiction in some cases. For example, the Court is the first and only court to hear cases involving disputes between two states, such as boundary disputes.

Today, the U.S. Supreme Court is composed of one chief justice and eight associate justices. When deciding to hear cases, the U.S. Supreme Court has a large amount of discretion, unlike the courts of appeals. The Court hears oral arguments in only a fraction of cases petitioned for review each year. In fact, out of approximately 7,000 cases on the Court's docket each year, only about 100 are selected for oral arguments (a link to a website illustrating this fact and the court's docket can be found on the textbook website at http://www.oup.com/us/labessentials). The U.S. Supreme Court only hears cases that involve what it considers to be the most important policy issues. Cases that come to the Court come from the U.S. Courts of Appeals (for cases involving federal law) and state supreme courts (for cases involving conflicts with federal law or state violations of the U.S. Constitution).

U.S. Courts of Appeals. The Judiciary Act of 1789 also established the appellate courts of the federal system. The country was divided into federal court circuits—southern, middle, and eastern—and an appellate court was established for each. The courts were staffed by two U.S. Supreme Court justices and a lower federal court judge (called a "district judge," which will be examined later). The lower court judge was responsible for establishing the court's caseload, and the Supreme Court justices traveled to each circuit to hear cases at the appellate level, a practice known as "circuit riding." This practice was grueling for the justices and the caseload of the appellate courts increased, especially after the Civil War, making the existing system ill equipped to handle a mounting workload. This system of hearing appellate cases continued until 1891, when Congress passed the Evarts Act. This act created nine federal appellate courts, one for each judicial circuit at the time, that were to hear appeals from the lower federal trial courts. Each appellate court, called a "circuit court," was staffed by newly created circuit court judges, thereby relieving the U.S. Supreme Court justices of their circuit-riding duties. This created a more uniform system of hearing appeals.

The U.S. Courts of Appeals have **appellate jurisdiction**, which means that cases do not originate there and these courts only hear cases that are brought up on appeal, after a lower court has decided an outcome. When federal appellate courts were established in 1789, the country was divided into three appellate circuits. Today, there are 11 appellate circuits, and each circuit consists of multiple states.

BOX 4.1

Key U.S. Supreme Court Rulings During John Marshall's Tenure as Chief Justice

Marbury v. Madison (1803)

This case established the Court's practice of judicial review. In this case, President John Adams, during his lame-duck presidency, created numerous federal judgeships. The judgeships were approved by the Senate but, when President Thomas Jefferson took office, four of the judicial appointees had not received their commissions. The secretary of state, James Madison, refused to deliver the commissions, as he and the new president disapproved of the newly created judgeships. The four judicial appointees asked the U.S. Supreme Court to force Madison to deliver the commissions, relying on a writ of mandamus, a federal provision that allows a court to compel a public official to perform a duty. The U.S. Supreme Court refused to intervene, finding that the federal provision gave the Court a power that the U.S. Constitution did not give it; that is, unless the U.S. Constitution states that the Court can or must enforce a writ of mandamus, any law that says otherwise is unconstitutional. Thus, the U.S. Supreme Court struck down the federal provision as unconstitutional and established the practice of judicial review—the ability to declare laws unconstitutional.

McCulloch v. Maryland (1819)

This case dealt with the powers of the federal government over those of the states. In 1791, Secretary of the Treasury Alexander Hamilton wanted Congress to charter a national bank called the Bank of the United States. Thomas Jefferson, who was secretary of state at the time, opposed the national bank, claiming that the U.S. Constitution did not give Congress the power to charter one. Hamilton disagreed, claiming that the "necessary and proper" clause in Article I gave Congress the authority to enact policies for the good of the nation. The bank was created and given a 20-year charter. When the charter expired in 1811, it was not renewed. After the War of 1812, it was evident that a national bank was needed to handle the business of the nation. As a result, the second Bank of the United States was chartered in 1816. State and local banks did not agree with the creation of the national bank, so state legislatures looked to restrict the bank's business. In Maryland, a tax was imposed on bank operations. James McCulloch, a cashier at the Baltimore branch of the Bank of the United States, refused to pay the tax and the case went to court. Ultimately, the U.S. Supreme Court ruled that the national bank was constitutional and that the federal government has broad powers to enact laws for the good of the nation. In effect, this case allows the federal government to trump state governments on issues in which the governments conflict.

Barron v. Baltimore (1833)

This case involved the power of the U.S. Supreme Court to become involved in cases in which state governments violate the rights of their citizens. In Baltimore, Barron owned a profitable wharf. The city of Baltimore wished to repave the streets near the wharf, and when the streets were excavated, the debris slid into Barron's

(continued)

BOX 4.1   *(continued)*

wharf, rendering it useless. Barron objected, claiming that, since the city of Baltimore had ruined his business, he should be compensated. He claimed that the just-compensation clause of the Fifth Amendment required the government to pay for any damages. Initially, Barron won his case in lower court, but the U.S. Supreme Court ruled against Barron, deciding that the just-compensation clause of the Fifth Amendment applied only to the federal government. In effect, the U.S. Supreme Court refused to apply the just-compensation clause to Barron's case, finding that, if state or local governments violate one's rights, one must look to the state or local courts for a remedy, not the federal courts. This ruling set the stage for a century of cases in which the U.S. Supreme Court refused to apply the protections of the Bill of Rights to state actions. Ultimately, the U.S. Supreme Court applied, or incorporated, these rights to the states and, now, states must offer the protections found in the federal Bill of Rights.

There is one U.S. Court of Appeals in each of these circuits, and these courts are identified by their circuit, for example, the U.S. Court of Appeals for the Eighth Circuit. There are two other federal appellate courts. One represents the D.C. Circuit (Washington DC) and one represents the Federal Circuit, which handles cases involving international trade and federal administrative law. See Box 4.2 for an illustration of the courts of appeals.

According to Neubauer (2004), approximately 57,000 cases are filed each year in the courts of appeals. Of these, only about 20 percent involve federal criminal law issues. Although decisions by the U.S. Courts of Appeals may be petitioned for review by the U.S. Supreme Court, these federal appellate courts are often the "court of last resort" for federal law because the U.S. Supreme Court rarely reviews decisions made by these courts.

Most of the cases heard by the courts of appeals come from the federal district courts. Defendants must appeal their cases in the courts that cover their states. The federal courts of appeals have no control over the cases they hear; that is, there is no discretionary authority to reject appeals. When deciding cases, the courts of appeals usually utilize three-judge panels, which rotate membership periodically. A majority of the panel is sufficient for a ruling. In rare instances, all of the judges in a circuit may sit to hear a case. This is called an **en bane proceeding**.

U.S. District Courts. The trial courts of the federal system, 13 district courts, were established by the Judiciary Act of 1789. The 11 states in the union at the time and the territories of Maine and Kentucky were considered districts, so the organization of the federal trial courts was entirely state-contained; that is, no federal district crossed state lines. Each district court was staffed by one district court judge who, as mentioned earlier, also had a role in hearing appellate cases. As new states entered the union, more district courts were created.

After the creation of the lower federal courts in 1789, each state was considered a district with one district court. Today, some states are divided into multiple districts because they are simply too populated to have just one district

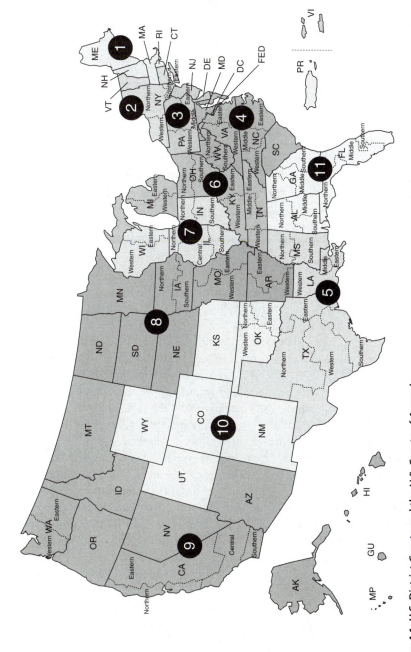

Figure 4.1 U.S. District Courts and the U.S. Courts of Appeals

SOURCE: Federal Judiciary website. http://www.uscourts.gov/images/CircuitMap.pdf.

court. There is at least one district court in every state. There are currently 90 district courts in the 50 states and the District of Columbia and four others in Guam, Puerto Rico, the U.S. Virgin Islands, and the Northern Mariana Islands. See Figure 4.1 for an illustration of the various district courts.

As mentioned above, district courts are the trial courts of the federal system. According to Neubauer (2004), approximately 67,000 criminal cases are filed in district courts every year, mostly for federal drug violations and various white-collar offenses. Despite this, civil cases compose the bulk of cases that move through the district courts. U.S. District Courts have **original jurisdiction**, which means that these courts have the authority to hear cases for the first time and decide an outcome.

History of State Courts

The federal court system is probably better known to the public, but state court systems were in existence before the federal court system was established. In colonial times, local courts, often called justice of the peace courts or magistrate courts, handled lower-level court matters. County courts were the trial courts of the colonies and appeals were handled by the royal governor (Carp and Stidham 1990). After the revolution, state court structure was largely the same as that of the colonial courts, although the royal governor was no longer present.

The various states had largely been left to their own devices when it came to the creation and administration of their court systems. Most states had systems for handling various levels of court procedures, such as trials and appeals, but encountered problems as industrialization and population increased after the Civil War. Local courts began to struggle with increased caseloads and different types of cases, which involved newly created laws dealing with issues such as business and child labor. As a result, state courts were forced to find innovative ways to deal with these issues, including creating more courts and specialized courts, although some states are still facing some of the same problems today.

State Supreme Courts. These courts are the courts of last resort for issues involving state law. Most states call these courts "supreme courts," but a few designate them as "courts of appeals" or other names. The number of judges who serve on state supreme courts varies depending upon the state, but the judges hear cases en banc. These courts have original jurisdiction in some matters, but largely have appellate jurisdiction. Like the U.S. Supreme Court, state supreme courts exercise a fair amount of discretion in deciding which cases to hear. As a result, appeals involving state law typically will end at the intermediate appellate court level.

State Courts of Appeals. These courts are often called "intermediate courts of appeals" because they compose the middle level of the court system between trial courts and the state supreme courts. Despite this, 11 states do not have intermediate courts of appeals; the appeal load is so low that this level of court is not needed. In these situations, the state supreme court is the only state appellate court. State courts of appeals primarily have appellate jurisdiction.

State courts of appeals do not exercise the same amount of discretion as the state supreme courts; they must hear all appeals that are filed with the court in order to provide a resolution to each. Because of this, the state supreme court is able to exercise much discretion because many appeals are resolved at the intermediate level. In those states that do not employ intermediate appellate courts, state supreme courts must hear all appeals and provide resolutions.

The number of judges serving on state courts of appeals varies depending upon the state. Like the federal courts of appeals, cases at this level are typically heard by three-judge panels. As stated earlier, most appeals end at this stage because the state supreme court is highly discretionary when selecting appeals to hear.

Trial Courts of General Jurisdiction. These courts are considered the major trial courts at the state level. These courts handle the more serious criminal and civil cases that arise in state courts. The actual names of these courts vary depending upon the state, but most **trial courts of general jurisdiction** are called "district," "circuit," or "superior" courts.

Generally, each state is divided into districts, usually counties, and each district employs one major trial court. In rural areas, these districts may encompass several counties and judges will travel to each county in the district to hear cases. In other areas, judges are assigned to specific courthouses and cases come to them. According to Neubauer (2004), over 30 million cases are filed each year in these courts, vastly outnumbering the number of cases filed in federal trial courts.

Trial Courts of Limited Jurisdiction. These courts compose the lowest level of courts in the state court system. These courts go by a variety of names, including "magistrate," "municipal," "city," and "justice of the peace" courts. They have limited jurisdiction because they are restricted to handling only certain types of matters: in effect, minor matters. In criminal cases, these minor matters include misdemeanors, but they also include the early stages of felony cases, such as first appearances, bail hearings, and appointment of counsel. These courts also handle cases involving traffic and small claims issues.

Although **trial courts of limited jurisdiction** are restricted in the *types* of matters they can handle, they constitute the bulk of court systems in the country— about 85 percent of all judicial bodies. As such, the *number* of cases that are handled by these courts has grown over time, now over 60 million cases per year (Neubauer 2004). This has resulted in overcrowding problems, when courts do not have the resources to handle the increasing numbers of cases coming into the system. The number of each of these courts varies from state to state and more populated areas have numerous courts of limited jurisdication in certain counties.

State courts vary in organization and structure. Additionally, state courts have different names for their courts. Box 4.2 illustrates three different court systems. California has a streamlined and organized court system; throughout the state, all courts of limited and general jurisdiction are called "superior courts." California's intermediate appellate courts are called "courts of appeal" and its court of last resort is called the "supreme court."

Ohio has four types of limited-jurisdiction courts, each handling similar cases. Counties and cities in Ohio vary as to which type of limited-jurisdiction court they will use. For example, municipal courts are found in 127 municipalities (cities) in

BOX 4.2

California
(Court structure as of Fiscal Year 2007)

Supreme Court   COLR

7 justices sit en banc   A

CSP Case Types:
- Mandatory jurisdiction in capital criminal, disciplinary cases.
- Discretionary jurisdiction in civil, noncapital criminal, administrative agency, juvenile, original proceeding, interlocutory decision cases.

                                                                     link

↑

Courts of Appeal (6 courts/districts)   IAC

105 justices sit in panels   A

CSP Case Types:
- Mandatory jurisdiction in civil, noncapital criminal, administrative agency, juvenile cases.
- Discretionary jurisdiction in administrative agency, original proceeding, interlocutory decision cases.

                                                                     link

↑

Superior Court (58 counties)   GJC

1,548 judges, 423 commissioners and referees   A
Jury trials except in appeals, domestic relations, and juvenile cases

CSP Case Types:
- Tort, contract, real property ($25,000–no maximum), miscellaneous civil. Exclusive small claims (up to $5,000), probate/estate, mental health, civil appeals. [Limited jurisdiction: tort, contract, real property ($0–$25,000).]
- Exclusive domestic relations.
- Exclusive criminal.
- Exclusive juvenile.
- Exclusive traffic/other violations.

                                                                     link

SOURCE: National Center for State Courts website. Retrieved May 20, 2009, from http://www. ncsconline.org/D Research/Ct Struct/state inc.asp?STATE=CA

Ohio
(Court structure as of Calendar Year 2007)

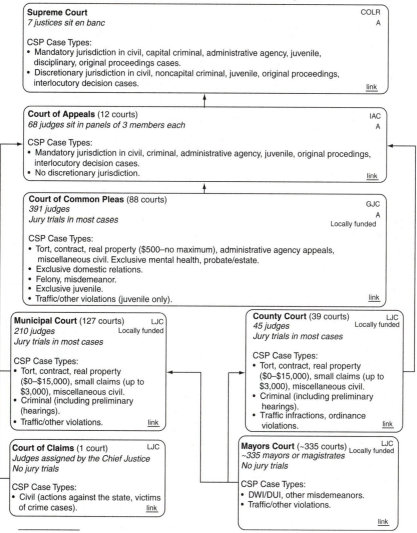

Supreme Court   COLR
7 justices sit en banc   A

CSP Case Types:
- Mandatory jurisdiction in civil, capital criminal, administrative agency, juvenile, disciplinary, original proceedings cases.
- Discretionary jurisdiction in civil, noncapital criminal, juvenile, original proceedings, interlocutory decision cases.   link

Court of Appeals (12 courts)   IAC
68 judges sit in panels of 3 members each   A

CSP Case Types:
- Mandatory jurisdiction in civil, criminal, administrative agency, juvenile, original procedings, interlocutory decision cases.
- No discretionary jurisdiction.   link

Court of Common Pleas (88 courts)   GJC
391 judges   A
Jury trials in most cases   Locally funded

CSP Case Types:
- Tort, contract, real property ($500–no maximum), administrative agency appeals, miscellaneous civil. Exclusive mental health, probate/estate.
- Exclusive domestic relations.
- Felony, misdemeanor.
- Exclusive juvenile.
- Traffic/other violations (juvenile only).   link

Municipal Court (127 courts)   LJC
210 judges   Locally funded
Jury trials in most cases

CSP Case Types:
- Tort, contract, real property ($0–$15,000), small claims (up to $3,000), miscellaneous civil.
- Criminal (including preliminary (hearings).
- Traffic/other violations.   link

County Court (39 courts)   LJC
45 judges   Locally funded
Jury trials in most cases

CSP Case Types:
- Tort, contract, real property ($0–$15,000), small claims (up to $3,000), miscellaneous civil.
- Criminal (including preliminary hearings).
- Traffic infractions, ordinance violations.   link

Court of Claims (1 court)   LJC
Judges assigned by the Chief Justice
No jury trials

CSP Case Types:
- Civil (actions against the state, victims of crime cases).   link

Mayors Court (~335 courts)   LJC
~335 mayors or magistrates   Locally funded
No jury trials

CSP Case Types:
- DWI/DUI, other misdemeanors.
- Traffic/other violations.   link

SOURCE: National Center for State Courts website. Retrieved May 20, 2009, from http://www. ncsconline.org/D Research/Ct Struct/state inc.asp?STATE=OH

(continued)

BOX 4.2   *(continued)*

New York
(Court structure as of Calendar Year 2007)

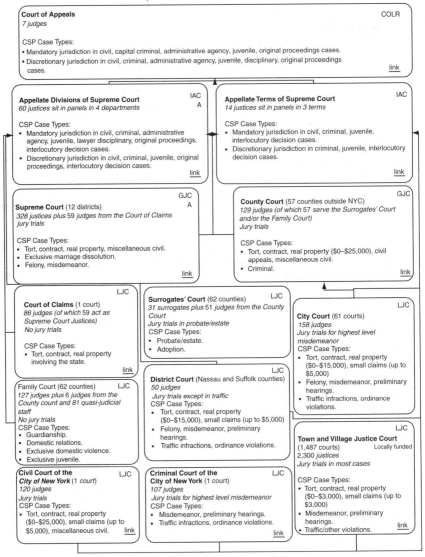

SOURCE: National Center for State Courts website. Retrieved May 20, 2009, from http://www. ncsconline.org/D Research/Ct Struct/state inc.asp?STATE=NY

Ohio, but there are only 39 county courts statewide. Generally, a particular county will have only one or the other operating within the county. Additionally, Ohio's trial courts of general jurisdiction are called "courts of common pleas," which is a unique name for this type of court. This name is a holdover from British common-law courts in existence in England until the 1800s. Most states call these courts "superior courts," "district courts," "circuit courts," and the like. Ohio's court of last resort is called the "supreme court."

Finally, New York provides a good illustration of a state court structure in need of organization. New York has eight limited-jurisdiction courts; again, the county or city will determine which court it will use. Additionally, New York has two trial courts of general jurisdiction—called a "supreme court" and a "county court"—with county courts operating outside of New York City. New York also has two inter-mediate appellate courts; counties in New York are combined into "departments" and each department has an appellate court that serves those counties. The first intermediate appellate court, the "Appellate Divisions of Supreme Court," serves departments outside of New York City. The second appellate court is called the "Appellate Terms of Supreme Court" and this court handles appeals from depart-ments representing the counties encompassing New York City. Finally, New York's court of last resort is called the "court of appeals." As can be seen, states differ widely in the way they structure their courts.

TRENDS IN THE COURT SYSTEM

Specialized Courts

In many areas, the court systems have had to devise ways to handle the increasing numbers of people coming into contact with the criminal justice system, especially those with special needs. Special-needs offenders are those who are repeatedly seen in the system due to issues such as drug and alcohol abuse and mental illness. Court systems have created specialty courts that deal exclusively with certain types of offenders.

Drug Courts. Due to the increased enforcement and punishment of drug offenses in the past 20 years, court systems have become bogged down with large numbers of relatively minor drug offenders. As a result, many court systems created **drug courts** to process these cases efficiently without taking up the time and resources of the lower courts. Drug courts have been in existence since the mid-1980s and are in operation or are being planned in every state. Despite this, drug courts are not utilized statewide, either because particular areas have no need for them or because states simply cannot afford to operate them.

Drug courts emphasize treatment of lower-level drug offenders. A lower court typically identifies these offenders and transfers the cases to a drug court. The drug court then establishes a treatment program that entails drug treatment, counseling, and employment and life-skills training. The offenders are usually released into the community and must meet with judges periodically. This is similar to probation, but it is not a probation sentence. The offenders are monitored by judges, not probation officers, and the judges ensure that the offenders are progressing through the treatment program.

The success of drug courts has been mixed. The research that has been conducted has found that offenders who were processed through drug courts and successfully completed their treatment programs had lower recidivism rates than offenders who were not processed through drug courts. This success is tempered, however, by the fact that being processed through drug courts and undergoing treatment is largely voluntary on the part of offenders. In effect, the success of drug courts could be explained by the possibility that offenders who volunteer to go through the drug court process want help for their problems and are willing to go through treatment (see Arnold et al. 2000).

Mental-Health Courts. It has been estimated that 5–15 percent of incarcerated offenders suffer from some form of mental illness. Many jails and prisons do not provide adequate treatment of mental illness while offenders are incarcerated, and fewer establish procedures for aftercare once the offenders are released. As a result, the mental illness, which may have contributed to the offenders' criminal behavior, remains untreated and the offenders are in no better position than they were before incarceration. This has led to the creation of **mental-health courts** in some areas. These courts establish guidelines for mental-health treatment in lieu of other punishments. Typically, mental-health courts place restrictions on the types of offenders that they process; for instance, these courts may prohibit eligibility for violent offenders.

Mental-health courts work with community-treatment programs to establish appropriate procedures for both the treatment of the offenders and the safety of the community. Offenders are closely monitored throughout their treatment programs, which usually consist of not only mental-health treatment, but also life-skills and vocational training. If an offender successfully completes the program, some courts authorize removal of the original criminal charges from the offender's record (see Slate 2000).

Research on the effectiveness of mental-health courts has found some success. An assessment of Seattle's mental-health court found that the court is successfully identifying offenders in need of treatment and that the treatment program itself has reduced recidivism (see Trupin et al. 2001).

ACTORS IN THE COURT SYSTEM

Each level of the court system in state and federal courts consists of individuals who are responsible for processing defendants through the system. This chapter has already mentioned judges with regard to their presence at the various levels of the court system, and the judge is perhaps the most visible actor in court. There are two other prominent actors, the prosecutor and the defense attorney, who occupy equally important positions. The judge, prosecutor, and defense attorney compose the **courtroom workgroup**, a concept used to illustrate how each individual actor works with the other actors to move cases through the court system. Although the criminal justice system is considered an adversarial system, there are no true adversaries in practice. Generally, prosecutors and defense attorneys work together to create mutually beneficial case outcomes, and judges are on hand to assist in the negotiations. This process is typically seen in overcrowded court systems, when all participants are eager to move cases off of their dockets and out of the system quickly through the use of practices such as guilty pleas or dismissals. In addition to the major actors in the court system, there are other actors such as clerks of court, court administrators, bailiffs, probation officers, and others who serve important functions in the court system.

Judges

As mentioned, **judges** are perhaps the most visible actors in the court system. They are also considered the most powerful, since they make many important decisions at all levels of the court system. They also exercise a large amount of discretion, as evidenced by the many roles that judges undertake. In lower courts, judges conduct bail hearings, assign counsel, accept guilty pleas, conduct misdemeanor trials, sentence defendants, conduct preliminary hearings, issue warrants, and rule on the admissibility of evidence. In trial courts, judges preside over felony trials and sentence defendants. At the appellate level, judges review decisions of lower courts and issue rulings based on the merits of the case. Judges are present at every level of the court system and issue important rulings on every aspect of a case.

Federal Judges. The path to becoming a judge in the federal court system is fairly straightforward. Federal judges are called "Article III" judges because their appointment is outlined in Article III of the U.S. Constitution. The president nominates a person for a federal judgeship, and that person must be confirmed by the Senate. Federal judges serve no specified terms of office; instead, they have life tenure and leave the federal bench through either retirement, death, or impeachment. There are no formal qualifications for becoming a federal judge, such as a minimum age requirement or minimum experience practicing law. There are, however, informal qualifications that can determine whether an individual is appointed to the federal bench. Typically, nominees have distinguished law careers or have actively supported the political party in office. As such, federal judges are considered political appointees and must endure a highly political process to be confirmed by the Senate.

An advantage of judicial appointment is that it leaves the decision to individuals who are able to judge the qualifications of a particular candidate. It also allows judges to make their decisions a little more freely, in that they are not subject to the will of the public and election cycles. A disadvantage is that the appointment is quite political, with ideology overshadowing qualifications in some cases. In addition, federal judges who make unpopular decisions cannot be removed from the bench easily. Life tenure enables judges to stay on the bench for an extended period of time.

State Judges. There are varying routes to becoming a state judge. Over half of the states utilize an election process, where voters decide who will be the next judge in their community. One type of election is called a **partisan election**, in which candidates declare a political affiliation. Other states utilize the **nonpartisan election**, in which the candidates' political affiliations are not specified. Despite this, a judicial candidate's party affiliation usually becomes known because the state's political parties contribute money to their candidates' campaigns. Elected judges usually serve a term of office and must be reelected after the term is complete.

An advantage of judicial elections is that the public can choose judges it feels are best qualified to serve. Also, judges can be held accountable for their rulings and voted out of office if the public feels they are not performing well. A disadvantage of judicial elections is that they are often not as publicized as other elections, and the public may not educate itself on the qualifications of a particular candidate, voting instead on criteria that have little to do with a judge's ability to serve.

Another selection method found in some states is called **merit selection**. This method involves a group of lawyers and citizens who make recommendations to the governor about qualified nominees. The governor ultimately appoints the judge, who serves a short term of office, perhaps a year, and then is placed on the ballot for a "retention election." This retention election asks voters if they wish to retain the judge for a full term of office. The vast majority of judges are retained by voters.

An advantage of merit selection is that it takes partisan politics out of the process: lawyers and citizens hold the cards in the selection. Also, merit selection gives voters a chance to see a judge in action before he or she is retained: voters do not have to wait for a full judicial term (usually six years) to vote someone out of office. A disadvantage is that, although power is taken away from political parties, it gives more power to the legal profession, which may reward its own.

A final selection method for state judges is gubernatorial or legislative appointment. Only a handful of states allow either the governor or legislature to appoint judges. In this system, the governor or the state legislature has the sole authority to appoint judges; there is usually no other entity (such as the Senate in federal cases) to approve the choice of the governor or legislature. The governor or legislature is also responsible for reappointment after the term of office is complete.

As with the federal system, politics comes into play with gubernatorial and legislative selection. Governors may give appointments to those who have supported their campaigns or those who could help them politically. According to Carp and Stidham (1990), legislatures often appoint former lawmakers to the post; in fact, the authors claim that legislatures appoint their former members as judges in 80 percent of cases.

Prosecutors

While judges are considered the most visible actors in the court system, prosecutors often work behind closed doors. Much of what prosecutors do is not readily visible to the public; as a result, the role of the prosecutor is cloaked in mystery. **Prosecutors** are most often seen by the public in courtrooms arguing cases on behalf of the state, but this constitutes only a small portion of their time. In the early stages of a case, prosecutors make bail recommendations to judges, file charges against defendants, conduct preliminary hearings and grand jury proceedings, file motions with judges, engage in plea agreements, represent the state at trial, and make sentencing recommendations.

Critical Thinking Exercise

Similar to the earlier issue of lifetime appointments, political appointments to the bench are not without controversy. Do you believe this is an appropriate means for seating judges? Does this process guarantee quality judges, or does it open the door for less-than-qualified judges? If the latter, what problems can this create? What changes (if any) should be made in this system?

Federal Prosecutors. Prosecutors in the federal court system work for the U.S. Department of Justice. As head of this department, the U.S. attorney general is nominated by the president, confirmed by the Senate, and serves as a member of the president's cabinet. The position of attorney general is largely an administrative one, directing the work of those who work for the department. As such, he or she is not involved in everyday federal court matters. This responsibility is given to U.S. attorneys and their assistants.

As mentioned earlier, the country is divided into federal court districts, and each district is assigned a U.S. attorney and multiple assistant U.S. attorneys. U.S. attorneys are nominated by the president and confirmed by the Senate, and assistant U.S. attorneys are appointed by the attorney general. These individuals have the responsibility of prosecuting cases in federal court and defending the United States when it is sued in civil court. U.S. attorneys are able to exercise tremendous discretion in their jobs; there is no real formal oversight of U.S. attorneys in their respective districts.

State and Local Prosecutors. The role of prosecutors at the state and local levels is not that much different than their role at the federal level, although the route to becoming a prosecutor at the state level differs. Like the federal system, states have attorneys general, who are usually selected by voters in statewide elections. The role of the state attorney general differs from state to state, but one main characteristic is the lack of authority over local prosecutors. In effect, the state attorney general does not have much authority to get involved in matters at the local level, limiting his or her role to providing legal advice and defending the state when it is sued in civil court. In recent years, state attorneys general have become increasingly involved in civil matters, especially matters that involve consumer protection.

The individuals responsible for prosecuting violations of criminal laws are the local prosecutors. Local prosecutors are usually elected at the county level, and they represent the county in which they are elected. These prosecutors are called by a number of titles; the most common are "district attorney," "chief prosecutor," and "county attorney." The chief prosecutor's job in a county is both administrative and prosecutorial, in that he or she organizes and directs the responsibilities of assistants as well as going to court and prosecuting criminal defendants in higher-profile felony cases. The assistants, often called assistant district attorneys or assistant prosecutors, are largely responsible for the early stages of a criminal case and minor criminal offenses. These assistants are typically hired by the chief prosecutor and are not subject to election by voters. It has been noted by Neubauer (2004) that assistant district attorneys are usually hired right out of law school, work only a few years at a prosecutor's office, and use the office as a stepping-stone into private practice or upper-level positions in the criminal justice system (such as judge).

Defense Attorneys

Defense attorneys have the (largely) thankless job of defending the accused against prosecution by the government. Although defendants in the criminal justice system have the right to be represented by an attorney, many cannot afford their services. As a result, the U.S. Supreme Court has ruled in a number of decisions that poor individuals have the right to an appointed attorney in certain cases. The various forms of defense attorneys are discussed below.

Private Attorneys. Private attorneys, or retained counsel, are hired by defendants, who pay for the attorneys' legal services. Defendants who can afford them may have their attorneys represent them in any type and at any stage of a criminal case. In these instances, defendants literally get what they pay for and are able to have continuous representation if they can afford it. However, the bulk of criminal defendants cannot afford to pay for their own attorneys and must use attorneys provided by the government. In fact, in some areas, up to 80 percent of felony defendants are considered too poor to hire an attorney (Smith and DeFrances 1996).

Appointed Attorneys. As mentioned earlier, a number of U.S. Supreme Court rulings have insisted that defendants can have appointed attorneys represent them if they cannot afford one. In *Gideon v. Wainwright* (1963), the Court ruled that poor defendants charged with felonies have the right to court-appointed counsel. In the subsequent cases *Argersinger v. Hamlin* (1972) and *Scott v. Illinois* (1979), the Court extended the right to court-appointed counsel to defendants who face imprisonment. Although this seems like a victory for poor defendants, in reality, defendants do not have the right to court-appointed attorneys if they do not face imprisonment; thus, defendants who are subject only to probation or fines are not entitled to court-appointed counsel. In addition, although private attorneys can represent their clients at any stage of a criminal case, court-appointed counsel is generally not guaranteed at stages that are not deemed "critical," such as lineups, grand jury proceedings, and some appeals.

At both the state and federal levels, the methods of providing and appointing counsel vary. At the federal level, Congress is responsible for organizing and appropriating funds to the various districts for provision of counsel. In the states, most methods are organized and financed by the state and/or county. In general, there are three methods of providing counsel to poor defendants: assigned counsel, public defenders, and contract systems.

One of the appointed counsel systems involves the appointment of private attorneys who volunteer their services to the court. This **assigned counsel** system is primarily utilized in areas with smaller caseloads, since it is more economically feasible to provide counsel on a case-by-case basis. Typically, a judge maintains a list of eligible attorneys and chooses one when a case arises. These attorneys are usually paid on an hourly or per-case basis, but the rate of compensation is generally low, so low that critics question their ability to provide effective representation. In fact, in 2000, the New York County Lawyer's Association successfully sued the city of New York to increase the compensation of court-appointed attorneys. Since 1986, court-appointed attorneys had been paid $40/hour for in-court work and $25/hour for out-of-court work, the third-lowest compensation in the nation. As a result of the lawsuit, court-appointed attorneys were able to restructure their compensation to be paid $75/hour for felony cases and $60/hour for misdemeanors. This compensation is quite small when compared to private attorneys, who can charge hundreds of dollars per hour for their services (Caher and Riccardi 2000).

A second type of appointed counsel system is the **public defender**. The public-defender system is usually a state- or county-administered organization that specializes in defending the poor. A public defender's office is usually staffed by numerous attorneys who are paid a yearly salary for their services. This system is typically found in medium- and large-sized urban areas that have considerable caseloads. Some proponents of a public-defender system claim that the attorneys are able to provide expert criminal defense, because it is the only thing they do. Despite this, public-defender systems have long been criticized for providing inadequate representation due to the numbers of cases they must contend with. In effect, although they may be experts in their field, public defenders may not have the time to concentrate on cases the way they should.

A third type of appointed-counsel system is called the **contract system**, which is relatively new compared to the other two. In this type of system, private attorneys bid to represent poor defendants for a fixed fee and a specified period of time. This method is seen as a way to save money on indigent defense because the state or county will likely choose the attorney who puts in the lowest bid. A down side is that the quality of representation may be low, because the attorney has only a set amount of money to use when defending clients.

Although not considered a formal, government-sponsored method of providing indigent defense, legal aid societies are being formed in many larger cities to work in conjunction with the established method in that area. **Legal aid** societies are usually supported by private contributions, which provide payment for the services performed by the attorneys who work for the organization. In addition, some attorneys work **pro bono**, donating their services out of what they see as a professional obligation. Finally, criminal defendants are allowed to represent themselves (called **pro se**), provided they meet certain requirements established by the judge in a particular case.

Regardless of the type of criminal defense, all attorneys are required to provide effective assistance of counsel, according to the U.S. Supreme Court's ruling in

McMann v. Richardson (1970). Since this ruling, the U.S. Supreme Court has established guidelines for defendants to meet if they claim that their attorney provided ineffective assistance of counsel. In general, defendants must prove that the outcome of their case would have been different if their attorney had been effective, which is extremely difficult to prove (see *Strickland v. Washington* [1984]).

Critical Thinking Exercise

Debate over the quality of legal representation often involves the relative merits of hired versus appointed counsel. Many critics claim that those who can afford to hire their own counsel fare better in court. Do you believe that this is true? Investigate this claim. What evidence is there to support this position? What evidence is there that this position is false?

Other Court Actors

Many individuals work in the courtroom besides the various types of attorneys discussed above. **Bailiffs** are responsible for maintaining order in the courtroom, and law enforcement officers—usually deputies—transport detained defendants between the courthouse and jail. Probation officers work with the court to monitor those individuals who are sentenced to probation. In addition, probation officers are often responsible for completing a presentence investigation of a defendant. This involves providing the sentencing judge with detailed information about the defendant and the crime so that the judge may consider a number of issues before imposing a sentence.

There are numerous individuals who are responsible for the administrative aspects of the court. **Clerks of court** are the record keepers of the case files that come before the court every day. **Court reporters** create a transcribed record of proceedings as they occur. **Court administrators** are responsible for supervising court staff and working with the judge on issues such as budgets and personnel.

Besides formal court personnel, there are others who appear in court from time to time. Victims and witnesses often come to court for official proceedings or to inquire about the state of their cases. Victims may also utilize **victim advocates**, who assist victims when their cases are processed by the criminal justice system.

MOVEMENT OF CASES THROUGH THE COURT SYSTEM

Most criminal cases follow a general trajectory as they move through the court system. As mentioned earlier, the court is involved in many cases before official arrests have been made, so the court's role is not relegated to dealing with cases after the police have completed their tasks. See Box 4.3 for an example of a criminal case's progression through the courts in Honolulu, Hawaii.

═══ BOX 4.3 ═══

Movement of Cases Through the Court System

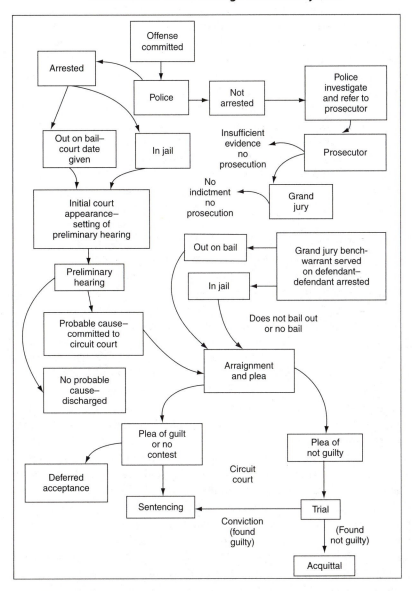

SOURCE: Office of Prosecuting Attorney, Honolulu, HI. http://www.honolulu.gov/prosecuting/flowchart.htm.

Initial Stages to Formal Charging

One of the constitutional requirements of police work is to secure a warrant prior to making an arrest. Despite this, the U.S. Supreme Court has authorized many types of arrest without a warrant; these are typically reserved for circumstances in which it is not feasible to take the time to secure a warrant. In other circumstances, police must secure a warrant from a judge in order to make an arrest. Police must go to a judge in a limited-jurisdiction court and support the information in the warrant (probable cause, evidence, etc.). Once the judge approves the warrant, the police may make a formal arrest. Police may also ask a lower-court judge to approve a search warrant in order to search a specific place for evidence.

After an arrest has been made, suspects are brought before a lower-court judge for their **initial appearance**. At this stage, defendants are informed of the charges against them, a bail decision is made, representation by a defense attorney is arranged (if applicable), and a date is set for the next stage in the case. In most misdemeanor cases, defendants plead guilty to the charges against them and are sentenced immediately. In many states, those charged with felonies are not allowed to plead guilty at this stage; instead, they plead not guilty and await the next stage of their case.

When a **bail** decision is made, the judge examines a number of variables to determine if a defendant is to be released into the community pending the resolution of his or her case. The primary variables are seriousness of the offense, prior record, and flight risk. Generally, the more serious the offense, the more extensive the prior record, and the higher the flight risk, the greater the likelihood that bail will be high or will be denied altogether. For some offenses, such as first-degree murder, bail is denied outright; a defendant has no chance to secure his or her release. In addition, the U.S. Supreme Court has upheld the denial of bail for purposes of **preventive detention** (*U.S. v. Salerno* [1987]). Regardless of the offense, prior record, or flight risk, if a defendant is deemed by the judge to be too dangerous to be released into the community, bail is denied. For most offenses, bail is granted; if a defendant pays the amount (called a bond), he or she is released and must return to court when his or her next court date is scheduled. Upon return, the bond is refunded to the defendant. If the defendant does not return to court, the bond is forfeited. Some courts will accept only a cash bond, while others will accept a collateral bond as well. In these cases, the defendants put up assets such as cars or property as collateral in return for release. In most cases, however, defendants are unable to pay the bail amount, so they use the services of bail bondsmen. Bail bondsmen usually require that the defendants pay a fee of 10 percent of the bail amount to the bondsmen; in return, the bondsmen pay the rest of the bond to the court, usually in the form of insurance, and guarantee the court that the defendants will appear for the next scheduled court date. The bondsmen keep the 10 percent of the bail amount as payment of services and can utilize any legal means at their disposal to ensure that the defendants appear for court.

The next stage of a case is usually a **preliminary hearing**. This occurs when a lower-court judge (not the judge at initial appearance) views the evidence against the defendant to determine if there is enough probable cause to proceed to trial. In many states, the preliminary hearing is the only chance for a judge to view the evidence before a trial. In these cases, a prosecutor will issue an "information" to indicate that probable cause has been met and the defendant is formally charged with a crime.

In other states, a **grand jury** hearing takes place after the judge has ruled in a preliminary hearing that a case will proceed. A grand jury hearing is required in all federal prosecutions, but not state prosecutions, although 19 states require the procedure in felony cases. A grand jury is composed of citizens who serve for a set period of time during which they consider numerous cases. The prosecutor alone provides evidence of the crime—the defendant has no right to present a case—and the grand jury must find that there is probable cause to proceed to trial, usually by majority vote. If probable cause has been met, the grand jury issues a "true bill of indictment," the equivalent of a prosecutor's "information." If probable cause has not been met, then a "no true bill" is issued. The idea behind a grand jury is that the public is allowed to provide a check on the power of the prosecutor and judge, in effect, to be a watchdog over the courts to prevent malicious prosecutions. However, most states do not utilize a grand jury, since it has not been required by the U.S. Supreme Court, and the vast majority of cases brought before grand juries end with indictments.

After formal charges have been filed, the next stage of a case is the **arraignment**. At this stage, the defendant is required to enter a plea to the formal charges against him or her. Defendants who have not yet pleaded guilty are likely to do so at this stage, since formal charges send a message that the criminal justice system has a strong case against the defendant. If a defendant pleads guilty, a sentence is then imposed. For those pleading not guilty, a trial date is set.

Plea Agreements. It is necessary to discuss plea agreements in a separate section due to the frequency of the practice in the court system. It has been estimated that 90 percent of cases in which charges are filed result in plea agreements (Carp and Stidham 1990). Plea agreements are often viewed as a necessary evil in a system that is ill equipped to take every case to trial. Plea agreements are a method of disposing of a court's caseload while trying to dispense justice at the same time.

A defendant can engage in a plea agreement at most stages of a criminal case. With few exceptions, such as felony defendants at first appearance, a defendant can decide to plead guilty if he or she feels it is warranted. As mentioned earlier, most misdemeanor defendants plead guilty and are sentenced at their initial appearance. Other defendants may plead not guilty and wait and see how their case progresses. There is always a chance (however slim) that the case will be dismissed later. Regardless of when the plea agreement occurs, most charged defendants plead guilty before a trial commences.

Plea agreements typically involve some sort of leniency on the part of the prosecutor and judge. Thus, a **plea bargain** occurs when the defendant makes a deal with the court to plead guilty in exchange for a charge/count reduction or a sentence reduction. In a charge/count bargain, a prosecutor may agree to reduce the charge from a felony to a misdemeanor or reduce the number of counts a defendant is charged with. In a sentence bargain, the prosecutor may agree to argue for a more lenient punishment at sentencing provided the defendant pleads guilty as charged. Some plea agreements involve no bargain at all, and defendants plead guilty as charged and are sentenced without any promised leniency.

Some argue that plea agreements, particularly plea bargains, allow defendants to "get off the hook" because their punishments do not fit their crimes. In fact, some communities have proposed or enacted bans on plea bargaining because of the sense that it allows criminals to escape harsher punishment. Critics also argue that plea agreements negate the adversarial process that is the cornerstone of the criminal justice system. In effect, plea agreements are orchestrated by the courtroom workgroup because the agreements are beneficial to everyone involved. Supporters argue that plea agreements are needed to help dispose of cases in crowded courts and that they result in sure convictions and punishment for defendants whom everyone knows are guilty. Regardless of the views on the practice, the use of plea agreements is something that will continue in the court system for a long time.

Assembly-Line Justice and Case Attrition. In the early stages of a criminal case, the court system is often accused of engaging in **assembly-line justice**, a term used to illustrate the movement of cases through the courts. In areas with large caseloads, it may not be possible for the courtroom workgroup to spend much time on cases, so each case is handled in a quick and efficient manner in order to move on to the next. This is especially seen in the lower courts, where initial appearances and plea agreements are handled much like a manufacturing assembly line. As mentioned earlier, in these crowded courthouses, it is not possible to devote a large amount of time to ordinary, run-of-the-mill cases, so they are handled in this fashion in order to concentrate on other, more serious cases, such as those that go to trial.

The handling of cases in such a manner is one of the reasons for **case attrition**, or the filtering out of cases from the court system. Case attrition is likened to a funnel, such that, as cases progress through the criminal justice process, the number of cases decreases. Although case attrition is most visible in the court system, police also engage in the practice. For instance, police may choose not to arrest or file charges against a suspect; as a result, these cases are filtered out of the courts even before they enter it. Largely, however, case attrition occures during the court process. Prosecutors may choose not to formally charge a suspect with a crime, due to lack of evidence or witness problems. Additionally, plea agreements contribute to attrition when cases are settled at initial appearance. As a case progresses, defendants may choose to plead guilty at a later stage, such as at arraignment, or a prosecutor may dismiss the charges. In effect, attrition for whatever reason is necessary because the court system is simply not equipped to take every case to trial. See Box 4.4 for an illustration of case attrition.

═══════ **BOX 4.4** ═══════

Example of Case Attrition

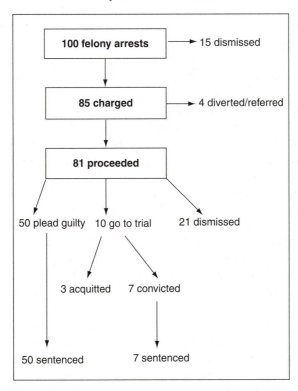

- 100 felony arrests → 15 dismissed
- 85 charged → 4 diverted/referred
- 81 proceeded
- 50 plead guilty   10 go to trial   21 dismissed
- 3 acquitted   7 convicted
- 50 sentenced   7 sentenced

Critical Thinking Exercise

Due to the increasing number of cases coming into the criminal justice system, the court system has become overcrowded and assembly-line justice has resulted. To remedy this, some have called for the decriminalization of certain offenses, particularly drug crimes, because they are considered "victimless." What are the advantages and disadvantages of such a strategy? Can you think of other mechanisms for reducing the influx of cases into the system?

Trial

After formal charges have been filed, a defendant enters a plea to those charges. If a defendant pleads not guilty, a trial date is set. According to the U.S. Constitution, a defendant has a right to a **jury trial**, but this right is limited to defendants who are charged with "serious" offenses—those that authorize a punishment of six months' or more incarceration. In addition, those defendants who are eligible for jury trials may opt for bench trials instead. A **bench trial** occurs when a judge alone hears the evidence against a defendant and renders a verdict. According to Neubauer (2004), a defendant may prefer a bench trial when the trial involves complex issues or when the case is emotionally charged.

If a jury trial is on the docket, the first step is to conduct jury selection. A **master jury list** is composed to identify potential jurors who are eligible to serve on a jury, usually people who are registered voters or who possess valid driver's licenses. Once the master jury list is created, a sample of potential jurors is selected from the list. This list is called the **venire**, or jury pool, and these individuals are notified by mail to report for jury duty. Once at the courthouse, the jury pool is questioned during a process called **voir dire**, in which the prosecutor and defense attorney (and sometimes the judge) question the individuals on their knowledge about the case or potential biases they may possess. If the prosecutor or defense attorney wishes to exclude an individual from jury duty, he or she may dismiss the juror using one of two methods. The first method, called a **challenge for cause**, allows attorneys to dismiss an unlimited number of jurors for legal reasons specified in state and federal statutes. An example of a challenge for cause would be that a potential juror is related to someone involved in the case. A second method of dismissing jurors is called a **peremptory challenge**, in which lawyers may dismiss a limited number of jurors based on reasons that do not need to be specified to the court. A lawyer may not feel that an individual juror "looks right" and may dismiss the juror based on a mere hunch. The use of peremptory challenges has long been challenged in the courts, as it provides opportunities for both the prosecution and defense to "stack the jury" in their favor. Historically, the use of these challenges allowed both sides to engage in discriminatory practices by removing jurors based on race or gender (see *Batson v. Kentucky* [1986]). Courts therefore have imposed a limited number of peremptory challenges, making it more difficult for either side in a case to stack the jury.

Once jury selection is over, the trial begins. The trial starts with opening statements by the prosecutor and defense attorney, each telling the jury what he or she hopes to show with regard to the evidence. The prosecution presents its case first and the defense has an opportunity to cross-examine the prosecution's witnesses. In a trial, the prosecution has the burden of proving the defendant is guilty beyond a reasonable doubt. This is called the **burden of proof**. The defense, on the other hand, only has to question the prosecution's case enough to instill doubt in a juror's mind—the defense does not have to prove a defendant innocent. In fact, the defense does not have to present any evidence at trial if it believes that the prosecution has not met the burden of proof. In reality, defense attorneys usually provide some sort of defense, calling witnesses who can support its case or call into question any evidence the prosecution presents. Like the defense during the prosecution's case, the prosecutor is able to cross-examine defense witnesses at this time. Both sides then have another chance to refute any evidence given by the other side, a process called rebuttal.

Once both sides have presented their cases, they are allowed to make closing statements to the jury. The prosecution emphasizes the evidence against the defendant and tries to convince the jury of the defendant's guilt. The defense also emphasizes its evidence, but stresses that the prosecutor must meet the burden of proof. After closing arguments, the judge provides instructions to the jury that outline the legal issues in the case (burden of proof, elements of the crime, possible verdicts, etc.). After instructions, the jury begins to deliberate the case. A unanimous vote is required for a verdict of guilty or not guilty. If the vote is not unanimous, there is no verdict and a **hung jury** is declared by the judge. If this occurs, the defendant may be prosecuted again on the same charge.

Sentencing

If a defendant has been found guilty by a judge or jury, the next stage is sentencing. Although the judge has formal sentencing responsibility, punishments for offenses are created by state legislatures and Congress (for federal cases). The various legislatures have adopted a number of sentencing schemes to achieve the goals that they consider important, whether they are retribution, deterrence, incapacitation, or rehabilitation. These schemes are addressed below.

Indeterminate Sentencing Schemes. In the past 100 years of punishment, **indeterminate sentencing** was the primary method utilized in the states. Indeterminate sentencing is usually associated with the goals of rehabilitation and incapacitation, tailoring sentences to the needs of individual offenders. In this scheme, a judge sentences a defendant to a minimum and maximum range of time; some states utilize indeterminate sentencing for incarceration sentences only, while others use it for incarceration and community supervision. The exact amount of time that is actually served by the offender is not specified at sentencing; instead, the parole board determines when and if an offender is eligible for release after the minimum term has been served.

Determinate Sentencing Schemes. In the late twentieth century, there was a shift away from indeterminate sentencing schemes due to an increased "law-and-order" approach to crime. In this scheme, a judge sentences an offender to a punishment for a specific period of time. Also referred to as "flat" or "fixed" sentences, **determinate sentencing** results in a defendant knowing how long his or her sentence will be when a judge imposes it. In effect, a judge declares what sentencing will be when a judge imposes it. In effect, a judge declares at sentencing that a defendant will serve X number of months or years of incarceration, probation, and so forth. In some states, prisoners can earn good-time credits for good behavior that decrease the amount of time spent in prison. Other states have abolished these credits, in hopes that defendants will serve their full sentences. Determinate sentencing schemes came about because many became skeptical of the rehabilitative aspects of indeterminate sentencing, feeling that defendants were not being punished for the crimes they committed.

Sentencing Guidelines. Regardless of the type of sentencing scheme, many states and the federal government have implemented **sentencing guidelines** to help curb what was considered to be inconsistent decision making on the part of judges and parole boards. In many areas, guidelines were established by a sentencing commission or a legislative body to assist judges and others in providing appropriate sanctions for similar defendants. The varying guidelines range between "suggested" sentences and mandated, specific sentences with little to no variation. Usually, the guidelines consider the seriousness of the offense and prior record, but some guidelines may take into account a defendant's legal status at the time of the crime—for instance, if the defendant was on probation or parole—and victim injury. Some guidelines allow limited judicial discretion by allowing a judge to impose less or more severe punishment on a defendant if circumstances warrant it.

Critical Thinking Exercise

The use of sentencing guidelines in some states has reduced the discretion exercised by judges with regard to imposing punishments for crimes. As a result, sentences have become offense based rather than offender based. Do you think that a judge should be able to consider the circumstances of the offender when imposing a sentence? In effect, should an offender's lack of education, home life, history of abuse, and so forth play a role in punishment? Explain.

Available Sanctions. State legislatures and Congress have authorized a number of sanctions that may be imposed by judges. Although prison is often the first punishment that comes to mind, it is not the most common punishment used for law violators. Jail, probation, fines, and other sanctions are far more common than prison. **Prison** is reserved for the more serious (i.e., felony) offenders. The United States has the highest incarceration rate in the world, housing approximately 1.5 million inmates in state and federal prisons (Harrison and Beck 2004). In recent years, legislatures have authorized longer and mandatory prison sentences for some offenses, including drug-related offenses. This has resulted in a dramatic increase in the incarceration rate (Blumstein and Beck 1999). Prisons are typically state controlled, but private prisons have been constructed in some states in hopes of defraying some of the costs it takes to operate state prisons. One sanction that is reserved for the most serious offenders is the **death penalty**, which is utilized in 38 states and in the federal system. The death penalty is rarely imposed, as it is restricted to individuals who have committed the highest form of murder, variously called first-degree, aggravated, or felony murder. At the federal level, the death penalty may also be imposed on those convicted of treason and drug kingpins.

Jail is a form of incarceration for individuals who have been convicted of misdemeanors. Approximately 700,000 people are housed in jails (Harrison and Beck 2004), which also house those who are awaiting trial; this is known as pretrial detention. In the states, jails are typically operated at the county level; the federal government operates its own jails.

The primary alternative to incarceration is **probation**. Over 4 million offenders are on probation at the federal and state levels (Neubauer 2004). The justification for probation is that incarceration is simply too much punishment for some offenders, but they simply cannot be released back into the community unpunished. Lower-level felony offenders and upper-level misdemeanor offenders are those typically placed on probation. Probation allows an offender to remain in the community as long as he or she abides by certain conditions, such as finding or maintaining employment, avoiding alcohol, submitting to drug tests, and meeting with a probation officer for a specified period of time.

For some offenders, probation is not a severe enough punishment, but incarceration is considered too harsh. A remedy to this is the use of **intermediate sanctions**, so named because they lie somewhere between prison and probation. Various intermediate sanctions include intensive supervision probation, electronic monitoring, house arrest, and boot camps. Intermediate sanctions tend to be used less frequently than regular probation, although the exact number of offenders serving intermediate sanctions is not known.

Fines are one of the oldest types of sanctions used and are typically reserved for traffic offenses or in conjunction with other types of punishment, usually probation. Fines are not utilized as extensively in the United States as in other countries, simply because most offenders in the U.S. criminal justice system cannot afford to pay them.

Regardless of the types of sentencing schemes and available sanctions, there has been a trend of increased legislative involvement in the sentencing of offenders. This involvement has led to reduced discretion on the part of judges, who were often viewed by legislators and the public as being too lenient in their sentencing practices. This law-and-order approach to crime and justice has led to increased supervision of more offenders by the criminal justice system, something that has cost considerable sums of money.

Appeals

After an offender has been convicted and sentenced, he or she has the right to one **appeal**. This means that the offender has the opportunity to have his or her case reviewed by an appellate court in order to fix any problems that may have occurred during the case. These problems typically involve issues such as improper jury selection, defects in jury instructions, or admission of illegally seized evidence. Prosecutors, on the other hand, cannot appeal a finding of not guilty.

The right to one appeal carries with it certain constitutional requirements by which the state or federal government must abide. Offenders who appeal have the right to free transcripts of their trials and the right to appointed counsel. Despite this, many offenders do not appeal their convictions or sentences, simply because they view it as a waste of time and energy, especially when they will have completed their sentences before their appeals get through the appellate stage. In addition, appeals are rarely sucessful; in fact, Neubauer (2004) estimates that only one in eight appellants find some sort of victory from their appeals. Most of these victories are minor, however. Convictions are typically upheld and sentences may be modified only slightly, or offenders are subjected to retrial only to be reconvicted the second time around.

After the first appeal is finished, offenders have the opportunity to file other appeals if they wish. Called **postconviction review** or a **collateral attack**, prisoners can challenge their convictions or sentences in a different proceeding. Collateral attacks are typically filed in federal court and are civil matters, not criminal appeals. They raise constitutional questions only, not errors in interpretation or application of the law, which are seen mostly in the first appeal of right. Offenders are not given free trial transcripts and are not provided with appointed counsel in these appeals. As a result, few offenders take advantage of the opportunity to file a collateral attack. A common type of collateral attack is habeas corpus, in which prisoners claim that they are being detained illegally. In recent years, Congress and the U.S. Supreme Court have greatly restricted the filing of habeas corpus appeals in a number of ways. Now, offenders have a one-year deadline to file an appeal and are limited in the number of appeals that can be filed, among other things (see Antiterrorism and Effective Death Penalty Act 1996).

Use of Court Technology

Many courts are using new and updated technology to assist with court operations. One of the uses of this technology is to create a more efficient case management process through an increased use of computerized files, in essence, creating an "e-court." Case files move among many individuals and offices within a court, so the use of case management technology is essential to keep the flow of cases moving. Although the court system is a long way from becoming paperless, case management technology allows all individuals involved in a case (the judge, prosecutor, clerk of court, defense attorney, probation officer, etc.) 24-hour access to case files. Thus, there is no longer the need to wait for a file as in a traditional paperwork scheme. Additionally, courts can measure their performance with the use of Courtools, an online measure instituted by the National Center for State Courts. These tools include such measures as access to the courts, fairness, length of case, and reliability of case files, among others. These tools allow courts to measure their performance and enact changes, if necessary.

Increased Victim Involvement

In addition to special-needs offenders, courts are increasingly allowing victims to become involved in the resolution of their cases. Traditionally, the court system has excluded victims from case processing; in effect, once the victim has reported a crime, the criminal justice system takes over and represents his or her interests. The criminal justice system views crime as an offense against the state or federal government, not against an individual victim. Because of this, victims have felt excluded from the criminal justice process, feeling that their interests are not taken into account during the course of the case. As a result, the court system has become more sensitive to the needs of victims and has devised new methods of taking victims into account.

Restorative Justice. This philosophy posits that the criminal justice system needs to address the real victims of crime—not only the actual victims themselves, but also offenders, family members, and the community. The idea is that crime affects more than the government entity whose laws have been broken and that the system must, in effect, restore the injured parties to where they were before the crime occurred. **Restorative justice** enables offenders to understand the harms they have caused and gives them the chance to try to make things right. Victims are able to provide input and participate in the process, meeting with criminal justice personnel and community leaders to outline the best course of action for a particular victim. One common requirement in restorative justice is victim restitution, which involves the offender offering monetary compensation for the harm caused. In addition, the criminal justice system works with community programs to address offenders' needs for the purposes of integrating them back into the community and reducing future criminal conduct.

Alternative Dispute Resolution. Though most common in civil cases, **alternative dispute resolution (ADR)** is also used in criminal cases, usually misdemeanors. As the name suggests, ADR seeks to settle disputes in ways besides the formal court process. One common form of ADR is mediation, which involves a neutral individual (not a judge) who works with the parties involved to come to a mutual agreement as to a resolution. For example, in civil cases, lawsuits may be settled through mediation without ever having to go to court. In criminal cases, mediation resembles aspects of restorative justice, in that the victim and offender can work out their issues to the mutual benefit of both. Usually, some sort of victim restitution is the aim of mediation. Some would argue that ADR is a form of restorative justice; however, offender reintegration does not occupy as predominant a position in ADR as it does in a true restorative justice program.

CONCLUSION

As evidenced above, the court system is involved in many aspects of the criminal justice system. Courts can become involved in cases before an arrest is made and after an offender has served a sentence. The courts are primarily responsible for ensuring that the laws are followed properly, both by citizens and government entities, and seeing to it that law violators are punished. Although many cases never formally enter the criminal justice system, the numbers of cases that courts have to process has increased in recent years due to law-and-order policies that have increased the numbers and types of offenders who come to the attention of the system. State and federal legislatures have also reduced the discretion of judges by authorizing longer and mandatory prison sentences, which have dramatically increased the incarceration rate. Courts are trying to find a balance between the demands of politicians and the public that offenders should be punished and caseload issues that pressure the courtroom workgroup to get cases out of the system quickly and efficiently, often with punishments that do not fit the crime. This can be an incredibly difficult task, so actors in the court system must measure the ideological goals of retribution and deterrence against the practical goals of not allowing the courts to fall apart as caseloads mount.

KEY WORDS

adversarial system
alternative dispute
    resolution (ADR)
appeal
appellate jurisdiction
arraignment
assembly-line justice
assigned counsel
bail
bailiffs
bench trial
burden of proof
case attrition
challenge for cause
clerks of court
collateral attack
contract system
court administrators
court reporters
courtroom workgroup
crime-control model
death penalty

defense attorneys
determinate sentencing
drug courts
dual court system
due-process model
en banc proceeding
fines
grand jury
hung jury
indeterminate sentencing
initial appearance
intermediate sanctions
jail
judges
jurisdiction
jury trial
legal aid
master jury list
mental-health courts
merit selection
nonpartisan election
original jurisdiction

partisan election
peremptory challenge
plea bargain
postconviction review
preliminary hearing
preventive detention
prison
probation
pro bono
pro se
prosecutors
public defender
restorative justice
sentencing guidelines
trial courts of general
    jurisdiction
trial courts of limited
    jurisdiction
venire
voir dire
victim advocates

SUGGESTED READINGS

Carp, R., and Stidham, R. (1990). *Judicial process in America*. Washington, DC: Congressional Quarterly Press.

Eisenstein, J., Flemming, R., and Nardulli, P. (1999). *The contours of justice: Communities and their courts*. Lanham, MD: University Press of America.

Mays, L., and Gregware, P. (2004). *Courts and justice: A reader*. Prospect Heights, IL: Waveland Press.

Tarr, A. (2003). *Judicial process and judicial policymaking*. Belmont, CA: Wadsworth Publishing. ✦

CHAPTER 5

Institutional Corrections

CHAPTER OUTLINE

Institutional correctional facilities have been used for centuries, ever since the Roman Catholic Church made use of confinement at the abbey during the Middle Ages. Even though there were precursors to the modern jails and prisons, reliance upon corporal punishments such as flogging, branding, and other forms of torture were widespread across the world. The American colonists followed suit with these punishments over the centuries, but soon came to realize that such sanctions were inhumane and inappropriate for some behaviors. Soon thereafter, the penitentiary became the primary method by which convicted offenders would be punished.

HISTORY OF PUNISHMENT

Punishment for the violation of group norms, rules, and laws is a common element across human history and societies. Whether the response is informally handed out by the head of a household or reflects the official commands of a modern-day court, social life imposes various restrictions on behavior and violations carry the possibility of a negative response. Punishment may be justified for a variety of social, political, moral, or religious reasons. In ancient times, punishment for a violation of a social norm or law was often handled locally, by either the family, clan, or head of the community. Larger and more organized societies typically used more formal procedures for investigating, prosecuting, adjudicating, and punishing offenders. There was considerable variation, however, in the response depending on the type of law or custom that was violated, who the offender and victim were, the specific geographic location of the incident, and the exact historical time period.

Nearly every society has had some arrangements for the temporary confinement of offenders. Some ancient civilizations, such as the Greeks and Romans, also had facilities designed to hold offenders for longer periods of time. In general, however, punishment in premodern Western societies and colonial America primarily involved the use of monetary compensation or corporal punishments. This is not to suggest that imprisonment did not occur, but it was far from the most common or most important form of punishment. When incarceration did occur, it was for the purpose of holding the offender until the corporal or capital sentence was to take place, usually within a day or two.

Modern societies are structured by the formal organization and routinization of social tasks and social life. One of the social tasks that has been increasingly controlled and managed has been the enforcement of laws and punishment of law violators. With the spread of democratic values and market capitalism came growing criticism of the use of physical punishment. In the late 1700s, severe forms of punishment were being questioned by those adhering to the Classical school. Furthermore, existing punishment and facilities of the day were perceived as ineffective and counterproductive. As society shifted from a top-down power structure to one based on the sovereignty of the people, new forms of punishment were needed to reflect these new social relations. It was during this time that the modern-day penitentiary was born, and with it the beginning of formal organizational structures designed to carry out punishments (see Morris and Rothman 1995; Rothman 1971).

Several major penal institutions were created in the United States between 1790 and 1830. Although there were differences in the design and operation of these early penitentiaries, they were more similar than not. In less than 100 years, punishment changed from the rather arbitrary use of physical punishment to a model emphasizing the confinement and correction of individual offenders through segregation, regimentation, and control. Offenders were increasingly separated based upon personal characteristics. As a result, female offenders, juvenile delinquents, and the mentally ill were placed in facilities independent of male adult criminal offenders.

ERAS OF PUNISHMENT

The purpose of punishment and the use of different types of punishment have largely reflected the needs of a particular society. As a result, there have been different eras of punishment in the United States that utilized varying mechanisms for punishment.

The Era of the Penitentiary

Incapacitation and deterrence were the philosophies that dominated the purposes for confinement in the 1800s to 1860s. This was known as the **penitentiary era**, so called because of the development of a formal penal system and a heavy reliance on incarceration. Two different styles of penitentiaries became symbols of this era: separate and congregate. These styles are more commonly known as the Pennsylvania and Auburn systems, respectively.

The Eastern State Penitentiary in Philadelphia, Pennsylvania, was said to be a separate system because of its heavy reliance on silence and the separation of inmates from one another in individual cells. Eating, working, and sleeping were performed in the confines of the cells. The purpose of silence and solitude was reflected in the belief that the only way to repent and reform for one's wrongdoings was to reflect silently on one's deeds. Inmates were also denied visits from family members and friends and access to newspapers, and correspondences of any kind were forbidden (Rothman 1971).

The Auburn Prison in New York also operated under the rule of silence, but differed from its western neighbor in that inmates could congregate with one another during the day while eating or working. Auburn prisoners returned to separate cells at night and silence, even while in the presence of other inmates, was strictly enforced. Inmates in New York were also secluded from the outside world; there was no sight, sound, or contact with anyone or anything beyond the prison walls (Rothman 1971).

Penitentiaries sprang forth in other parts of the United States following the procedures and philosophies of their predecessors, despite the criticisms lodged against the imposition of silence, corporal punishments to keep inmates under control, and restriction of access to the external society. This so-called old prison discipline led some inmates to suffer from mental, emotional, and physical illness and, in some cases, even death.

The Era of Reform

The Civil War detracted attention from the plight of prisoners housed in the penitentiaries that were built in the 1800s. By 1870, however, the harsh environment of these institutions again came to be scrutinized. A more humanitarian approach to the practice of incarceration was advocated based more on the philosophy of rehabilitation rather than pure incapacitation or deterrence. The National Prison Association, which is known today as the American Correctional Association, was formed in 1870 to address the problems of the penitentiary system. Prison administrators, members of Congress, and prominent citizens from the United States and abroad gathered in Cincinnati, Ohio, and issued a set of declarations by which the prison would be reformed. These principles emphasized the value of treatment for inmates based on their individual needs, an indeterminate sentencing scheme by which inmates could earn their way out of prison, vocational and educational training, labor that was purposeful rather than punishment oriented, and noncorporal methods of discipline that made use of rewards rather than punishment for conformity (Pisciotta 1994). In addition, the reformers abolished the rule of silence. A system whereby released inmates could continue their treatment in the community was also introduced during the **reform era**. Today, this practice is better known as parole, and it will be discussed in more detail in the following chapter.

The Elmira Reformatory in New York was the prototype institution whose mission was to carry out the aforementioned principles. Inmates were classified based on their conduct and success in the interventions available at the facility, such as training for trade and academics. Similar to Elmira's predecessors, the reformatory was criticized for the means used to control inmates, inhumane working and living conditions, and rigid order. Thus, the intentions of the reforms appeared to be sound but, in the end, poor implementation and a lack of funding required a new approach to the use of institutions for punishment.

The Era of Industry

The idea of convict labor was not new to the world of incarceration. Both the Pennsylvania and the Auburn systems required inmates to engage in craft-oriented or factory-oriented labor, respectively (Conley 1980). The goods produced by inmates were often sold in the open market. Inmates at the Auburn Prison actually built Sing Sing Prison, New York's second state institution for the incarceration of convicted offenders. Chain gangs were developed during this era, with inmates working on road or canal projects and prison construction for the states. Inmates were also tied to the private sector by being employed contractually with private-sector businesses in the making of furniture, clothing, brooms, baskets, and hosiery. In addition, some inmates were contracted out to work in the stone quarries and coal mines (Mancini 1978; Sellin 1976).

These latter practices, known as **convict leasing**, were a Southern development, and some authors have purported that convict leasing was basically another way to enslave blacks following the Civil War (Johnson 2002; Sheldon 2001). Convict leasing of inmates often led to illness, suffering, and even death. For example, in Georgia, convicts were beaten if they did not produce the designated amount of coal per day (Mancini 1978).

Despite such horrific consequences associated with convict labor during the **industrial era**, states and their officials continued their labor programs for inmates until the 1930s, when state legislatures and Congress passed a number of measures banning the sale of inmate-produced goods to the public (Sexton 1995). The major impetus for such legislation was complaints advanced by workers in the organized labor force that inmate-made goods negatively affected the price at which free-market products could be sold. Once the Great Depression hit in the 1930s, pressure from workers increased considerably to prohibit inmate labor from interfering with their profits; thus, inmate labor was curtailed.

Legislation was reintroduced in the late 1970s that permitted products produced by prison industries to be sold in the open market once again. Today, inmates continue to work while doing their time in various industries connected to the private and public sectors. Inmates have been involved in such jobs as assembling graduation gowns for Jostens, Inc., making embroidered emblems for Lyon Brothers Manufacturing Company, and even sewing garments that were later purchased by J.C. Penney and Victoria's Secret for retail sale for Third Generation, Inc. (Sexton 1995).

The Era of Rehabilitation

By the early 1930s, there was a strong sense of urgency to do something about the harsh punishments faced by inmates in U.S. penal institutions. The Depression contributed to discontent among the general public, and dissatisfaction in prisons was also on the rise. Several major prison riots in Illinois, Colorado, New York, and Kansas City prompted the government to take notice. Even prison officials began to understand the hopelessness that prisoners experienced. With a report issued by the Wickersham Commission in 1931, inmate grievances were officially recognized. State prisons did not provide anything more than capricious rules and coercive punishments for inmates, and meaningful programs to assist inmates in their reformation were lacking. In fact, inmates spent most of their time inactively engaged in simply doing their time.

The Wickersham Commission called for a new philosophy to guide the prison system; the philosophy of **rehabilitation** soon replaced the philosophies of deterrence and incapacitation that had dominated since the inception of the penitentiary. The major players in the move towards more rehabilitative efforts were the progressives, who were most active during the first couple of decades of the twentieth century. The progressives were known for their indeterminist view that social problems, including crime, were often beyond an individual's control, much like having a disease that needs treatment. The medical model dominated the **rehabilitation era** with a focus on the needs of the individual offender and less reliance on prisons to carry out the criminal sanction. Probation, indeterminate sentences, classification systems, vocational and educational training, and release from prison based on treatment success were some of the significant practices devised and implemented to carry out the goal of rehabilitation. Many of the recommendations from the 1870 National Prison Association finally came to fruition.

Corrections would follow the rehabilitation philosophy for over 40 years with reported success in some jurisdictions and failure in others. It appeared that states were just not equipped to carry out the rehabilitative ideals. This latter statement especially held true for prisons where the correctional officers were mandated to keep order within the institution while simultaneously attempting to create an environment that was amenable to treatment (Rothman 1980). It soon became clear that the premise of rehabilitation could not climb over the hurdles blocking its proper implementation.

Coupling these ideological struggles with the social and political context of the 1960s and 1970s, it should come as little surprise that the philosophy of rehabilitation would soon be replaced with a more punitive philosophy, better known as the "get-tough" movement. Student uprisings over Vietnam, civil rights demonstrations, increases in poverty and crime rates, and the Watergate scandal led people to question the government, social institutions, law enforcement, courts, and corrections. The catalyst that provided further justification for abandoning the philosophy of rehabilitation was the publication of a report by Robert Martinson, which indicated that "with few and isolated exceptions, the rehabilitative efforts that have been reported so far have had no appreciable effect on recidivism" (Martinson 1974: 25).

The Era of Retribution

The "nothing works" doctrine associated with Martinson's publication provided the ammunition to close the book on rehabilitation. Now, sentencing and correctional policies are based on more punitive ideals such as an increased reliance on secure confinement for more offenders for longer periods of time, determinate sentencing models, and the abolition of parole. Offenders are now sentenced to a finite amount of time and release is not necessarily tied to reformation or rehabilitation. Under the auspices of "get-tough" practices, offenders who commit crimes will get their just deserts.

Now in the **retributive era**, during the past 25 years, there has been a general trend in the United States and western European countries to respond to law violators with more severe penalties and a decreasing support for rehabilitative efforts towards crime and offenders (Donziger 1996). In the United States, this has resulted in most jurisdictions enacting lengthier prison sentences, more punitive sanctions (such as "three-strikes" policies that stipulate life sentences for offenders convicted of their third felonies), and attempts to limit the discretion of judges or correctional administrators to reduce sentence lengths. Although these changes apply to a wide variety of behaviors, violent crimes and drug-law violations have been particularly affected by these changes (Blumstein and Beck 1999). Perhaps most important has been the increasing effort towards the "war on drugs" that has been fought during the past 30 years. As a result, drug-law violators make up a significant percentage of offenders in criminal courts and under correctional supervision. This is a considerable change from just 30 years ago (Blumstein and Beck 1999).

SIZE AND COSTS OF IMPRISONMENT

The results of heightened attention and more punitive responses to crime are indicated in Figure 5.1. In total, there are over 7.3 million individuals under some form of correctional supervision in the United States, be it prisons, jails, probation, or parole (Bureau of Justice Statistics 2007f). Perhaps the figure that stunned the nation most recently, however, was this: one out of nearly 100 adults is institutionalized in jail or prison at the state and federal levels (Pew Center on the States 2008). Alas, over 2.3 million people are incarcerated. This figure was released in early 2008 and made history for being the first time the United States has ever witnessed such an alarming incarceration rate. As a

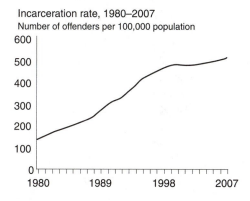

Figure 5.1 Sentenced inmates in state and federal facilities
SOURCE: Correctional Populations in the United States, 1997, and Prisoners in 2007 (Bureau of Justice Statistics, 2000 and 2007)

result, the United States has the highest incarceration rate of all industrialized countries. Four years ago, the United States followed Russia in the rankings. Look at Table 5.1 to see how the United States compares to other countries in the world in prison population. Which country has the lowest prison

Table 5.1 International country populations and persons in prisons and pretrial detainees as of January 2007

COUNTRY	COUNTRY POPULATION	PRISON POPULATION	% POPULATION DETAINED
United States	29,91,00,000	21,86,230	0.731
China	1,31,14,00,000	15,48,498	0.119
Russian Federation	14,23,00,000	8,69,814	0.611
Brazil	18,68,00,000	3,61,402	0.193
India	1,12,18,00,000	3,32,112	0.03
Mexico	10,83,00,000	2,14,450	0.198
Ukraine	4,68,00,000	1,65,716	0.354
Thailand	6,52,00,000	1,64,443	0.025
South Africa	4,73,00,000	1,57,402	0.333
Iran (Islamic Republic of)	7,03,00,000	1,47,926	0.21
Indonesia	22,55,00,000	99,946	0.044
Philippines	8,63,00,000	89,639	0.104
Pakistan	16,58,00,000	89,370	0.054
United Kingdom	6,05,00,000	88,458	0.146
Vietnam	8,42,00,000	88,414	0.105
Poland	3,81,00,000	87,901	0.231
Japan	12,78,00,000	79,055	0.062
Germany	8,24,00,000	78,581	0.095
Bangladesh	14,66,00,000	71,200	0.049
Rwanda	91,00,000	67,000	0.736
Turkey	7,37,00,000	65,458	0.089
Ethiopia	7,48,00,000	65,000	0.087
Spain	4,55,00,000	64,215	0.141
Colombia	4,68,00,000	62,216	0.133
Egypt	7,54,00,000	61,845	0.082
Italy	5,90,00,000	61,721	0.105
Myanmar	5,10,00,000	60,000	0.118
Cuba	1,13,00,000	55,000	0.487
Morocco	3,17,00,000	54,542	0.172
Argentina	3,90,00,000	54,472	0.14
France	6,12,00,000	52,009	0.085
Uzbekistan	2,62,00,000	48,000	0.183
Kenya	3,47,00,000	47,036	0.136
Korea (Republic of)	4,85,00,000	45,882	0.095

Table 5.1 (Continued)

Tanzania (United Republic of)	3,79,00,000	43,911	0.116
Algeria	3,35,00,000	42,000	0.125
Belarus	97,00,000	41,583	0.43
Nigeria	13,45,00,000	40,444	0.03
Chile	1,64,00,000	39,916	0.243
Malaysia	2,69,00,000	35,644	0.133
Peru	2,84,00,000	35,642	0.126
Romania	2,16,00,000	35,429	0.164
Canada	3,26,00,000	34,096	0.105
Congo (Democratic Republic)	6,27,00,000	30,000	0.048
Saudi Arabia	2,41,00,000	28,612	0.119
Uganda	2,77,00,000	26,126	0.094
Tunisia	1,01,00,000	26,000	0.257
Australia	2,06,00,000	25,353	0.123
Sri Lanka	1,99,00,000	23,613	0.119
Turkmenistan	53,00,000	22,000	0.415
Netherlands	1,64,00,000	21,013	0.128
Madagascar	1,78,00,000	20,294	0.114
Cameroon	1,73,00,000	20,000	0.116
Venezuela (Bolivarian Republic)	2,70,00,000	19,853	0.074
Czech Republic	1,03,00,000	18,950	0.184
Azerbaijan	85,00,000	18,259	0.215
Zimbabwe	1,31,00,000	18,033	0.138
Kyrgyzstan	52,00,000	15,744	0.303
Hungary	1,01,00,000	15,720	0.156
Singapore	45,000	15,038	0.334
Zambia	1,19,00,000	14,347	0.121
Yemen	2,16,00,000	14,000	0.065
Israel	72,00,000	13,909	0.193
Portugal	1,06,00,000	12,870	0.121
Ghana	2,26,00,000	12,736	0.056
Dominican Republic	90,00,000	12,725	0.141
Ecuador	1,33,00,000	12,251	0.092
El Salvador	70,00,000	12,176	0.174
Sudan	4,12,00,000	12,000	0.029
Libyan Arab Jamahiriya	59,00,000	11,790	0.2
Georgia	44,00,000	11,731	0.267
Panama	33,00,000	11,649	0.353
Honduras	74,00,000	11,589	0.157

(Continued)

Table 5.1 (Continued)

COUNTRY	COUNTRY POPULATION	PRISON POPULATION	% POPULATION DETAINED
Hong Kong, China (SAR)	70,00,000	11,580	0.165
Bulgaria	77,00,000	11,436	0.149
Tajikistan	70,00,000	10,804	0.154
Syrian Arab Republic	1,95,00,000	10,599	0.054
Mozambique	1,99,00,000	10,000	0.05
Greece	1,11,00,000	9,984	0.09
Malawi	1,28,00,000	9,656	0.075
Belgium	0.105	9,597	0.091
United Arab Emirates	49,00,000	8,927	0.182
Austria	83,00,000	8,766	0.106
Slovakia	54,00,000	8,493	0.157
Cambodia	1,41,00,000	8,160	0.058
Lithuania	34,00,000	8,124	0.239
Costa Rica	43,00,000	7,782	0.181
Bolivia	91,00,000	7,710	0.085
New Zealand	41,00,000	7,620	0.186
Sweden	91,00,000	7,450	0.082
Guatemala	1,30,00,000	7,227	0.056
Nepal	2,60,00,000	7,135	0.027
Mongolia	26,00,000	6,998	0.269
Uruguay	33,00,000	6,947	0.211
Latvia	23,00,000	6,676	0.29
Botswana	18,00,000	6,259	0.348
Switzerland	75,00,000	6,111	0.081
Lebanon	39,00,000	5,971	0.153
Niger	1,44,00,000	5,709	0.04
Nicaragua	56,00,000	5,610	0.1
Jordan	56,00,000	5,589	0.1
Senegal	1,19,00,000	5,360	0.045
Paraguay	63,00,000	5,063	0.08
Jamaica	27,00,000	4,913	0.182
Denmark	54,00,000	4,198	0.078
Papua New Guinea	60,00,000	4,056	0.068
Finland	53,00,000	3,954	0.075
Trinidad and Tobago	13,00,000	3,851	0.296
Haiti	85,00,000	3,670	0.043
Croatia	44,00,000	3,594	0.082
Kuwait	27,00,000	3,500	0.13
Albania	32,00,000	3,491	0.111
Chad	1,00,00,000	3,416	0.034

Table 5.1 (Continued)

Ireland	42,00,000	3,080	0.073
Guinea	98,00,000	3,070	0.031
Norway	47,00,000	3,048	0.065
Armenia	30,00,000	2,879	0.096
Sierra Leone	57,00,000	1,740	0.031
Bosnia and Herzegovina	39,00,000	1,526	0.039
Bahamas	3,00,000	1,500	0.5
Fiji	8,00,000	1,113	0.139
Barbados	3,00,000	997	0.332
Congo	37,00,000	918	0.029
Luxembourg	50,00,000	768	0.154
Bahrain	70,00,000	701	0.1
Cyprus	10,00,000	580	0.058
Saint Lucia	2,00,000	503	0.252
Grenada	1,00,000	237	0.237
Samoa	2,00,000	223	0.112
Saint Kitts and Nevis	50,000	214	0.428
Iceland	3,00,000	119	0.04

SOURCE: ICPS (International Centre for Prison Studies). 2007. World Prison Population List, Seventh Edition. London. For more details visit: http://www.kcl.ac.uk/schools/law/research/icps.

population? What is the median figure? How do countries on the other continents compare to the United States in incarcerated populations? Why do you think this is the case? To find out more about prison populations and related costs in your particular state, go to http://www.pewcenteronthestates. org and follow the links to the *One in 100* and *One in 31* reports.

To keep up with the constant flow of offenders formally processed in the criminal justice system due to the passage of "get-tough" policies, jurisdictions have had to increase the funding for various justice agencies. While the funding for all aspects of the criminal justice system has increased, the increase for correctional spending has been the most dramatic. Recent costs analyses observed that state correctional budgets in the United States total over $49 billion, which is six times greater than that allocated for higher education. Indeed, corrections is a costly business and states are grappling with both a high institutional population and budget crises (The Pew Center on the States 2008). To reduce prison over-crowding, many states and the federal government have greatly increased the bed space within their prison systems through massive prison construction pro-grams. The rationale behind the boom in building more secure places of confine-ment is the idea that, eventually, the more offenders we incarcerate, the less crime we will have (Austin and Irwin 2001). Unfortunately, it also appears that even with such a high incarceration rate, recidivism and crime rates have not been reduced as

---

Critical Thinking Exercise

Corrections has witnessed several eras in relation to the types of punishments used and for which purposes. What do you think the next era of corrections will be like? For example, will there be an even greater reliance on institutions for punishment? Will more rehabilitation programs be developed? Will special offender populations be effectively served? Will we see more technological advances and less human interaction between corrections officers and inmates? What will our future prisons look like? Who will be housed in them? How can you be confident that your predictions are accurate? Evaluate.

---

significantly as many policymakers and the public had expected. Indeed, we continue to incarcerate at levels disproportionate to actual offense counts (The Pew Center on the States 2008).

In 2005, the mean cost of incarcerating one person in prison for one year was $23,876 (Pew Center on the States 2008). Estimates from 33 states surveyed in 2008, however, indicated the price tag to be closer to $30,000 (Pew Center on the States 2009). Figured into these costs are expenditures for housing, feeding, clothing, and supervising inmates. If we include capital expenses and employee wages and benefits in the calculation, the total annual cost per inmate could run as high as $65,000 in a medium-security prison. To put these numbers in perspective, consider that, in the academic year 2004–2005, per-pupil expenditures in state schools averaged $9,266 (National Center for Education Statistics 2008). As you can see, states spend anywhere from three to seven times the amount per inmate as per pupil in a given year.

On a global scale the United States, although it is the number one country in incarceration, spends fewer dollars per inmate on average (using the $30,000 figure) when compared with other Western nations. For example, Canada's average per-person incarceration cost is $54,466 a year. England closely follows Canada at $54,306. Australia spends nearly $7,000 less per inmate than Canada and England. Yet, these three nations' total prison populations combined do not even compare to that of the United States, 147,907–2,186,230, respectively. Indeed, the United States prevails as the "winner" in the total number of persons imprisoned and expenditures on incarceration.

By this point in our discussion, it is obvious that corrections is big business with high overhead and human costs. Some states are beginning to realize that something must be done to curb the amount of money allocated to institutional corrections, especially with serious state budget crises that have occurred over the past few years. For example, Massachusetts, Michigan, Missouri, Arizona, New Mexico, and Mississippi legislators have either repealed minimum mandatory sentencing laws that were the cornerstone of the "get-tough" era in the 1980s and 1990s or are considering modifications to existing legislation (Shy 2004). Many of these laws targeted drug offenders and few, if any, states have observed significant decreases in the number of drug crimes occurring with the adoption of minimum mandatory sentences for these offenders. The proposed changes to these types of sentencing systems involve either a reduction in time spent in prison or widening the eligibility standards for parole. Thus, "get-tough" stances are being replaced by "smart-on-crime" strategies that enable states to conserve both monetary and material resources for already taxed social systems (Shy 2004: 1).

JAILS

Currently, there are over 3,300 jails in the United States. **Jails** and **detention centers** are facilities designed to hold a variety of offenders for a relatively brief period of time, usually for less than one year. The size of a jail varies depending on the geographic and legal jurisdictions that the facility serves. While jails in rural areas and small communities may hold relatively few prisoners, the facilities found in America's largest population centers can be quite immense. Counties or municipal governments operate most jails, while some jurisdictions such as the federal government have special facilities for their own detainees in certain areas of the country. There has also been a trend for small jurisdictions to combine their smaller jails into a single, regional center that serves several surrounding communities (Stinchcomb and Fox 1999).

Jails perform several important functions. First, jails are where most offenders are housed following arrest. After arrest, a local judge or magistrate reviews the offenders' charges and flight risk and sets a bail amount, orders the offenders held without bail, or releases the offenders on their own recognizance until their next court date. Second, jails house defendants who have been sentenced to less than one year of incarceration. Some jail sentences are served on weekends, or the offenders may be released to the community for work while residing in the jail. Finally, jails may serve as detention centers to temporarily confine a variety of offenders until their cases are resolved or until authorities from the proper jurisdiction assume custody. Therefore, juvenile and adult, misdemeanor and felony, and state and federal offenders may all be housed briefly in the same facility, but sometimes in different units within that facility.

Although there are exceptions, jails tend to be chaotic environments and face a number of problems. Jails have historically been the dumping grounds for the poor, deviant, and marginalized individuals in a community (Sheldon 2001). They seem to be continually under pressure from overcrowding, a lack of resources and training, and the issue of local politics. Many individuals processed into the jail are intoxicated or under the influence of behavior-altering substances, highly agitated, suicidal, or mentally unstable when they arrive. Jail personnel often do not have adequate information on an arrestee's needs and risks when he or she is first booked into the facility. This lack of knowledge may lead to otherwise preventable problems. Finally, the continuous movement of prisoners in and out of a jail facility presents logistical and safety challenges to jail staff and administration. Jail inmates are frequently moved for court hearings, community service work, and other activities. The high volume of visitors into these facilities can also provide opportunities for violence or smuggling of contraband.

Jail administrators are constantly facing a number of problems in the management of their facilities. Jails are often impersonal, with little contact between the guards and the inmates. Jails also lack necessary services such as medical, psychological, and substance abuse treatment for inmates. It should come as no surprise that stress levels are often heightened in the jail setting, with violence and safety issues in constant need of resolution. To overcome some of these problems, there has been a movement to replace existing jails with what are known as **new-generation jails (NGJs)**. Architecturally, these NGJs are built to house fewer inmates in what are known as pods or modules that contain anywhere from 16 to 30 separate cells with one or two inmates per cell. Inmates do not have access to other pods in the jail and the staff does not have to be concerned with managing more than 60 inmates at any given time. In other types of jails, staff may have to monitor hundreds of inmates at once, thereby decreasing safety for all involved. In the NGJs, inmates eat, sleep, make phone calls, and engage in activities such as game playing or television viewing all in the pod (Reichel 1997). The staff is in closer contact with the inmates and consistently monitors inmate behavior, which not only attenuates problems among the inmates and within the facility, but can also provide inmates with more positive social exchanges between inmates and staff (Bayens, Williams, and Smykla 1997). One evaluation of a NGJ found that recidivism of inmates housed in these facilities did not increase and, for some offenders, recidivism decreased when compared with inmates housed in traditional jails (Applegate, Surette, and McCarthy 1999).

While there are many persons housed in jails today, prisons house about twice as many offenders. In recent years, jails have seen a small decrease in their populations, but few prisons have seen a decline. In fact, between July 1, 2002, and June 30, 2003, on average, most local jails were actually less crowded than in years past (Bureau of Justice Statistics 2004d). Prisons, however, remained cramped.

MODERN PRISONS

While felony offenders in the United States are more commonly sentenced to community supervision rather than incarceration, prisons are financially and symbolically important forms of punishment. Prisons are also socially and politically important because they are used to house those individuals who are determined to be unresponsive to community supervision, who pose a considerable risk to the community, or who have committed offenses so serious that they deserve to have their freedom taken away for a given period of time. Prisons are also known as penitentiaries, correctional institutions, and penal institutions. To reduce confusion, the term *prison* will be used in this section.

Prison Types

In most American criminal justice systems, those offenders who have been convicted and sentenced to more than one year of incarceration for a felony offense are generally held in **prisons**. Although many jurisdictions have a juvenile version of a prison system, the majority of prisoners are adults held in state or federal institutions. At any one time, the prison population is composed of offenders sentenced for a variety of offenses as well as those sentenced to prison for probation violations and those returned for violations of their parole. Individual states and the federal government tend to have a number of prisons within their prison systems. Each prison has certain features that make it more suitable for particular types of offenders. Once an inmate is sentenced to prison, personnel from the corrections department usually conduct an initial **classification** review, in which the needs and risk of the offender are evaluated to determine the best placement of that individual within the prison system. Common topics evaluated in this assessment are the danger posed by the prisoner, the length of sentence, any gang affiliation, physical or mental health needs, and whether treatment programs are available and considered important for the prisoner. Based on this assessment, prisoners are sent to an institution that is classified by its security type.

Critical Thinking Exercise

Prisons house offenders who have committed a variety of different offenses. Investigate sources of information on the types of crimes for which offenders have been incarcerated and the demographics of offenders (the textbook website has some suggestions on where to look at http://www.oup.com/us/labessentials). Describe the types of offenses and offenders in prison. What does this suggest about crime that is committed and who commits it?

Most American jurisdictions have three to five different types of prisons, distinguished by their security level. **Supermax prisons** are primarily found in the larger jurisdictions and represent the most restrictive and secure prisons in the country. Because of their extremely high cost of operation and strict limitations on the number of prisoners they can hold, supermax prisons are generally reserved for the most incorrigible and dangerous prisoners in a correctional system. Prisoners in these facilities tend to be continuously confined to their cells except for very brief periods of exercise. Supermax prisons utilize the most sophisticated security systems and most rigorous safety procedures.

Maximum-security prisons represent the highest level of security in many states. These facilities tend to hold the most violent and disruptive prisoners in those jurisdictions without supermax facilities. Inmate movement within the prison is restricted by numerous checkpoints and gates. External barriers such as walled perimeters, several rings of razor-wired fencing, or armed guard towers are also common.

Some jurisdictions use a third security classification known as **close security**, which lies between maximum- and medium-security prisons. Such facilities may be used for individuals convicted of violent offenses who do not require a maximum-security setting or disruptive inmates who do not pose as great a physical threat to inmates or staff. **Medium-security prisons** hold a diverse inmate population and can have a variety of architectural styles. Inmates may have some degree of movement within the institution during certain times of the day and participate in a range of activities. However, the specifics of inmate life and the amount of security can vary considerably, even within different prisons of the same jurisdiction.

Finally, **minimum-security prisons** represent the most open and least restrictive type of institution. These can house prisoners convicted of nonviolent offenses, those who pose a minimal security risk, or those nearing final release. Minimum-security prisons tend to allow the greatest freedom of movement and offer a range of programs and services for inmates to participate in.

Some jurisdictions have **specialized prisons** that primarily house inmates with specific characteristics that pose unique challenges to institutions. These facilities offer treatment programs or services that are tailored to meet the needs and risks posed by particular populations. Examples of these institutions include those dedicated to substance-abusing prisoners, sex offenders, and mentally handicapped or psychiatric prisoners. Each jurisdiction typically has a facility dedicated to housing prisoners with severe psychological disorders because of the unique problems such inmates present to the operation of an institution.

Female offenders may be held in jails that house both males and females, but prisons are typically separated by sex. This was not always the case, however. Historically, females, juveniles, and adult male inmates were often housed in the same facility and perhaps even the same cell. Although females compose about 6 percent of all prisoners and less than 15 percent of all offenders under community supervision, in the past decade females have been one of the fastest-growing correctional populations (Bureau of Justice Statistics 2000). If this trend continues, correctional systems will have to respond to the increasing proportion of female offenders with more designated institutions and additional resources to serve this population.

Another characteristic that can distinguish prisons is whether they are privately operated or managed and staffed by a jurisdiction's own personnel. Historically, it has not been uncommon for some degree of private interest to be involved in the operation of jails and prisons. Since the birth of the modern penitentiary around the turn of the nineteenth century, American correctional systems have had a variety of relationships with private for-profit businesses and nonprofit agencies. However, during the twentieth century, the funding and operation of most American prisons has primarily been the responsibility of the public sector. During the push for increasing privatization of government services in the 1980s, American jurisdictions began increasingly to contract out some of their correctional services (Gowdy 2001).

To date, treatment services, community service, and smaller residential programs are more commonly privatized than major prisons. With rising incarceration rates, prison overcrowding, and increasing operating costs during the 1980s, governments were interested in alternatives that could increase the cost-effectiveness of correctional budgets. While the term **private prison** is often used to indicate a correctional facility that is managed and operated by a private corporation, the privatization of correctional services can take a number of forms. The authority to operate these facilities is granted through a contract awarded by a jurisdiction's government. There is considerable debate about the validity of incorporating a profit motive in the punishment of offenders (Gowdy 2001). There are also real questions about whether private prisons are actually more cost-effective and about the quality of services provided at those institutions. Despite this, punishment is a major for-profit enterprise and several states have private prisons that are used in conjunction with the state-run institutions. Only time will tell whether privatization becomes a permanent and growing feature of American corrections or a passing trend that is remembered primarily in history books.

Critical Thinking Exercise

Investigate the use of private prisons in your state. How many people are in private institutions (nationally and in your state)? Should states be turning over control and supervision of prisoners to for-profit companies? What advantages and disadvantages do you see?

Custody and Security Within Institutions

The primary goal of a prison is maintaining custody of inmates within the institution. So central is this need that nearly every decision affecting the operation of a prison must consider the safety and prison control consequences of that decision. Even within the most secure facilities, at any given time, inmates outnumber **correctional officers** (or guards) who supervise the prisoners. This is particularly true of large, lower-security facilities.

Secure **custody** of inmates actually involves several components. First, prisons must ensure that they are physically secure and can prevent the likelihood of escape and the introduction of contraband into the institution. Second, prison officials want to reduce the occurrence of inmate assaults on staff. Limiting the frequency of inmate-on-inmate violence is another important goal for both the safety of the inmates and the impact such events have on institutional operations. Finally, prison administrators want to secure the efficient functioning of an institution. There are a number of procedures such as head counts and activities such as the feeding, clothing, and work details that create a structure to prison life. The smooth operation of these various activities is vital to a manageable environment.

A symbiotic relationship is thought to exist between prisoners, correctional officers, and prison administrators. Though prison personnel have official (and unofficial) mechanisms at their control to ensure discipline, prisoners can create considerable disruption in the operation of a facility. Therefore, all sides tend to engage in activities and relationships that will maintain the status quo and reduce disruptions to daily life and routines. Clearly, the most destructive and disruptive event is a prison riot. Riots are circumstances in which prison officials lose all but the most basic control over some or all inmates and institutional operations. As a result, staff and inmate safety can be in serious jeopardy and considerable damage can be done to the physical structure of the institution.

Prison Violence and Prison Discipline

Violence, or at least the threat of violence, is a common concern among both inmates and staff. After all, prisons tend to be filled with people who have already demonstrated a willingness to engage in violent or otherwise unlawful acts. Knowledge about violence within prisons is limited by concerns over the validity and reliability of prison records and the limitations of other methodologies used to study **prison violence.** The level and extent of violence will greatly vary from prison to prison and for different prisoners. Different features of the prison, such as its architectural design, inmate freedom of movement, and group and individual dynamics, can affect the level of prison violence (Adams 1992; Bottoms 1999).

Research suggests that most prisons are not characterized by the systematic and rampant violence often portrayed in the popular media (Bottoms 1999). Of course, there have been and continue to be prisons and prison systems that are plagued by higher levels of violence. Coercion and the threat of violence appear to be more common than actual physical assaults. Coercion may be used by physically dominating inmates to obtain items such as food, money, personal services, and sexual favors. This threat of violence, including sexual assault, is very real to prisoners. Furthermore, prisoner assaults on staff and other prisoners do occur and can result in serious injury or death. Female prisons tend to have less explicit violence than male prisons, though violence and the threat of violence are clearly a reality in women's prisons as well. Similar to male prisons, there tend to be female "convicts" within any given institution who are more willing to use instrumental violence and cause disruptions within the facility (Johnson 2002).

Prison officials have a number of tools to deal with violence and other violations of institutional rules. For violations that are criminal offenses, administrators can refer the matter for criminal prosecution. However, the difficulty in obtaining a conviction in many of these cases and the logistical problems involved often discourage such attempts (Jacobs 1982). A more common response is to use one or more of the sanctions that prison officials have at their disposal. These include the loss of certain privileges such as visitation, solitary confinement (often called segregation) for a period of time, or a change in the inmate's classification status or location (Jacobs 1982). Prison officials may also have the discretion to reduce an inmate's good-time credit. In jurisdictions with indeterminate sentencing, parole officials will examine an inmate's behavior and may reject a parole application if an inmate has a history of disruptive behavior while incarcerated.

Prison Life

Prison life can be stressful for both inmates and staff. Research indicates that the unique nature of prison life results in a distinct subculture within prisons. Prison life can be both stressful and monotonous, and adapting to the new environment is essential for an inmate to successfully cope with the demands of prison. Perhaps the most important initial concern is an inmate's personal safety and how to deal with the violence that occurs within an institution.

Prison Subculture and Coping. Most of the research on prison subculture is from the study of maximum-security prisons (e.g., Sykes 1958). There is reason to believe that elements of a unique prison subculture exist even in less secure facilities. Based on the premises of the **deprivation model** used to explain the formation of prison subcultures and adaptation to the prison environment, the nature and impact of an individual prison's culture over its residents will vary across prisons and among residents (Adams 1992; Bottoms 1999; Johnson 2002). In an important work, Sykes (1958) identified several characteristics of prison life that contribute to the development of the prison culture and individual responses to imprisonment. These **pains of imprisonment** included the loss of liberty, deprivation of goods and services, the barring of heterosexual relations, limitations to a prisoner's autonomy, and concerns over personal security. These pains are thought to be central features of prison life and require adaptations by individual prisoners if they are to cope with their new environment in any positive manner (Johnson 2002).

The first pain, the deprivation of liberty, refers to the fact that inmates are confined to the total institution and within the institution. The second pain is the deprivation of goods and services, in which inmates are deprived not only of individual dress, but also of amenities such as televisions, radios, and favorite foods. The third pain is the lack of heterosexual relationships, which makes inmates experience a loss of identity. The fourth pain is the deprivation of autonomy or the lack of freedom to make choices for oneself. The final pain is the deprivation of security, in which inmates are housed together with the violent and the nonviolent, constantly living in fear of victimization.

Since Sykes's publication, the degree to which inmates experience these deprivations has changed. Some deprivations, such as the deprivation of goods and services, have been lessened somewhat with the opportunity to purchase some goods in the commissary. The deprivation of heterosexual relationships can be attenuated if prisoners are allowed conjugal visits with significant others. For example, some women's facilities have provided family "homes" in which family members can visit over a couple of days. These facilities, while still located on prison grounds, are usually set apart from the general prison population. This opportunity is a privilege, not a right; therefore, corrections officials can withhold these visits from inmates in order to gain compliance with directives.

Researchers also believe that individual characteristics, as opposed to the characteristics unique to the prison as detailed in the deprivation model, will affect a particular prisoner's ability to adjust. The **importation model** suggests that the skills, experiences, and attributes that individuals bring with them into a prison environment affect the prison culture and the ability of an individual to adjust to that environment (Adams 1992). Increasingly, researchers recognize that it is likely the interaction of individual attributes and the unique physical and social dynamics of a given institution that will determine the nature of the prison culture and how an individual is able to cope within that setting (Adams 1992). Whatever the specifics of a given institution's subculture, it is important that a prisoner become socialized into this environment by learning the norms or expectations of behavior and various techniques to cope and adapt to this environment.

Prison Programs. With the exception of the highest-security prisons, most prisons offer some **prison programs** promoted as helping with offender rehabilitation and increasing the structure and activities involved in an inmate's daily routine. The number and types of programs vary in different institutions and jurisdictions. In some jurisdictions, inmates can receive good-time credits by productively participating in approved activities. In states with indeterminate sentencing, inmates may consider that participation in certain programs improves their chances of an earlier parole release. Prisoners may be given a particular work assignment that constitutes a major part of their day. Many basic prison operations, such as food service, laundry, and groundskeeping, are carried out by prisoners with varying degrees of staff supervision. Other prison programs may be of a more voluntary nature. Participation in activities such as religious groups, substance abuse and counseling programs, educational classes, and charity and self-help groups may be offered for interested and eligible prisoners. While the funding for such programs tends to be a relatively low priority, many scholars and practitioners consider these types of activities important in helping prisoners cope with the stresses of prison life and improving prisoners' likelihood of successful reintegration after release (e.g., Gaes et al. 1999).

SPECIAL OFFENDER POPULATIONS

Similar to the general public, the prison population is composed of individuals with substance abuse problems, mental illness, physical disabilities, and diseases. There has also been an increase in the number of aging offenders in correctional institutions due to the "get-tough" sentencing policies adopted and implemented during the 1980s. Inmates are a unique population in that they are one of two groups in society that are entitled to medical treatment based on decisions handed down by the U.S. Supreme Court. The other group is the military. Although there are services available in society to deal with these issues and problems, the prison, its officials, and its "guests" are often forced to deal with such a wide variety of problems. It is important that we become better acquainted with special offender populations.

Inmates and HIV/AIDS

Since the 1980s, the prison population, like the general population, has witnessed an explosion of individuals diagnosed as HIV positive or with full-blown AIDS. Today, there are approximately 24,000 inmates in state and federal prisons who are HIV positive, and one-quarter of that number have confirmed cases of active AIDS (Maruschak 2004). Prior to 1999, it was estimated that prisoners were seven to nine times more likely to have confirmed cases of AIDS than the general population. The good news is that, since 1999, the number of inmates who have HIV/AIDS is decreasing. Despite this, AIDS is a leading cause of death in prison.

The number one method of transmission of HIV in the United States is through the sharing of needles or other equipment used to ingest illegal substances. The increase in mandatory minimum sentencing practices arguably led to an increase of substance users in prison, many of whom had already been exposed to HIV. In secure facilities HIV is most often spread through sexual contact between inmates who were most likely exposed prior to their incarceration via unclean drug-taking methods.

Correctional administrators and staff across the country have implemented several approaches to decreasing the number of new cases within the prison. Some institutions focus on education in terms of how the disease is contracted and treatment options available. A few institutions have provided condoms for those inmates engaged in sexual activities; however, this option is controversial, as sex between inmates is usually prohibited. Voluntary or mandatory testing to determine who is infected with HIV has also been used. Special housing for inmates at different stages of the disease has also been attempted. It has been proposed that, at a minimum, infirmaries should be established where inmates already confirmed to have AIDS can be held to protect them from airborne infections such as tuberculosis and pneumonia.

Many state corrections systems have been proactive in collaborating with public health agencies to increase the knowledge about how to take care of not only HIV/AIDS in the prison, but also other sexually transmitted diseases and tuberculosis, which are widespread among correctional populations disproportionate to the general population (Hammett 1998). Given that many inmates will eventually be released into society and the gravity of these communicable diseases, there is a definite need to provide appropriate treatment, prevention, and postrelease programs to curb further transmission of these conditions. Thus, it would be remiss to ignore what goes on in the prison merely because the population affected is made up of offenders.

Critical Thinking Exercise

What should be the response of prisons to HIV/AIDS and other sexually transmitted diseases? What alternatives make the most sense? What do institutions in your state do to deal with these problems?

Inmates and Substance Use

Nearly one-half of offenders housed in jails and prisons across the United States admit to having been under the influence of alcohol or drugs when they committed the current offenses that led to their incarceration. Drug and property offenders are more likely than other types of offenders to engage in crime to acquire money to feed their substance addiction. The mentally ill are more likely to be under the influence at the time of their offenses than those who are not mentally ill. Overall, approximately 70–80 percent of incarcerated offenders report that they have used drugs in their past. Younger offenders, particularly those who are first-time or minor drug offenders, make up a significant proportion of jail populations. Since the war on drugs in the 1980s, the United States has seen unprecedented increases in incarceration rates for drug crimes that carry longer sentences than was typically the case prior to "getting tough."

Given that kicking the habit is difficult for those seeking treatment in the general population and their success rates are low, the environment of the prison often complicates effective service delivery for inmates to rid themselves of their substance addictions. Treatment in correctional facilities can involve counseling, therapeutic communities, detoxification, and 12-step programs such as Alcoholics Anonymous or Narcotics Anonymous. Some institutions also provide aftercare services for released inmates to prevent relapse. The introduction of drug courts as alternatives to incapacitation since the late 1980s has provided yet another avenue for handling offenders with substance abuse problems.

Overall, some treatment programs have been found to be ineffective in reducing recidivism as much as would be desired. It is important to note, however, that only about 20 percent of inmates in secure confinement actually participate in alcohol or drug-treatment programs that are offered. If inmates do participate, they usually do so during the last six months of their sentences. The length of time in treatment could be one of the hurdles standing in the way of reducing recidivism. In fact, a review of the literature demonstrates that programs that do work are intensive, last 9–12 months, focus on offenders who are younger and more at risk, and maintain services upon and after release. They actually work quite well and save money, too. Several recent studies have observed that offenders who participate in treatment programs both in prison *and* in the outside community have fewer occasions of drug relapse and criminality (see McCollister et al. 2004).

Aging and Elderly Inmates

One prominent issue in the United States over the past 10 years has been a surge in the percentage of the population over the age of 55. News reports and politicians have often highlighted this fact with an emphasis on government programs in need of reform such as Social Security and Medicare, long-term care, and prescription drug costs. Special housing such as assisted-living communities and retirement communities has been a significant money maker for construction companies, investors, and real estate developers alike. Few cities over 50,000 residents are without such properties.

Recall that what happens in the general society soon occurs inside the prison walls. With the mandate to provide medical treatment for inmates, the costs and unique problems posed by an aging prison population is an ever-pressing dilemma for an institution that traditionally held convicted offenders between the ages of 18 and 49. Longer sentences, life-without-parole sanctions, and mandatory-minimum provisions have resulted in a corrections system that needs to allocate three times the expenditures to care for aging inmates compared to their younger counterparts (Faiver 1998). Some state prisons have created special wings that are essentially nursing homes to provide for their share of older prisoners.

When people age, in or out of prison, they change physically, socially, and mentally. For offenders who are aging behind bars, however, many of the issues associated with aging are aggravated and heightened. Although aging inmates are entitled to health care, the quality of that care may not be sufficient to take care of many of the problems associated with old age, such as dementia. In addition, older inmates may not be able to take care of themselves if they are harassed or assaulted by younger inmates.

Possible solutions to the above-noted problems involve early release on medical parole, sentences served in the community for older offenders who do not pose a significant risk to the community, increases in funding to serve aging inmates, and the creation of geriatric units within existing and proposed facilities. Certainly, the former two alternatives would be the most cost-effective for the administration of corrections, considering that offenders serving their time in the community are responsible for their own housing, medical treatment, and daily care. Government allocation of more funds to correctional budgets would be helpful, but not practical or economical based on recent fiscal crises over the past several years. In general, most states spend more on corrections than on education and other social programs.

Creating geriatric units is becoming the major approach for dealing with the aging inmate population. The public, at least for now, does not appear willing to give up on the philosophy of retribution, which is interesting given that there is also public support for rehabilitation efforts. Nonetheless, sanctions such as "three strikes, you're out" are still receiving support from the public and policymakers. For example, in November of 2004, citizens of California were given the opportunity to amend their "three-strikes" law to require giving longer sentences only to offenders who commit serious or violent felonies on their second or third offenses, rather than any felony, as the law then read. The proposal, known as Proposition 66, was not adopted. Thus, with sentencing strategies that require lengthy prison terms, the concomitant struggle of how to effectively provide services to an aging inmate population will not be easily resolved.

Inmates and Mental Illness

Historically, asylums held society's misfits, whether they were insane, poor, or criminal. In nineteenth-century America, asylums were institutions where the mentally troubled were held until a cure for their sickness could be found. Once tranquilizers became available, asylum patients were basically sedated into a stupor. Essentially, this practice continued into the twentieth century. Long-term institutionalization in a secure hospital setting became the primary method of care in the United States until the early 1970s. Family members of relatives confined in the mental hospitals were requesting lengthier periods of confinement for them. Something had to be done.

With the passage and implementation of community mental health acts by states across the country, patients housed in the asylums who were no longer considered to be a threat to themselves or others were released into general society, a process called **deinstitutionalization.** Soon, many city streets in America were occupied by thousands of mentally ill ex-hospital patients, many of whom were unable to function in ways that were deemed appropriate law-abiding behaviors. Most jurisdictions responded to the problem by confining these "offenders" in correctional institutions. This process is known as **trans-institutionalization**; the mentally ill were first placed in secure confinement in a hospital setting, then they were released, and then they were reconfined, this time under the auspices of the criminal justice system.

Today, it is estimated that 10–20 percent of inmates housed in jails or prisons can be classified as having a mental disability (Pollock 2004). Nearly all of the state public and private correctional facilities in the United States reported in 2000 that they provided some sort of treatment to cover inmates' mental health needs (Beck and Maruschak 2001). Treatment forms range from therapy or counseling services to psychotropic medications and separate care units within the facility.

Inmates with mental disabilities are often at most risk for victimization, both physically and psychologically. These inmates are also found to be difficult for staff to control because many correctional officers do not have the training or educational background to deal with the compounded problems inmates with mental illness face in correctional facilities, especially when officers must give inmates orders of compliance to maintain security and control within the institutions. For example, correctional officers may be required to distinguish between those inmates who truly do not understand the orders that they are given, and as a result act out irrationally, from those who understand the expectations but become upset because they do not want to comply (Pollock 2004).

Dual-disorder inmates are also becoming a major concern for management issues in the nation's prisons and jails. These inmates are those who can be classified as having both substance abuse and mental health problems. These inmates are especially problematic for jails, since the majority of these offenders are purportedly arrested more frequently for less serious offenses (Alemagno et al. 2004). In addition, some of these dual-disordered individuals may seek treatment in a traditional psychiatric center for their mental illness, but they are often turned away because some centers or programs prefer not to deal with patients who also have drug addictions.

Critical Thinking Exercise

To what extent should correctional institutions be responsible for handling mentally ill individuals? Why does the criminal justice system assume responsibility for these individuals? Should it continue? What alternatives exist (or should exist) for handling these individuals?

Secure institutions in the criminal justice system have been facing an increase in the number of inmates with characteristics that require special assistance and programming. There has been progress in providing services for the mentally ill in terms of screening for problems and treatment availability, but more needs to be done. The same can be stated for aging inmates, inmates with diseases, particularly HIV/AIDS, and inmates with substance abuse issues. These special populations, however, will continue to grow as long as legislation is supported that increases sentence lengths for various offenses and broadens the types of offenses punishable by incarceration.

PROBLEMS, RIGHTS, AND IMPLICATIONS IN MODERN PRISONS

In addition to the challenging composition of inmate populations, institutional corrections will continue to deal with the problems of crowding, violence, and decreased availability of effective programs to reduce recidivism. Of course, these issues existed in the past and, given the heavy reliance on institutional facilities for punishments over the past few decades, will most likely persist in the future. Many of these issues have been brought to the attention of the courts by prisoners seeking to lessen the impact that the unique features of prison have on their lives. Even though many decisions set forth by the courts could be considered in favor of such solutions as reducing inmate crowding, the reality is that changes to rectify these problems have been more the exception than the rule. Indeed, some argue that problems surrounding inmate rights, crowding, violence, and inmate social systems have actually worsened over time.

Inmate Rights

Traditionally, appellate courts took a hands-off approach to the problems and grievances of those incarcerated (Haas and Alpert 1989). The reasons for this hands-off approach were that (1) the courts felt that they should not interfere with the operations of the prisons; (2) the judiciary offered a type of checks and balances; and (3) the judiciary could not possibly understand the problems of prison administrators because judges lacked a coherent knowledge of penology (Haas and Alpert 1989). In 1941, the Supreme Court ruled in *Ex parte Hull* that the Fifth and Fourteenth Amendments to the Bill of Rights granted everyone, even inmates, access to the courts (Haas and Alpert 1989). However, not until 1964 did the courts really begin to lift the hands-off policy with the *Cooper v. Pate* decision.

Until the mid-1960s, most prisons were homogenous institutions in which strict control, sometimes rehabilitation, and structure were the rule (Sykes 1958). With the advent of the civil rights movement, many groups began to seek legitimacy for their grievances and remedies to their problems through court decisions. The courthouse door opened for inmates and granted them access to address their grievances similar to that of other groups in society. This hands-on approach to inmate rights has led to lessening a number of deprivations, but also paved the way for inequitable sentences, which could undermine other goals or philosophies of the criminal justice system in general and the corrections system in particular.

The prisoners' rights movement led to the establishment of certain privileges that were not previously available. For instance, inmates now could buy televisions or radios, wear what they wanted in some prisons, or have visitors bring in amenities (Carroll 1974). This led to a situation of the "haves" versus the "have nots" in which the "have nots" could burglarize or victimize the "haves" to obtain what they wanted. The purpose of utilizing correctional facilities for incapacitation is to prevent offenders from committing any further crimes. If crime continues in the prison, the goal of incapacitation is weakened.

Another result of the prisoners' rights movement is increased freedom of movement and the elimination of the requirement that inmates must participate in treatment programs. Lack of structure means idle time for some inmates, which occasionally leads to violence (Wooldredge 1994). This means that some inmates will experience a rougher time in prison than others because they are being victimized. Therefore, the philosophy of retribution is undermined in that no longer will punishment for similar crimes be the same for all inmates (Hawkins and Alpert 1989). Rehabilitation as a goal may be impossible to meet because inmates must be able to concentrate on their treatment and, if they are constantly worrying about being victimized, they cannot actively participate in their own reformation. Deterrence—the idea that imposing severe punishments will create enough fear that the costs will outweigh the benefits of committing crime—may also be undermined because some inmates will be victims and some will continue to be offenders. Correctional officers often look the other way for most infractions because they do not want to attract the attention of administrations that are primarily concerned about the effective control of prisons (Zimmer 1986).

Legislation passed by Congress in 1995, however, may change the current state of affairs for both correctional philosophies and prisoners' rights. The Prison Litigation Reform Act (PLRA) establishes that inmates must exhaust the internal prison grievance procedures before accessing the federal courts. The PLRA also requires inmates to pay their own court filing fees, thereby further limiting access to judicial review of complaints by inmates. In addition, the PLRA reinforces the right of the courts to dismiss any lawsuit deemed by judges to be frivolous or malicious or to state an improper claim. If an inmate receives three such determinations (i.e., three "strikes") regarding his or her petitions, the inmate is restricted from filing further lawsuits without paying court fees in advance. Prisoners also face the possibility of losing good-time credit if judges find that the purpose of their grievances was harassment or a presentation of lies or false information. Further, the PLRA has a provision mandating that inmates must show physical injury in order to file a claim for mental or emotional injury. State inmate petitions filed in U.S. district courts, for both civil rights and prison-conditions grievances, did decline after the passage of the PLRA. Despite these reductions in inmate lawsuits, several key cases did make their way to the U.S. Supreme Court and further affected life in prison and correctional operations. Table 5.2 summarizes these decisions.

Table 5.2 Key cases decided by the U.S. Supreme Court concerning prisoners' rights

CASE	DECISION
Shaw v. Murphy (2000)	Inmates do not have a special First Amendment right to provide legal assistance to fellow inmates.
Booth v. Churner (2000)	Inmates must still exhaust prison administrative remedies before going to court to seek monetary damages even in those situations where such damages are not part of the administrative process.
Overton v. Bazzetta (2003)	Department of Corrections can withdraw visitation privileges for a limited period without violating inmates' due-process rights under the Fourteenth Amendment or their Eighth Amendment protections against cruel and unusual punishment.
Garrison S. Johnson v. California (2004)	Racially segregating all new inmates must be subjected to judicial scrutiny to determine whether the practice is a violation of the equal protection clause or serves a compelling governmental interest such as institutional safety and security.
Cutter v. Wilkinson (2004)	Inmates are free to practice their religion as they wish as long as the safety, order, and security of the prison are not compromised by these practices, even if the religions are considered bizarre or nonmainstream.
Beard v. Banks (2006)	Prisoners held in long-term segregation can be denied access to nonreligious newspapers and magazines because doing so promotes rehabilitation and ensures institutional safety.
Jones v. Bock (2006) consolidated with *Williams v. Overton* (2006)	Judicially created rules (e.g., requiring inmates to demonstrate how they exhausted the administrative processes per the PLRA of 1995) that seriously obstruct an inmate from bringing grievances to federal court are not permitted.

Crowding

Due to the growing trend of incarcerating and managing large numbers of offenders because of the fall of rehabilitation, more punitive sentencing policies, and increasing the number of offenses eligible for incarceration, crowding has become an endemic problem in the United States. For example, it is estimated that 44 percent of the prison population can be accounted for due to the war on drugs (Blumstein 1995). The rise in prison populations is indicative of the trends that can be attributed to judges and prosecutors in convicting more persons and sending them to prison. Prison populations will vary according to (1) how many people are sentenced to prison; (2) how long offenders are sent to prison; and (3) the rate at which they return (Joyce 1992).

Crowding leads to a number of problems within the institution, such as elevated blood pressures, more trips to clinics, difficulty sleeping, suicides, homicides, and other types of assaultive behaviors (Gaes and McGuire 1985; Harer and Steffensmeier 1996). In addition, crowding adds to the uncertainty, apprehension, and cognitive overloads of inmates. These emotional difficulties can interfere with treatment because inmates need to concentrate on their reformation; if they are constantly living in fear, this becomes a near-impossible task. Crowding can also undermine rehabilitation, in that classification of inmates into appropriate housing, programs, and the like is made more difficult and can deplete resources, leaving some inmates to be placed on treatment waiting lists or leading to the eradication of rehabilitation programs altogether.

In addition, crowding can undermine incapacitation due to early release mechanisms relied upon to reduce the population. In effect, inmates are on the streets sooner and may return to crime due to shorter sentence lengths. Inmate crowding can also weaken the goal of general deterrence because would-be offenders see that crowding has led to limited space in facilities, which means that they may not receive prison sentences at all. Crowding can also weaken the objectives of specific deterrence due to the harsh living conditions of the prison environment. Finally, crowding can negatively affect retribution because no two sentences will be served equitably due to crowding.

Violence

As noted, violence in prison has become more and more pervasive due to the ever-changing composition of the prison population, such as the entrance of gangs and the mentally disordered, and the pervasive impact of the prisoners' rights movement (Irwin 1980). Inmates are free to move around the facilities, which leads to more opportunities for victimization. In addition, due to increased crowding, classification efforts may be ineffective at separating violent inmates from the nonviolent (Van Voorhis 1994). Further, because inmates are not required to participate in treatment programs, they have plenty of free time. It has been found that inmates who spend less time in educational activities are more likely to commit personal crimes (Wooldredge 1994). In addition, the impact of determinate sentencing, the entrance of younger inmates into the prison, decreases in furloughs, lack of visitation, and longer time until parole dates can lead to increases in violence (Burke 1995).

Violence undermines retribution because some inmates are offenders and some are victims; this is not equal time for equal crimes. Violence weakens the goals of deterrence and incapacitation because the mere existence of violence in prison means that threats of punishments and preventing further crimes are ineffective at suppressing violence. Rehabilitation efforts may also be unsuccessful because some inmates live in fear of being victimized, and inmates must feel in total control of their beings and safety in order to gain anything from treatment efforts.

Critical Thinking Exercise

You are the director of the Department of Corrections for your state. The governor has just informed you that you need to devise a plan to reduce prison crowding by 30 percent in year one, by 40 percent in year two, and by 10 percent each year thereafter until prison crowding in your state's facilities is near 0 percent. How will you accomplish this task? What policies would you propose to reduce incarceration rates? Why do you think these would work? What are some of the problems you might face when implementing your policies? Remember to take into account special offender populations when designing your plan.

Inmate Subcultures

Inmate subcultures originally developed out of the pains of imprisonment. Subcultures can help us understand the socialization of inmates, can help us determine how inmates are adapting to the prison environment, and can provide insight for correctional officers to control the prison environment. Before the prisoners' rights movement, prisons were more homogenous and every inmate suffered the same deprivations (Sykes 1958). After the prisoners' rights movement, many deprivations were weakened. For example, inmates are able to move around facilities more freely, and this liberty can lead to more cohesiveness among inmates. In the mid-1970s, life within the prison walls began to look like life on the outside: racially, politically, and religiously divided (Carroll 1974; Irwin 1980).

The traditional subculture of inmates versus correctional officers became inmates versus inmates. The black population became politically and religiously centered around the rally of white oppression and racism, often divided across racial and ethnic identities. Whites, on the other hand, only looked out for number one when it came to surviving in prison (Carroll 1974). These events broke the solidarity-in-numbers factor inherent in the traditional inmate subculture. In addition, gangs began to enter prisons, which made it easier for new inmates to adapt to prison life when their gangs were already established within a facility (Irwin 1980). See Table 5.3 to learn the characteristics of the six major prison gangs affecting U.S. prisons today. Further, inmates from the mentally ill population led to more problems and more stratification of the inmate population (Irwin 1980).

Table 5.3 Characteristics of Six Major Prison Gangs in U.S. Prisons

GANG	DATE & LOCATION OF ORIGINATION	RACIAL/ETHNIC COMPOSITION	COMMON IDENTIFIERS	RIVALS	WAY OF LIFE
Aryan Brotherhood	1967 in San Quentin State Prison, CA	White	Swastikas, shamrock clover leaf, initials "AB", numbers "666", double lightning bolts	Black Guerrilla Family, Crips, Bloods, El Rukns	Hold white supremacy ideologies, introduce contraband, drugs, and shirking rules and regulations while in prison, work with Mexican Mafia
Black Guerrilla Family	1966 in San Quentin State Prison, CA	Black	Cross sabers and shotgun, black dragon overtaking prison or prison tower, antiauthority mentality shown by display of "BGF" initials	Aryan Brotherhood, Texas Syndicate, Aryan Brotherhood of Texas, Mexican Mafia	Most political of prison gangs, work with La Nuestra Familia, Black street gang members are recruited upon imprisonment, history of violent acts
La Nuestra Familia	Mid-1960s in Soledad Prison, CA	Mexican-American (traditionally rural, young)/Hispanic	Red rags, large tattoos often on their backs, initials "NF", "LNF", "ENE", "F", number 14 for "N" standing for Norte or Northern California, sombrero with dagger symbol	Mexican Mafia (primary rival), Texas Syndicate, Mexikanemi, F-14s, Aryan Brotherhood	Started to protect members from Mexican Mafia, membership extends beyond prison, drug trafficking, extortion, and pressure rackets
Mexican Mafia	Late 1950s at Duel Vocational Center (young offender facility), CA	Mexican-American/Hispanic	"EME" initials, eagle and snake with "EME", black single handprint, "MM" or "M" initials, EME symbol of eternal war	La Nuestra Familia (primary rival), Northern Structure, Arizona's New Mexican Mafia, Black Guerrilla Family, black street gangs	Ethnic solidarity and supremacy, drug trafficking, most active gang in federal prisons, extortion, and pressure rackets, will kill to punish or gain respect

Neta	1970 Rio Pedras Prison, Puerto Rico	Puerto Rican-American/Hispanic	Red, white, and blue, sometimes black for blue, are colors, wear beads, clothing, rags, and other items in these colors, Puerto Rican flag, have Neta identification cards, emblem of heart pierced by two crossing Puerto Rican flags and a shackled right hand with middle and index fingers crossed	Latin Kings, Los Solidos	Started to halt violence between inmates in the Rio Pedras Prison, claim to be a cultural organization, very patriotic, call for independence of Puerto Rico, view themselves as oppressed, not willing to be governed by U.S. authorities, keep low profile, drug trade and extortion, known danger to staff and inmates
Texas Syndicate	Early 1970s, Folsom Prison, CA	Mexican-American/Hispanic	Tattoos with "TS" located on back of right forearm or outside neck, chest, or calf areas	Aryan Brotherhood, La Nuestra Familia, Mexican Mafia, Mexikanemi, Mandingo Warriors	Started to protect native Texas inmates from CA prison gangs. Membership increasing, considered to be a security threat in prisons due to violent acts, drug trafficking, extortion, and pressure rackets

SOURCE: Florida Department of Corrections (n.d.) Gang security and threat group awareness. Retrieved April 30, 2009, from http://www.dc.state.fl.us/pub/gangs/index.html.

Even though the inmate subculture is often considered a phenomenon of the past, pockets of unified groups and gangs exist behind prison walls; they are essentially the same gangs found outside of prison (Jacobs 1976). The mere existence of unified groups in prison can undermine rehabilitation because some pockets are more cohesive than others, which places non-gang members in the path of victimization. The constant worry of being harassed and maltreated is counterproductive to meeting individual treatment goals. It is also difficult to meet the goal of deterrence because offenders who are members of a gang or group may not be deterred from prison if their group is in a position of power in the facility. Retribution can be weakened much in the same way for inmates whose gang or group is in prison, because their time will be more easily spent. Therefore, no two sentences will be proportional. Finally, incapacitation goals may be impossible to achieve because there will be crime within the prison due to the tension between rival gangs or between inmates who belong and those who do not.

Solutions

Possible solutions to these problems have been studied and found to be promising. For example, architecturally smaller, more efficiently designed prisons are better able to alleviate the problems posed by violence, inmate subcultures, and crowding. New designs used in jails such as the new-generation or direct-supervision jails have already been witnessed. Such facilities make better use of design to promote a safer and more controlled environment for correctional officers. Smaller facilities may also encourage inmates to engage in activities such as treatment, vocational training, or education in a manner that can be replicated on the outside when they are released. Housing inmates in huge, dark, noisy prisons is not beneficial for any goal, let alone the well-being of inmates.

If classification systems, which have been found to be valid in dividing prison populations into manageable subgroups, are utilized more effectively, there may be reductions in violence and crowding (Van Voorhis 1994). Arguably, some inmates do not belong in prison in the first place, and classification systems can dictate which offenders would be better served in the community. More emphasis might be placed on separating the violent from the nonviolent, the aging from the young, and the mentally disabled from the general population. These types of separation could reduce levels of violence, dilute the inherent inequities that resulted from the prisoners' rights movement, and counterbalance the emergence of gangs in correctional institutions.

In addition to classification systems, alternatives to incarceration such as intensive supervision probation and home confinement coupled with treatment interventions could be utilized. Better use of administrative good time and sentencing guidelines to reduce sentence lengths may also help alleviate crowding as well as violence and other problems (Joyce 1992). Perhaps limiting parole supervision to one year could be implemented if prison is used as the sanction of choice or if community corrections are used. The conditions required of offenders could be limited to those that are necessary to ensure public safety.

FUTURE DIRECTIONS FOR INSTITUTIONAL CORRECTIONS

Like all components of the criminal justice system, correctional systems reflect the characteristics and environment of the society that they serve. It is only natural that, as society changes, so will the institutions designed to reinforce and protect it. While there is inadequate space to cover the considerable number of important issues facing corrections in the next few decades, the following discussion will briefly touch on some of these issues.

Perhaps the most compelling issue is what will happen with the prison population and incarceration rate, which has seen a fourfold increase over the past 30 years. The wars on crime and drugs have taken an enormous toll on government budgets, often to the detriment of other human services such as education and social services. It is unclear whether jurisdictions can maintain the level of spending on corrections indefinitely or whether public and political support will continue for such expenditures. The wars on crime and drugs have also had a considerable impact on the social fabric of communities and society in general that we are only beginning to understand (Hagan and Dinovitzer 1999). Removing such a large number of persons from society will have an observable impact on the children, families, and communities of offenders. This impact will likely include a number of negative consequences. Expanding the prison population also increases the number of prisoners who will eventually return to the community with additional burdens. What steps are taken to reintegrate this population into the community and the success of those efforts will be important issues for the country as a whole.

A second major issue is how institutional supervision will deal with the special-needs offenders who are increasingly becoming part of the correctional population. One population demanding special attention is the growing number of substance abusers and addicts in jails and prisons. Although prisons have always had a disproportionate number of substance abusers among their populations, quality drug-treatment programs have never been a high priority within correctional budgets. Most programs tend to be understaffed, underfunded, poorly designed and implemented, and simply too short in duration to adequately address the multifaceted problem of substance abuse. The relatively high percentage of HIV-positive inmates presents another set of unique legal, medical, and operational challenges to correctional institutions. How prisons respond to HIV-positive inmates and the measures they take to limit the spread of the virus within institutions will require balancing the needs and rights of the individual with the needs of the other inmates and the institutions. Medication and treatment for illnesses related to HIV also increase medical costs for correctional budgets.

A third population that will increasingly become a fixture in institutions is the elderly. As jurisdictions have increased sentence lengths and decreased the discretion to reduce those sentences, the percentage of older inmates has increased. Incarcerated elderly inmates will require additional medical resources and have special physical and psychological needs.

CONCLUSION

Clearly, there are problems and challenges that correctional systems face. The nature of the problems is a function of the society that a correctional system serves. Exploring alternatives to secure confinement and methods to improve existing conditions within institutions should be seriously considered. Currently, it could be argued that none of the goals of the criminal justice system has been achieved due to the problems and characteristics of current correctional environments. Crowding, violence, gangs, and even the unforeseen consequences of the prisoners' rights movement have helped to further diminish the prospects for effective rehabilitation, retribution, incapacitation, and deterrence. These realizations should be at the heart of policies and reforms; there are no short-term solutions to problems that have lasted for decades, especially when they were exacerbated during periods when crime rates were decreasing.

KEY WORDS

classification
close security
convict leasing
correctional officers
custody
deinstitutionalization
deprivation model
detention centers
dual-disorder inmates
importation model
industrial era
jails

maximum-security
  prisons
medium-security prisons
minimum-security
  prisons
new-generation jails
  (NGJs)
pains of imprisonment
penitentiary era
prisons
prison programs
prison violence

private prison
punishment
reform era
rehabilitation
rehabilitation era
retributive era
specialized prisons
supermax prisons
trans-institutionalization

SUGGESTED READINGS

Jacobson, M. (2005). *Downsizing prisons: How to reduce crime and end mass incarceration.* New York: New York University Press.

National Center for Education Statistics, U.S. Department of Education. (2008). *Digest of Education Statistics, 2007* (NCES 2008–022), Table 171.

Pew Center on the States. (2008). One in 100: Behind bars in America in 2008. *Public Safety Performance Project.* http://www.pewcenteronthestates.org.

Pew Center on the States. (2009). One in 31: The long reach of American corrections. *Public Safety Performance Project.* http://www.pewcenteronthestates.org.

Pratt, J. (2002). *Punishment and civilization: Penal tolerance and intolerance in modern society.* Thousand Oaks, CA: Sage Publications.

Pratt, T.C. (2009). *Addicted to incarceration: Corrections policy and politics of misinformation in the United States.* Los Angeles, CA: Sage.

Santos, M. (2004). *About prison.* Belmont, CA: Thomson/Wadsworth.

Terry, C. (2003). *The fellas: Overcoming prison and addiction.* Belmont, CA: Thomson/Wadsworth. ◆

CHAPTER 6

Community Corrections

CHAPTER OUTLINE

Community corrections constitutes the various sanctions and forms of supervision that occur within the community rather than in an institutional setting. Contemporary forms of community corrections include probation, intermediate sanctions, and parole supervision. Although some types of **intermediate sanctions**, such as boot camps and community residential programs, occur in institutional settings, such programs are generally brief in duration and include an element of community supervision. Therefore, they are typically included in discussions of community corrections. Although institutions such as jails and prisons are commonly identified as the prototypical punishment in the United States, far more offenders are supervised in the community than in institutions (Bureau of Justice Statistics 2008b). In fact, 70 percent of the American correctional population is supervised in the community (Bureau of Justice Statistics 2008b). Thus, community corrections is an important aspect of the criminal justice system and one that requires further discussion.

Correctional agencies and institutions are responsible for administering the penalties imposed on convicted offenders by the courts. Generally considered to be the end of the criminal justice process, the correctional agencies actually provide a range of services to the criminal justice system and participates in collaborative activities with a variety of criminal justice and human service agencies. For example, probation officers in many jurisdictions are responsible for conducting court-ordered investigations on defendants, such as presentence investigations, and submitting reports to assist in judicial decision making. In their community supervision efforts, community correctional officers may have informal or formal arrangements with drug-treatment programs, area schools and aftercare programs, and local law enforcement.

Similar to the various types of detention and prision facilities, community correctional services are provided by a number of different agencies depending on the legal and geographic jurisdiction. The federal government has a number of community correctional programs, and local and state governments have various community correctional programs for both juveniles and adults. The decentralized nature of criminal justice in the United States makes it difficult to generalize about specific practices and policies. Because the purpose of this text is to be an introduction to the essential features of the criminal justice system, this chapter discusses community corrections generally, with an emphasis on sanctions and supervision of adults in the community (see Chapter 7 for discussions about juvenile sanctions). While specific practices and the types of sanctions that are available will differ across jurisdictions, many of the underlying principles and issues are quite similar.

HISTORY OF COMMUNITY CORRECTIONS

For most of human history, punishment has been "community" based. With the exception of banishment, most punishments were carried out in a public setting or in a manner that involved community members (especially victims) to a far greater extent than today. The most common punishments in Western societies typically had a monetary or corporal nature, such as whipping, stocks, and stoning, and either sought to reinforce community norms and obedience or attempted to restore relations between private individuals (in the form of restitution). Punishing offenders by removing them from the community and incarcerating them for a specified period in a facility built specifically for that purpose is largely a modern practice. Chapter 5 described the numerous changes in the later eighteenth and early nineteenth centuries that were associated with the birth and development of the penitentiary and its use. However, by the middle of the nineteenth century, additional changes were occuring that led to an increased use of **community supervision** for offenders. Many of these community correctional practices had their roots in historical practices, such as judicial reprieve and release on recognizance, that were designed to mitigate the severity of criminal punishment (Clear and Dammer 2003).

By the nineteenth century, the ideas of the Enlightenment, the growth of capitalism, and democratic values were influencing attitudes about crime and society. These changes led to new approaches to dealing with problems of social order in the new American republic. In particular, the impact of the social environment on morality and behavior was increasingly identified as a source of crime and disorder (Rothman 1971). Within this context, the notion of individual reform, whether based on moral repentance or changing environmental factors, was incorporated into views about what to do about criminal behavior, especially among less serious offenders. Such ideas would have a direct impact on the development of two of the major forms of community corrections: probation and parole.

Of increasing concern in the new republic was drunkenness and the perceived problems associated with it (Rothman 1971). During the nineteenth century, those arrested for public drunkenness were frequently sentenced to periods of confinement in local jails, which were often overcrowded and characterized by filth and disease. It was in just such a case that John Augustus, a Boston boot maker and philanthropist, asked a Boston court to release an offender into his custody in 1841. Motivated by humanitarian interests, Augustus allowed the defendant to reside in his home and assisted him in securing employment while requiring that the offender abide by certain conditions. It was from this humble beginning that **probation** started. After returning to court with the defendant several weeks later, the court was impressed with the apparent change in the offender and agreed to continue to suspend his sentence as long as he remained in good conduct. Augustus soon returned to court to select additional offenders whom he supervised under certain conditions in exchange for the court delaying the imposition of the original sentences (Abadinsky 1997).

For the next 18 years and until his death in 1859, Augustus developed a system of interviewing defendants to determine their suitability for release. In addition, he developed a set of conditions for offenders, reported on released offenders' progress, and notified the court if offenders violated a condition of their supervision (Clear and Dammer 2003). These remain essential features of probation nearly 150 years later. In 1878, the Massachusetts legislature created a paid position for a probation officer who was to be assigned to the Boston court (Abadinsky 1997). By 1925, formal probation organizations existed in numerous state and local jurisdictions, including a federal probation system and, by 1956, probation was available for adult felony offenders in all U.S. states and under the federal government (Abadinsky 1997).

During the same time that probation was in its inception, dissatisfaction with the new American penal system and the apparent failure to achieve its initial goals was spreading (Rothman 1971). In particular, innovations by prison administrators in Australia and Ireland had a considerable impact on American criminal justice systems. In 1840, Alexander Maconochie became administrator of the Norfolk Island penal colony off the coast of Australia (Abadinsky 1997). Maconochie arrived at a penal colony that had experienced a number of disruptions and set about to institute changes to encourage individual reform. The system he developed was based on "marks" that prisoners earned towards early release. Prisoners would pass through stages of increasing liberty on the island after periods of good conduct and could eventually earn an early conditional release from the colony. While the experiment appeared to result in improved prisoner conduct, it was politically unpopular and Maconochie was removed as superintendent of the colony in 1844 (Abadinsky 1997).

Although Maconochie's mark system lasted for only a few years, news of his experiment reached Britain. Soon after, laws were passed that allowed for awarding "tickets of leave" for those prisoners who earned early release, during which time they were to be supervised by the local police (Abadinsky 1997). In 1854, Walter Crofton became head of the Irish prison system and instituted policies based on Maconochie's earlier experiment. Under the Irish system, prisoners progressed through four stages of incarceration, each providing a greater level of freedom within the institution, resulting ultimately in early release through a ticket of leave. Importantly, released prisoners were given conditions of release and were supervised by either local police or a civilian who was assigned this responsibility (Abadinsky 1997).

The policies implemented by Maconochie and Crofton were rooted in a penal philosophy emphasizing individual reform that held prominence among many leading American prison experts during this period. The notion of individualized punishment by use of an indeterminate sentence was promoted at an important conference of the National Prison Association in 1870. Dissatisfied with the current state of prison operations, scholars and practitioners called for a system of incarceration that encouraged reform through offering incentives for early release dependent upon evidence of good conduct and individual reform (Clear and Dammer 2003). Based on these ideas, New York passed an indeterminate sentence law in 1876 to be used for inmates sentenced to the Elmira Reformatory. The superintendent, Zebulon Brockway, assisted in drafting legislation that required sentences to a maximum term of incarceration but allowed inmates to earn early release after demonstrating good conduct and accumulating a specified number of marks by participating in various activities. This became the first official version of parole in American corrections (Abadinsky 1997). Released prisoners were supervised by appointed guardians (rather than the police officers of the Irish system), and failure to abide by certain conditions of release could result in their return to prison (Abadinsky 1997).

The notion of the indeterminate sentence spread slowly to other states, who used it initially only for youthful offenders and those sentenced for less serious offenses. By the early part of the twentieth century, the majority of states used indeterminate sentences for at least some types of offenders. As Rothman (1980) notes, the growth of the use of parole was likely as much a matter of convenience as principle. Urbanization, the increasing immigrant population, and the Great Depression contributed to prison overcrowding and strains on correctional resources (Abadinsky 1997). The increasing use of and support for parole, while consistent with penal theories of the day, was also perceived as a mechanism for controlling both inmate behavior and prison overcrowding (Bottomley 1990). By the middle of the twentieth century, the indeterminate sentence and parole had become standard features of American criminal law and corrections.

CONTEMPORARY COMMUNITY CORRECTIONS

There have traditionally been several philosophies or justifications for punishment. The justification utilized in a given jurisdiction may depend on recent social and political forces as well as the circumstances of a particular case. Different types of sanctions are often justified by different rationales. Some penalties may be viewed as utilitarian in nature, with goals such as deterrence, rehabilitation, or incapacitation (Harris 1996). Other penalties have a retributive component in the sense that the penalty is viewed as a sufficient response to the severity of the original crime. From this perspective, a concern is that offenders receive their just deserts for their crimes without regard to the consequences of that punishment. Though these rationales are philosophically distinct, in practice, criminal justice sanctions tend to be justified by a number of rationales. For example, proponents of intermediate sanctions such as boot camps have used rationales based on the perceived deterrent, rehabilitative, and retributive elements of such programs. During certain periods, however, some justifications garner increasing public and political support.

As described in Chapter 5, there has been an increase in punitive sanctions and a decrease in rehabilitative efforts in the past 25 years. While there is an increasing call for more attention to the problems associated with mass incarceration and to the attempts to improve prisoner reintegration (e.g., Maruna and Immarigeon 2004; Petersilia 2003; Travis and Waul 2003), there has not yet been widespread public and political support for such changes. Furthermore, ongoing efforts in the international war on terrorism, concerns about homeland security, and the recent economic crisis have put a strain on public resources and redirected political and public attention. It is unclear what impact these forces will have on criminal justice policy. History suggests, however, that the economic implications and political feasibility of any changes will be more important than philosophical considerations of criminal justice policy. Recent state budget crises have resulted in many government agencies, including corrections, making budget cuts. In corrections, resources dedicated to rehabilitation efforts typically suffer most during periods of budget problems.

While a number of sanctions are involved in community corrections, offenders on regular probation and those under parole supervision constitute the largest population. Although the various intermediate sanctions to be discussed have the potential to affect criminal punishment, to date they are used sparingly compared to traditional probation or prison sentences. As Figure 6.1 indicates, of the estimated 7.3 million persons under some form of correctional supervision in 2007, slightly over 4 million were under probation supervision and another 800,000 were under parole supervision. The populations on probation, parole, and within jails have increased at rates similar to or higher than the prison rate. Interestingly, these changes have occurred during a period that did not see a dramatic increase in crime rates or the rate of reported drug use.

Since the 1980s, correctional departments have experienced significant increases in their funding while other social and human service agencies and activities have seen dramatic decreases in their budgets (Blumstein and Beck 1999). Even though community correctional populations have increased at generally the same rates as the prison population, the vast majority of correctional budgets has been directed at institutional corrections (Petersilia 1997). The result is that community corrections agencies have generally been forced to do more with less.

Though there may be similarities, each jurisdiction has its own model for organizing its criminal justice system. The federal government has a specific criminal justice system for defendants arrested and prosecuted for violating federal criminal statutes and a correctional system to carry out the punishments ordered by the federal courts. When it comes to violations of state law, the picture becomes more complex, as each state has its own criminal justice system and various

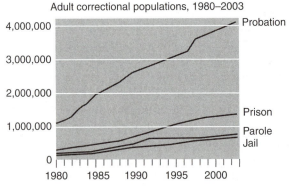

Figure 6.1 Persons under correctional supervision. Adult correctional populations, 1980–2003. http://www.ojp.usdoj.gov/bjs/glance/corr2.htm
SOURCE: Bureau of Justice Statistics (2009)

subsystems within that larger framework. Defendants convicted of state felony statutes and sentenced to prison are generally sent to facilities run by state correctional agencies. Defendants convicted of misdemeanors and sentenced to time in jail are primarily held in facilities funded and run by city or county governments. On the other hand, responsibility for supervising defendants convicted of misdemeanor or felony offenses and sentenced to nonprison sanctions is greatly varied. In some jurisdictions, supervision of defendants sentenced to community supervision is the responsibility of court employees, while other jurisdictions use state agencies (such as departments of corrections) to handle supervision duties. There are also combination or hybrid models of organizing correctional services in which the sanction imposed or the jurisdiction determines who supervises an offender. In addition, the supervision of parolees or those released to a form of supervised release may be the responsibility of a department that also supervises probationers or an agency that exclusively handles parolees. Therefore, the following discussion emphasizes common features and general principles of community corrections.

Jurisdictions vary greatly in the number and types of sanctions that they can use for law violators. The term *sanction* is often used interchangeably with *punishment* and refers to a specific punishment (e.g., fine, probation, prison) imposed by a court. Although prison is the first punishment that comes to mind for many Americans, it is actually not the most common punishment used for violations of the law. Incarceration in a state correctional institution is typically reserved for the most serious offenders and those who cannot abide by the rules of other previously imposed penalties. On a daily basis, courts that deal primarily with misdemeanor crimes handle a far greater volume of offenders than courts that deal exclusively with felony offenders. However, even among offenders convicted of felonies, a probation sentence is imposed in over one-fourth (28 percent) of all such cases (Bureau of Justice Statistics 2008b).

Available sanctions for felony offenders include a range of penalties that vary in severity. Figure 6.2 provides a brief description of the range of sanctions found in the United States. While not all of these sanctions are available in every jurisdiction, the variety of sanctions in most jurisdictions has increased in the past several decades. Futhermore, courts may use a variety of punishments rather than simply relying on one sanction. It fact, it is quite common for offenders to receive a combination of sanctions. Courts may use a variety of punishments rather than simply relying on one sanction.

It is quite common for offenders to receive a combination of sanctions. Parole supervision is not a sanction imposed by a court; instead, prisoners are released from incarceration to parole supervision by a correctional agency (e.g., a parole board). Perhaps the most important distinction is that parolees remain under the jurisdiction of the correctional system while probationers and others on community supervision remain under the legal jurisdiction of the original sentencing court. In practice, parolers and probationers may have many of the same conditions and may even have the same officer in a given jurisdiction. Violations of the conditions of

Probation	A term of supervision in which offenders can remain in the community provided that they follow a set of rules (conditions of probation) in lieu of incarceration.
Fines	Fines are often a part of a larger probation sentence. Some jurisdictions have developed more rigorous monetary penalties called "day fines" that require payment of a percentage of an offender's income over time rather than a flat fee.
Community Service Work (CSW)	CSW requires that a set number of volunteer hours be completed within a specified period of time. Some jurisdictions use CSW as a stand-alone punishment, especially for misdemeanor offenders. CSW for felony offenders is usually a requirement of their probation sentence.
Day Reporting Center (DRC)	A form of community supervision requiring offenders to report to a DRC on a daily basis, or at least very frequently. DRCs may house a variety of services and programs that offenders are required to participate in, such as drug testing, GED courses, and counseling.
Intensive Supervision Probation	A form of supervision involving frequent contact (up to several times a week) between offenders and probation officers. Some jurisdictions may require offenders' confinement to their residences when not engaged in approved activities (house arrest) and may use electronic monitoring devices.
Community Correctional Facilities	A wide variety facilities designed to hold offenders for relatively brief periods of time. May serve as work-release facilities in which offenders go into the community for work or other approved activities, but are otherwise required to remain in the facilities. May also serve as halfway house facilities for prisoners.
Jail	Offenders who are sentenced by the court to less than a year of incarceration (the maximum may be less in some jurisdictions) usually serve their sentences in jails or detention centers run by the county or municipality. Jail sentences may involve work-release provisions or may be followed by a period of community supervision.
Shock Incarceration	Some states give judges or correctional authorities the authority to grant early conditional releases to eligible offenders who have been sentenced to a period of regular incarceration. This release typically follows a brief period of confinement (30–180 days) and is conditional upon the offenders' remaining on community supervision for a specified time upon release.
Boot Camps	Also referred to as shock incarceration programs in some jurisdictions, boot camps involve a brief (less than 6 months) confinement in a secure facility in which inmates go through a period of drill and instruction modeled on basic military training. Common features include the use of physical exercise and instruction in an attempt to instill discipline, self-control, and normative behaviors. May be followed by a period of community supervision.
Prisons	Also referred to as penitentiaries or correctional institutions. Typically hold felony offenders sentenced to incarceration for more than one year and those returned to prison for parole violations. Security levels and the types of services and offenders they are designed to accomodate vary among prisons. Prisoners under sentences of death are typically held on "death row," a wing in a high-security institution in or near where executions are carried out.

Figure 6.2 List of sanctions

supervision for either group require that the offender answer to the authority that retains jurisdiction in his or her case. Parole is considered a form of community corrections because it involves the supervision of the offender in the community (or a community-based facility) and the use of community resources. Therefore, parole supervision is included in this chapter.

Jurisdictions have sought new sentencing options that are less expensive than incarceration but more punitive than regular probation. Often referred to as **intermediate sanctions**, these sanctions provide an alternative to either traditional probation or prison. Referring to Figure 6.2, sanctions such as intensive supervision probation and community residential centers are forms of intermediate sanctions that are increasingly used for a variety of offenders. Such programs are touted as more cost-effective than prison and more restrictive and punitive than regular probation and as offering a better opportunity for a rehabilitative or deterrent impact on offenders (Tonry and Lynch 1996; also see Byrne, Lurigo, and Petersilia 1992; Ellsworth 1996). Some scholars have also argued for the expanded use of fines and community service work in a manner that would be more punitive than regular probation (e.g., Morris and Tonry 1990). The remaining sections describe several of the more common sanctions used by criminal courts and the major issues associated with their use.

In 2007, there were approximately 5.1 million adult offenders under some form of community supervision in the United States (Bureau of Justice Statistics 2008b). Nearly one-half of all probationers had been convicted of a felony. Currently, intermediate sanctions represent only a small fraction of all offenders sentenced to community supervision, though the exact number of offenders serving intermediate sanctions is not known. There are another 800,000 offenders in the community on parole supervision or postrelease supervision (Bureau of Justice Statistics 2008b). As seen earlier, the size of the correctional population (including jail, prison, probation, and parole populations) has dramatically increased in the past 25 years.

Critical Thinking Exercise

Examine the different types of criminal sanctions found in Figure 6.2. What is the best justification for each of these sanctions? Is there more than one possible justification for some of the sanctions? If yes, how might having multiple justifications be a potential problem?

COMMUNITY SUPERVISION

Offender Responsibilities

Offenders who are placed under some form of community supervision or in an intermediate sanction residential program are given a list of conditions that they must meet in order to remain in good standing with the court or parole board. These **conditions of supervision** state the behavioral expectations for offenders while under supervision. Failure to conform to these rules constitutes a violation of the offenders' supervision and may result in a supervising officer or staff member submitting a violation report to either the court of jurisdiction or the parole board. As a consequence, offenders' supervision may be revoked and they can receive more severe sanctions or be returned to prison.

Conditions of supervision can be divided into standard or special conditions. **Standard conditions** are rules that all offenders placed on this type of supervision must follow. Standard conditions represent the minimum expectations for offenders to obey while under supervision. The most prevalent standard condition requires offenders to obey all laws. Other common standard conditions include informing a supervising officer of a change in address or work, not leaving the state or jurisdiction without the approval of a supervising officer, and in some jurisdictions, submitting to drug testing.

Courts and parole boards impose **special conditions** depending on the nature of the crime or characteristics of the defendant. Such conditions are individualized to respond to the needs and risks of a particular defendant. Examples of special conditions include sex-offender treatment, substance-abuse counseling, work towards the completion of a GED, and the payment of restitution to a crime victim.

Officer Responsibilities

In many jurisdictions, officers who supervise offenders in the community perform a range of duties. The two major responsibilities involve conducting investigations and supervising offenders. The most important investigation conducted by probation officers is the court-ordered **presentence investigation**. Normally conducted after a defendant has been found guilty through a plea or trial, a presentence investigation results in a document that summarizes facts about the offender, the offense, and other relevant information used by the court to determine an appropriate sentence. Typically, information about the defendant's education, employment, substance abuse, and criminal history, as well as information about the offense and harm caused to any victims, is reported. Through their investigation, probation officers may identify special conditions that the court should consider imposing on the offender if he or she is to be placed on a form of community supervision. Although the courts are not required to follow either the sentencing or special condition recommendations found in the presentence investigation report, there tends to be a close association between the probation officer's recommendations and the final sentence (Abadinsky 1997). A postsentence investigation may be conducted in cases that did not have a presentence investigation completed. Supervising agencies frequently use the pre- or postsentence report to assist in the needs and risk assessment for the offender. Other investigations conducted by community supervision officers include helping the court to determine if it is appropriate to reduce a defendant's bail and verifying an offender's plans for transferring supervision to or from another location.

The most important role of a community supervision officer is to ensure that offenders abide by the conditions of supervision. Depending on the type of supervision and jurisdiction, officers may have little personal contact with offenders, or they may have regular office, work, or home contacts. Officers are responsible for verifying that offenders are attending all required programs; making regular payments towards their court costs, fees, and restitution; and abiding by the law while under supervision. Officers may also conduct drug tests on those offenders who are required to submit to drug testing as a condition of their supervision.

Probation officers may also be given the responsibility to supervise offenders who have been placed in diversion programs prior to adjudication of guilt. **Diversion programs** offer offenders the opportunity to temporarily halt the prosecution effort against them. Some jurisdictions have a special form of proba- tion that is imposed prior to adjudication of guilt. If the offender successfully completes the requirements of the program, the prosecutor's office typically dis- misses the charges against the offender, avoiding an official conviction on his or her record. Violation of the conditions of the program can result in the prosecutor deciding to proceed with a criminal prosecution against the defendant. Diversion programs are usually reserved for juveniles, youthful offenders, or first-time offen- ders. Offenders with previous felony convictions or those arrested for violent or serious offenses are typically not eligible for participation in diversion programs.

Supervision Violations

Supervision violations are violations of probation, parole, or an intermediate sanction's program conditions. Such violations are usually categorized as either new offenses or technical violations. **New-offense violations** occur when offenders under supervision commit new crimes. In such situtions, offenders have to appear before the appropriate court for the new crimes and will likely appear before the courts or parole boards that originally released the offenders to com- munity supervision to address the violation of supervision conditions (i.e., viola- tion of the conditions to obey all laws). **Technical violations** are violations of conditions of supervision that do not involve violations of criminal statutes. These are violations of rules that regular citizens are not required to follow but have been made a condition of an offender's release to the community. A positive drug test, failure to attend treatment meetings, and failure to make a good-faith effort towards paying restitution are common technical violations.

How officers respond to a violation of supervision conditions depends on the nature of the violation, the offender, and the officer's perception of the appropriate response (e.g., Clear, Harris, and Baird 1992). Minor technical viola- tions are often handled informally, perhaps with verbal or written warnings to the offender. More serious violations require officers to consider the nature and context of the violations, the probationers' progress and likelihood of successfully completing supervision, and organizational and office dynamics (McCleary 1992). New-offense violations, especially felonies, are nearly always reported to the court or parole board. Serious technical violations, such as those that potentially represent a threat to public safety, are also commonly reported to the appropriate agency. Prosecutors, judges, and parole boards have considerable discretion in their response to condition violations, but supervising officers' recommendations can play an important role in the final disposition of the case. For new-offense violations or serious technical violations, offenders' supervision may be revoked, and offenders may be sentenced to new terms of supervision, more restrictive forms of community supervision or intermediate sanctions, or terms of incarceration in jail or prison.

PROBATION AND INTERMEDIATE SANCTIONS

Probation

All forms of probation represent a term of conditional supervision imposed by a sentencing court. The frequency of contact required between the offender and the probation officer varies depending on the jurisdiction, the offender, and the specific type of probation supervision that the court imposes. Although traditional probation is frequently the subject of political and media criticism, it remains the most frequently imposed penalty for criminal offenders (Petersilia 1997). In recent decades, a recurring theme has been the lack of proper funding for regular probation that has resulted in increasing caseload sizes and a reduction in the amount of contact between offenders and officers (Petersilia 1997, 2002).

While there is no universal level of supervision for offenders placed on regular probation, a common practice is that offenders must report once a month to their probation offices. In addition, officers may be expected to have direct contact with offenders at least once a month, whether in the office or in the field. However, due to budgetary constraints and concerns about officer safety, in some jurisdictions officers may go several months between direct contacts. Furthermore, some departments utilize a form of nonsupervised probation that does not require personal contact between offenders and officers except for special problems or concerns. Such circumstances have led many to question the effectiveness or meaningfulness of regular probation as a response to any but the most minor of offenses (Morris and Tonry 1990). In particular, scholars and practitioners are skeptical of either the deterrent or rehabilitative function of probation when so little supervision actually takes place or when there are few consequences for technical violations (Petersilia 1997, 1998). Although traditional probation continues to have potential as a meaningful sanction for certain offenders, increased resources and a larger variety of intermediate sanctions may improve both the deterrent and rehabilitative goals of traditional probation.

Intermediate Sanctions

Intermediate sanctions are promoted as achieving a number of often competing goals (Tonry 1990). These stated goals include decreasing costs, increasing offender accountability and public safety, and increasing rehabilitative effectiveness (Tonry and Lynch 1996; see also Petersilia, Lurigio, and Byrne 1992). Intermediate sanctions can also be justified by both retributive and utilitarian penal philosophies; however, the targeted population and function of the sanctions may differ depending on the perceived value of these goals (Harris 1996; von Hirsch 1998). Although scholars and critics are correct to point out the challenges intermediate sanctions face, support for alternatives to traditional probation and reducing our overreliance on prison remains strong (e.g., Byrne 1996; Petersilia 1997, 2002; Tonry and Lynch 1996). The following sections discuss some of the more important intermediate sanctions currently utilized. Not every intermediate sanction is discussed here (see Clear and Dammer 2003, Chapter 7). For example, the use of community service work and fines, although potentially important forms of intermediate sanctions, are far more commonly used as a special condition of community supervision rather than a stand-alone penalty as many advocate (e.g., Morris and Tonry 1990).

Net Widening. A frequent goal of intermediate sanctions is to divert offenders from a sentence that is considered too severe or expensive for a particular offender. In fact, a number of intermediate sanctions are justified on the premise that such programs can divert less serious offenders from prison into less expensive sentencing options. While such sanctions offer the potential to provide more appropriate penalties and reduce costs, scholars have questioned how new sanctions are utilized by the courts in practice. Research and experience indicate that intermediate sanctions are often applied to offenders who would have received a *less* severe sanction prior to the availability of the intermediate sanction. As a result, some offenders receive a more severe sanction than they originally would have received prior to the creation of this new sanction. Meanwhile, many offenders who were the targets for diversion by the new intermediate sanction continue to be sentenced to the more punitive sanctions that existed prior to the new program. In other words, the new program is used for less serious offenders, rather than the originally targeted population. This is referred to as **net widening**, when a punishment is used on a larger or different population than that originally intended.

Although some may see net widening as simply an appropriate increase in the severity of punishment for offenders, this ignores a primary rationale for intermediate sanctions and poses a problem for several reasons. First, net widening increases costs rather than decreasing them by placing offenders who would have received a less expensive sanction (generally, the closer the supervision, the higher the costs) on a more expensive form of supervision without similarly diverting prison-bound offenders. Second, because closer supervision programs generally have higher revocation rates for technical violations (Petersilia and Turner 1993), a percentage of the offenders who might have succeeded under a less restrictive program will likely end up in prison because of violations of the stricter rules of the intermediate sanctions.

This could add to operating costs rather than reduce them. A third major concern is the larger issue of social control. By using new sanctions to impose more severe penalties on offenders rather than diverting those who do not require a prison sentence, the criminal justice system is expanding its sphere of control over society and the lives of individual members of that society (Cohen 1985). As noted previously, recent trends have already demonstrated a dramatic increase in the amount of social control that the correctional systems exercise—both in severity and in the numbers of persons under that control—despite no correlating increase in crime. Such increases represent a potential threat to the democratic values and justice of a society that places so many of its citizens under legal constraint and supervision.

Front-End Versus Back-End Programs. Traditionally, the notion of intermediate sanctions applies to penalties imposed by the courts that fall between probation and prison in severity. Such programs are described as "front-end" because the courts determine who will receive these sanctions at sentencing. A major goal of this approach is to use intermediate sanctions as a diversion from jail or prison sentences. However, as previously noted, research indicates that such diversion is difficult to achieve. Inevitably, some net widening occurs and these programs include unintended populations. One method to minimize net widening is to use intermediate sanctions as a "back-end" mechanism to facilitate early release from incarceration. A major goal of this model is to reduce prison overcrowding by releasing inmates to intermediate sanction programs that are cheaper than incarceration but have more supervision than regular parole. The benefit of this approach is that the decision to place an offender in a particular program is made by correctional personnel rather than by prosecutors and judges, who are susceptible to using such programs in a manner resulting in net widening. To some extent, this increases the likelihood that the sanctions are used for more serious and high-risk offenders. A drawback to this approach is that the sanctions can only be used for offenders initially sent to incarceration, and it does not affect the available sentencing options for the courts.

Critical Thinking Exercise

Front-end and back-end approaches to intermediate sanctions are two competing strategies for using intermediate-type sanctions. Which do you believe makes the most sense and why? What suggestions would you make for addressing the issues related to each?

A third option that has been promoted is the inclusion of intermediate sanctions in a structured sentencing system (Tonry and Lynch 1996). Ideally, this could increase the sentencing options for the courts by using a front-end approach while reducing the likelihood of net widening statutorily by restricting the use of intermediate sanctions to offenders who fall within a predetermined criteria based upon existing guidelines. A challenge for structured sentencing systems such as sentencing guideliness is to ensure that the actual sentencing criteria reflect such goals. Ideological arguments and biases rather than rational deliberation frequently drive criminal justice policymaking. Thus far, the construction of sentencing systems that reflect intended policy goals has been difficult.

Intensive Supervision Probation. After early experiments with intensive supervision in the 1960s, the notion of **intensive supervision probation** (ISP) gained increasing support in the 1980s. Today, ISP is perhaps the most common intermediate sanction and is available, in some form, in many jurisdictions around the country (Clear and Dammer 2003). Some jurisdictions use intensive supervision exclusively for parolees (and thus as a "back-end" program), while other jurisdictions have ISP available as both a sentencing option for the courts and a form of early release. Most ISP programs have several common features. A central premise of ISP is that it provides closer supervision by frequent contact between offenders and officers and greater restrictions on the freedom of offenders. An offender on ISP has far more contact with his or her officer than those on regular probation. They may be in contact several times per week, with interactions at the probation office and their offender's home and place of employment. Due to the increased supervision, ISP officers have smaller caseloads than regular probation officers. Although the exact number may vary, ISP officers typically have fewer than 40 offenders under their supervision, whereas regular probation officers may supervise more than 100 offenders, depending on the jurisdiction. ISP conditions are more restrictive, and violations tend to be dealt with in a more immediate and punitive manner.

ISP is frequently promoted by supporters as a "real" form of supervision and contrasted with the comparatively lenient requirements of regular probation. A primary goal of many ISP programs is the reduction of institutional overcrowding by diverting appropriate offenders from prison and jail. Proponents claim that ISP can improve community safety by increased surveillance and contact with offenders and provide a more meaningful opportunity for rehabilitation. Despite calls for ISP to incorporate more rehabilitative elements and evidence that ISP can increase participation in treatment programs (Petersilia 1997; Tonry and Lynch 1996), in many jurisdictions, ISP is used primarily as a more restrictive and punitive form of probation.

Critical Thinking Exercise

The fact that intensive supervision programs are more restrictive and provide much greater contact and oversight of offenders means that more technical violations are uncovered in these programs. As a result, a higher percentage of ISP offenders generally fail to satisfactorily complete their supervision. If a goal of ISP is to keep offenders *out* of prison, what should officers and courts do when violations become known?

Home Confinement and Electronic Monitoring. In some jurisdictions, offenders placed on ISP may be given special conditions that impose a period of home confinement and/or electronic monitoring. Other jurisdictions may use these as penalties independent from ISP. Also referred to as "house arrest," **home confinement** is literally a specified period of time during which offenders may not leave their places of residence except for previously approved activities such as work, participation in treatment programs, food shopping, visits to the doctor, reporting to the probation office, and other approved activities. Offenders are typically required to submit in advance a weekly schedule, and any activities outside the home must be preapproved by supervising officers. Officers can use this schedule to make random field contacts to verify that offenders are at home or at an approved activity. The rationale behind the use of home confinement is fairly simple—the likelihood of offenders violating their supervision can be reduced by greatly restricting their movement and freedom by confining them to their residences. The state essentially incarcerates the offenders, except for approved activities, without accruing the costs associated with incarceration. Of course, like any form of community supervision, offenders can easily choose to ignore the requirements of the program. In particular, home confinement (and electronic monitoring) cannot prevent crimes and violations that occur within residences. Confined to their residences, however, offenders are less likely to have access to targets and opportunities for many types of crimes.

Electronic monitoring is the use of technology to improve compliance with home confinement. Electronic monitoring has also been used as a condition of pretrial release. The primary types of electronic monitoring systems currently used are either programmed contact or continuous signaling devices (Clear and Dammer 2003). Programmed contact devices use random automated telephone or beeper calls that require offenders to contact a centralized call center within a limited period of time. Offenders then must verify their identities by voice identification, use special bracelets that are attached to their legs or wrists that transmit a signal over the telephone line, or insert similar bracelets into special receivers placed in the offenders' homes that transmit a signal to verify their presence. Continuous contact devices utilize bracelets that emit a continuous signal to receivers that are placed within offenders' residences. Such bracelets typically have a limited range (e.g., 200 feet) and, once a bracelet is taken beyond that radius, the receiver automatically contacts a centralized computerized system to note that the offender left the premises. The computer system is thus able to keep records of when offenders leave their residences and when they return, which officers can compare to approved schedules (Clear and Dammer 2003). Bracelets are typically tamper-proof and, if removed, result in an automatic notification to the computer system.

Several jurisdictions have experimented with the use of Global Positioning Systems to have even more specific information about the location of offenders in the community. Such systems use satellite technology to monitor the specific location of offenders and can also be programmed with information about the community to indicate whether offenders are entering problematic or restrictive areas, such as when sex offenders approach schools (Clear and Dammer 2003). The use of such technology for criminal offenders is still very rare and has several challenges such as signal strength and high costs. There are additional concerns about the unforeseen social consequences of such invasive surveillance in a democratic society. If there is sufficient political and public support for the use of these new technologies, regardless of such drawbacks, the use of such sanctions may increase.

Critical Thinking Exercise

Many scholars are concerned about the impact of increasing surveillance on the American public. In particular, technological advances continue to make surveillance less expensive and less noticeable. But does that make it any less obtrusive? How do we determine the line that separates beneficial and cost-effective supervision from an oppressive intrusion into the lives of American citizens? When is it too much?

Day Reporting Centers. First instituted in Great Britain, the initial American **day reporting centers** were begun in Massachusetts and Connecticut in 1985 (Clear and Dammer 2003). Today, day reporting centers are found in a number of jurisdictions, and similar to other community correctional programs, day reporting centers can actually be used for a variety of populations. For example, Cook County (Chicago) has a day reporting program for offenders released prior to trial that the courts may order as a condition of pretrial release (McBride and Vander Waal 1997). While the intial program in Massachusetts was designed to serve newly released inmates, there are programs in the United States. (e.g., Vaas and Weston 1990) that are conceptualized as intermediate sanctions intended to divert appropriate offenders from incarceration.

Despite the variety of populations they serve, most day reporting centers have several common features. First, they are nonresidential programs that require offenders to report on a daily or very frequent basis to a reporting center. The specific frequency of reporting may vary across programs and individual offenders. Offenders in these programs, however, report to their centers far more frequently than regular probationers or parolees report to their supervising officers. Second, these centers house a number of the required programs and services for offenders, such as drug testing, substance abuse treatment, job training, and education courses. Because offenders given a day reporting sanction are also considered to be under community super-vision, offenders' probation or parole officers may be stationed at the center as well. Thus, day reporting centers can serve as a centralized location for offenders to fulfill a variety of their program and court-ordered conditions, such as drug testing, restitution payments, community service orders, and treatment programs (see Clear and Dammer 2003). While the amount of contact between participating offenders and program staff tends to be quite high, the emphasis of many day reporting centers is to provide a range of services to offenders with identified treatment needs.

Residential Programs. Residential programs that serve as temporary housing for released inmates as they adjust to living in the community are referred to as **halfway houses** because they serve offenders who are halfway between prison and complete freedom in the community. While the public is familiar with such programs, less commonly known is that similar programs exist for offenders *before* they are sentenced to incarceration. The term **residential community correctional program** (Latessa and Travis 1992) is increasingly used to designate those residential programs that serve a variety of offender populations for a relatively short period of time (typically less than one year) in facilities designed to assist in offender reintegration into the community. Specific programs may target particular offender needs and specialize in providing services to those offenders. For example, some programs may focus on substance abuse treatment, while other programs serve as work release centers that assist offenders in securing employment and making payments towards their financial obligations, such as child support and restitution.

The level of freedom and security in residential correctional programs varies. Some programs require offenders to remain at the facility except for approved activities, while others allow more freedom of movement. The types and intensity of the services provided at these facilities depend to some extent on the population they serve. It is not uncommon, however, for such programs to offer education and employment training, cognitive thinking and life-skills courses, and substance abuse treatment. Residential programs, especially those emphasizing employment, are frequently located in urban or suburban areas with accessible employment opportunities and public transportation.

Although the evidence is unclear about the impact of such programs on recidivism, most residential programs serve a relatively high-need population that tends to be at higher risk for substance abuse and/or recidivism than comparison populations (Latessa and Travis 1992). There is evidence that residential community correctional programs may have the most impact on those at highest risk for substance abuse and recidivism (Lowencamp and Latessa 2002). This would suggest that programs targeting the highest-risk offenders are more likely to see a return on their correctional investment, though given the high-risk nature of the population, offender failure would not be unusual.

Boot Camps. Certainly one of the more publicized and well known of the community correctional programs, **boot camps** have been subject to critical scholarly attention since they began to be used as a correctional sanction in the late 1980s. The use of boot camps for offenders has intuitive appeal for American society. Most adults are familiar with the premise of military boot camps, and many American males associate their own military experience with numerous benefits that could translate into a meaningful sanction for offenders. Some jurisdictions and scholars identify boot camps with **shock incarceration**. Not all shock incarceration programs, however, incorporate a boot-camp experience (Clear and Dammer 2003). Some jurisdictions retain the option of early release to community supervision for eligible inmates. The idea is that offenders' brief experience in prison will "shock" them into a desire to abide by community supervision requirements and remain crime free. The evidence concerning such programs suggests that they do little to reduce recidivism rates and may actually result in higher technical violations and other problems (National Institute of Justice 2003; Wilson, Mackenzie, and Mitchell 2005). Programs that utilize a boot-camp experience have been subject to far more public and scholarly attention. Therefore, the following comments are directed at such programs.

Although there are considerable differences across boot-camp programs, the central premise is that the highly structured environment of military-like training can provide a unique experience for offenders. In particular, the emphasis on discipline, strict adherence to program rules, and physical conditioning is thought to provide an opportunity for constructive change in offender attitudes and behavior (National Institute of Justice 2003). The most characteristic feature of boot camps is the quasi-military atmosphere created by physical conditioning, drills, and manual labor that are enforced with strict rules and program staff who act in a manner consistent with military boot-camp training. Recent modifications to early programs have included incorporating more rehabilitation and treatment services to inmates and increasing educational and life-skills training components (Clear and Dammer 2003; National Institute of Justice 2003).

The physical nature of the boot-camp experience naturally limits such programs to eligible youthful offenders. Some boot camps are exclusively for juvenile offenders, while other programs accept young adult offenders. Many programs target offenders with a history of substance abuse and most exclude offenders with a significant history of personal violence. Furthermore, despite the existence of several boot camps for female offenders, the majority of boot-camp programs are designed for male offenders (Clear and Dammer 2003). The unique characteristics of female offenders (e.g., history of abuse, status as primary child caregiver, etc.) have provided serious challenges to the use of boot camps for females and the validity of such a response to female criminality is questionable (see National Institute of Justice 2003). Boot camps may be used as an early release program for younger inmates or may be an intermediate sanction for offenders sentenced by a court. Nearly all boot-camp programs have a period of aftercare and supervision in the community. In fact, a common finding has been that boot camps with longer and more intensive aftercare services have been associated with more positive outcomes among their graduates (National Institute of Justice 2003). Support for boot camps, however, may be diminishing. Several high-profile incidents (see the material available at http://www.oup.com/labessentials) and the overwhelming evidence that there is little difference between the recidivism rates of boot-camp graduates and offenders sentenced to other sanctions have led many states to modify their existing programs. Some jurisdictions, most notably the federal government, have closed their boot-camp programs. Boot camps for offenders, however, remain popular in some jurisdictions, especially for juvenile offenders.

Critical Thinking Exercise

Despite the considerable evidence that boot-camp graduates do not have lower recidivism rates and that such programs fail to result in meaningful cost savings, such programs remain popular with some politicians and the public. Why do you think this is the case? What explains the apparent disconnect between research on the value of such programs and continuing support for them? What is the impact of such factors on criminal justice policy in general?

THE EFFECTIVENESS OF PROBATION AND INTERMEDIATE SANCTIONS

Research has found a variety of community supervision programs to be only modestly successful in reducing recidivism (see Petersilia 1997; Tonry and Lynch 1996). Given the wide variety of sanctions discussed and the meaningful differences in the same type of sanction across jurisdictions, any conclusions about the impact of various sanctions should be tempered with caution. Furthermore, some programs have been found to be successful with particular types of offenders. Despite these caveats, there appear to be some common themes in the research on a variety of community correctional sanctions. Interested readers are encouraged to review the more comprehensive reviews of the research literature found in Petersilia (1997) and Tonry and Lynch (1996).

Depending on the jurisdiction and the exact outcome measure, research has found considerable variation in the effectiveness of regular probation (see Morgan 1996). In general, research has found that probation is moderately effective at achieving several goals. A major issue in evaluation research is determining how program effectiveness will be measured. Measurements of offenders' behavior while under supervision could include the number of offenders who successfully complete the program, the number of new-offense or technical violations during supervision, or the number of new arrests at the end of a follow-up period after the completion of their sentences. How "success" is measured will greatly impact how successful a program appears. The percentage of those on probation and other intermediate sanctions who complete their sanctions without having them revoked by the court is much higher than the percentage of those same offenders who have not been arrested within a year or more after release from supervision. Morgan's (1996) review of probation research reported that various studies have found 15–50 percent of probationers "failed" under community supervision. Many probation failures are the result of technical violations. The majority of new-offense violations are for misdemeanors, and most studies have found that violations for new felony offenses are less common than other violations (e.g., Gray, Fields, and Maxwell 2001). Probationers tend to have a lower failure rate than those released from prison (whether supervised or not), though this is not particularly impressive given the high failure rate of these populations. Those on misdemeanor probation appear to have a much higher success rate than offenders placed on probation for felonies, but this could be due to the lower risk posed by misdemeanor defendants or the less intense nature of the supervision for those convicted of misdemeanors (Petersilia 1997).

An important question in evaluating the effectiveness of intermediate sanctions is "in comparison to whom?" Determining the appropriate comparison group for offenders sentenced to intermediate sanctions is often a challenge and may affect conclusions about the utility of such sanctions. To some extent, the identification of a comparison group depends upon the goals of a specific program. Despite the diversity of programs across different jurisdictions and the variety of program goals, there are some common themes found in the research on the impact of intermediate sanctions to achieve a variety of goals (Lurigio and Petersilia 1992). One goal that is consistently met with most intermediate sanction programs is the closer supervision and control over offenders compared to regular probation (Petersilia 1998). In many jurisdictions, new intermediate sanctions have been incorporated into sentencing options, providing more appropriate penalties between probation and prison (Harland 1998). Additionally, a common finding is that offenders sentenced to intermediate sanctions generally have higher levels of participation in treatment programs than offenders sentenced to regular probation or imprisonment (Tonry and Lynch 1996). Interestingly, programs that emphasize treatment services are typically found to be more effective at reducing recidivism than similar programs that focus primarily on surveillance and control (Tonry and Lynch 1996; National Institute of Justice 2003).

Intermediate sanctions, however, have also been found to suffer from a number of problems that challenge their ability to reduce recidivism or correctional costs. Perhaps the most significant problem is that net widening plagues front-end programs where offenders are sentenced by the court (Tonry and Lynch 1996). Although the previous discussion identified ways to minimize net widening, many programs continue to be used for a population different from the one originally intended, resulting in higher costs, limited impact on prison overcrowding, and expanded social control over offenders. Generally, most evaluations have found little difference in the recidivism rates of similar offenders who receive intermediate sanctions versus those who receive either probation or imprisonment. Probationers tend to have the lowest recidivism rates, followed by offenders placed on intermediate sanctions. Released inmates have the highest recidivism rates. However, when offense seriousness and other relevant characteristics are controlled for, the difference in recidivism rates between intermediate sanctions and other populations becomes marginal (Petersilia and Turner 1993; Tonry and Lynch 1996). This suggests that it is the characteristics of the offenders, more than existing programs, that primarily explain offender success.

While probationers and those on intermediate sanctions may have comparable new-offense violations, offenders placed in intermediate sanctions typically have higher revocation rates. The increased restrictions and closer supervision involved in intermediate sanctions have resulted in considerably higher technical violation rates than regular probation. The stronger control and surveillance orientation of most intermediate sanction programs also means that such violations will likely be dealt with more severely and result in revocation and possible imprisonment (Tonry and Lynch 1996). A result of higher technical violation rates is that offenders who could have "slipped by" on probation are possibly having their intermediate sanctions revoked and being sentenced to prison. As a result, research has also questioned the ability of intermediate sanctions to reduce offender recidivism or correctional costs (see Tonry and Lynch 1996).

Critical Thinking Exercise

Although intermediate sanctions do not appear to have met many of their utilitarian goals (cost-effectiveness, reduction of prison overcrowding, reduction of recidivism), some argue that such penalties may serve a retributive function of simply being a more appropriate (deserved) punishment and offering the courts an additional sentencing option. However, a consequence of this is the certain increased costs to the criminal justice system. Is it appropriate to spend more money on the criminal justice system, especially given the fact that state budgets are increasingly tight and reported crime and drug use are declining? How do we balance the budgetary needs of the criminal justice system and other public goods (such as education, health care, highways, etc.) that governments provide?

POSTRELEASE SUPERVISION AND REINTEGRATION

Types of Release

Over 90 percent of all prisoners will eventually be released from prison (Petersilia 2003). Approximately 600,000 prisoners are released each year to the community. This means that a significant number of convicted offenders will need to transition from the highly structured prison environment to the relative freedom of open society. Upon release, most prisoners must identify new ways to meet basic needs such as food, shelter, employment, and clothing that were previously provided by the institution. Failure to adequately secure these will decrease the likelihood that a released offender will be able to successfully reintegrate into the community (Petersilia 2003).

Depending on the jurisdiction and the particular inmate, prisoners may be released from prison in four ways. Perhaps the most important distinction is whether the prisoner will be under any form of supervision after release. First, a small portion of offenders serve their maximum sentences and are released due to an **expiration of sentence**. Such inmates, who may be in either indeterminate or determinate sentencing systems, have "maxed out" their sentences and all supervision is terminated upon released from the institution. Although only approximately 20 percent of inmates are released without any supervision, this is a dramatic increase from 30 years ago, when only 5 percent of prisoners were released in this manner (Petersilia 2003). Second, some prisoners may be sentenced to **spilt sentences**, in which they serve a period of probation following their release. Third, several jurisdictions with determinate sentencing models have created a period of supervision for released prisoners called **supervised release**, or postrelease supervision. Released prisoners are required to report to community supervision offices located near where they will reside and are assigned to supervising officers. Similar to probation and parole, prisoners are required to abide by certain conditions following their release to the community. The length of supervision may vary depending on the nature of the crime that the defendants were convicted of or the length of time they were incarcerated. A violation of these conditions may result in offenders' return to prison for a period of time. Finally, prisoners given an indeterminate prison term may be considered for release by the parole authority to **parole supervision** by the parole authority once they have served their minimum sentence. Prisoners must agree to abide by parole conditions in order to obtain their release. Parolees are assigned to parole offices and officers near where they will reside after release. Parolees are supervised until the expiration of their maximum sentences or until the parole authority terminates their supervision. Failure to comply with the conditions of release may result in parolees being returned to prison until the parole authority grants a new parole release or until the expiration of their sentences. In some jurisdictions, officers who supervise probationers are also responsible for supervising parolees in their geographic area. In other jurisdictions, distinct agencies provide parole officers who supervise only parolees and those released from prison to mandatory supervised release.

Prisoner Reentry and Reintegration
The sheer numbers of prisoners returning to American communities each year has forced correctional administrators and policymakers to reevaluate their efforts in reducing the likelihood that released prisoners will return to prison. Prison has not

demonstrated itself as being very effective at preventing future criminal behavior by offenders (through rehabilitation or deterrence). It is an unfortunate reality that a significant percentage of released prisoners will eventually return to prison. A recent study of prisoner recidivism found that over 60 percent of released prisoners are rearrested for serious misdemeanors or felonies within three years of release, and one-half of released prisoners return to prison within three years (Langan and Levin 2002). The consequences of the recent imprisonment binge (Austin and Irwin 2001) are becoming apparent in the reallocation of public resources and the problems high recidivism rates cause the criminal justice system. In addition, scholars are increasingly discovering the often unintended negative consequences of mass incarceration and failed prisoner reentry on communities (e.g., Rose and Clear 2003), families (e.g., Travis and Waul 2003), and offenders themselves (Petersilia 2003). Recent works have discussed the challenges of prisoner reentry (Maruna and Immarigeon 2004; Petersilia 2003) and major policy efforts in several jurisdictions have been initiated (see the textbook website at http://www.oup.com/us/labessentials for an example plan for prisoner reentry).

Prisoners face a multitude of problems and challenges that they must overcome if they are to avoid returning to prison. Research indicates that lack of adequate and meaningful employment is one of the major characteristics associated with a return to prison (Petersilia 2003). In addition, offenders may face difficulties because of the "ex-convict" label that can negatively impact their occupational and housing opportunities. A lack of sufficient education, job skills, or life skills may present difficulties in obtaining basic amenities, services, and material goods. Another major concern is reestablishing family and social networks. Offenders may be estranged from family and friends who could assist with reintegration back into the community. Though not all former associates will have a positive influence on offenders' lives, social isolation can lead to stress and negative behavioral adaptations such as substance abuse and crime. Research indicates that an increasing percentage of inmates have histories of substance abuse and/or mental health problems. At the same time, the availability of prison programs and participation in such programs has been diminishing (Petersilia 2003). Therefore, prisoners increasingly need access to meaningful treatment services inside prison and upon release.

Prisoner reentry (also referred to as prisoner reintegration) efforts are those activities and programs designed to assist offenders in adjusting to a law-abiding lifestyle after returning to the community from prison (Petersilia 2003). There are a variety of reentry efforts currently in operation throughout the country. Some of these are informal programs run by nonprofit and faith-based agencies, while other jurisdictions have very structured programs that may involve a variety of organizations, including correctional staff and resources (see Petersilia 2003; Travis and Waul 2003). To reduce the stress and problems of release, many offenders are released into halfway house facilities. Such facilities may be privately operated or run by correctional departments. Similar to the community residential programs discussed earlier, there is considerable diversity in the types of halfway houses. They typically provide inexpensive housing and offer only basic amenities. Prisoners may be placed in these facilities as a condition of their release or may elect to reside there because of a lack of housing options and a shortage of money. More structured facilities may provide a range of services and resources such as substance abuse counseling, life-skills training, or other relevant services and may place a number of restrictions on residents.

Perhaps the clearest measure of successful reintegration is whether a released prisoner is rearrested or returns to prison following release. While there is evidence that prisoners who participate in targeted, problem-specific prison programs have significantly lower recidivism rates upon release, the percentage of offenders participating in such programs has diminished (Petersilia 2003). Many of the recent reentry programs have not yet been subject to thorough evaluation. However, released prisoners who participate in long-term, well-designed, and well-implemented postrelease programs tend to have lower recidivism rates than inmates released without such services. The extent to which reentry continues to be a politically viable investment remains to be seen. The history of criminal justice policy suggests caution in assuming long-term commitments to particular policy initiatives, especially those with treatment or rehabilitation components. Evaluation research indicates that the continuing allocation of sufficient resources and proper implementation greatly affect the overall effectiveness of such programs. It is too early to determine how such issues impact the future of reentry efforts. Given the tremendous number of inmates released each year and the direct and collateral consequences of imprisonment, however, the benefits of improving prisoner reintegration could be tremendous. On the other hand, the failure of the criminal justice system, social service agencies, and communities to assist this population could have serious long-term negative implications that we are only beginning to appreciate.

Critical Thinking Exercise

Many studies find that most violations of supervision are technical violations and not for new offenses. If most violations are technical, should they be considered in determining the success or failure of a program? What are the justifications for sanctioning an individual for a technical violation when no one is hurt by the violation? What should the courts or parole boards do in such cases?

SPECIAL-NEEDS POPULATIONS AND COMMUNITY SUPERVISION

It is no surprise that many offenders have characteristics that place them at considerable risk for recidivism or create additional barriers to successful reintegration. Scholars have identified several characteristics that pose unique or particularly difficult challenges for offenders, often referred to as *special-needs populations*, and those responsible for supervising them. Research has begun to focus on how these traits affect offenders' behavior and their ability to meet the conditions of supervision. Examples of such groups include substance abusers (e.g., Center for Substance Abuse Treatment 2005), elderly persons under supervision (e.g., Aday 2003), female offenders (e.g., Belknap 2001), and offenders with mental health problems. While not all individuals with these traits experience difficulty in completing their sentence, research has found these to be associated with a variety of problems including higher rates of recidivism and other negative behavioral outcomes. Those responsible for the supervision of these offenders should be aware of the challenges and problems they commonly experience.

For example, it is generally acknowledged that the criminal justice system has been increasingly responsible for supervising individuals with mental health problems and that the percentage of the correctional population with identifiable mental health disorders has been growing over the past 30 years (Ditton 1999; James and Glaze 2006; Prins and Draper 2009). To date, correctional agencies have been unable to adequately provide for the increasing demand for mental health services for institutional or community-based offenders (Ditton 1999). Offenders with mental health problems have considerable challenges in abiding by the conditions of their supervision. In addition to the challenges of obtaining and maintaining a stable residence and employment, mental health problems can make complying with seemingly simple conditions of supervision (such as reporting to the probation office) difficult. Furthermore, these offenders often have co-occurring disorders of mental health and substance abuse problems. Such conditions exacerbate already difficult circumstances and place real constraints on offenders' personal and social resources and the skills to utilize those limited resources.

The criminal justice system has taken steps to improve the success of offenders with mental health problems. Many probation departments have officers with special training who are responsible for supervising such cases. Also, mental-health courts exist in some communities. These courts are designed to provide a holistic response to match the challenges facing these offenders (e.g., Justice Center 2008). While considerable variation exists, mental-health courts seek to coordinate the variety of social services thought necessary to improve the lives of individuals with mental health problems that come to the attention of authorities. They often utilize a problem-solving and team approach to participant services and supervision. For those cases under community supervision, the probation officer may have an active role in case management (Justice Center 2008). While many mental-health courts are in the experimental stage, results are encouraging. Furthermore, the use of evidence-based treatment strategies and protocols has been found to reduce a variety of negative outcomes for this population (Justice Center 2008; Prins and Draper 2009).

INCORPORATING "BEST PRACTICES" INTO COMMUNITY CORRECTIONS

Responding to criticisms about the effectiveness of correctional interventions, a growing body of research has focused on those practices that have demonstrated success in reducing offender recidivism (e.g., Andrews and Bonta 2006; Bernfeld, Farrington, and Leschied 2001; McGuire 2001). Based upon evaluations of a wide range of correctional practices, scholars have identified important principles for correctional treatment programs (Andrews and Bonta 2006); examples of programs and programmatic elements associated with offender change (e.g. Latessa and Cullen 2002); and insights into implementing these in real world settings (Bernfeld et al. 2001; McGuire 2001). For example, recent studies have demonstrated that more intensive programs (whether surveillance or treatment components) should be reserved for the most at-risk offenders (Lowenkamp and Latessa 2005). The use of intensive programs for low-risk offenders can actually *increase* offender recidivism rates, thereby decreasing public safety and increasing costs. Correctional agencies are increasingly developing and implementing programs consistent with these *correctional best practices* and *effective correctional interventions*. Websites for many community correctional agencies highlight initiatives organized around the principles of "what works" (e.g., Crime and Justice Institute 2004; Ohio Department of Rehabilitation and Correction 2007; White 2005).

While some offenders will fail to positively respond to even the best-designed programs, the knowledge base about how to improve program success rates has grown considerably in the past two decades. The challenge is how to translate such knowledge into politically, fiscally, and operationally meaningful action. Politically, public officials remain very cautious about supporting policies that may be interpreted as "soft on crime." The use of correctional resources has historically been focused on control and surveillance activities. Even within community corrections, where officer caseloads are often high and resources limited, there is often real skepticism about the development and resource allocation to new programs and strategies. Finally, research has demonstrated that new programs are often not implemented in a manner consistent with important underlying principles. Whether the result of budget shortfalls, a lack of staff training or commitment, or changes in administrative philosophy, it is difficult to maintain long-term program integrity in human service organizations.

CONCLUSION

Community corrections are increasingly recognized as a vital component of American criminal justice systems. Unfortunately, community corrections continue to be viewed by the public and political decision makers as of secondary importance compared to institutional corrections. A result has been that community correctional programs have been required to do more with less: supervise more offenders without a similar growth in the funding to provide adequate supervision and services to those populations. Every day, thousands of community correctional professionals try to achieve the difficult balance of helping offenders maintain a crime-free lifestyle and reintegrate back into the community while identifying and responding to supervision violations and threats to public safety. The trend appears to be to increase both the surveillance and the treatment requirements for many (though not all) offenders placed under community supervision. It is unclear if the funding necessary to sustain such changes will continue to be available. Recent attention to the challenges and long-term consequences of prisoner reentry may provide an opportunity for meaningful dialogue about offenders in the community and efforts to reduce the likelihood of their engaging in dysfunctional behaviors. It is certain that community corrections will continue to be an important component of American criminal justice and serve a vital role in the criminal justice process and the communities it serves.

Critical Thinking Exercise

The recent economic crisis has required many state and local governments to make significant cutbacks in government services. Although the criminal justice system is often protected from substantial cutbacks, this may not be the case under current circumstances. As noted earlier, community corrections is often far more susceptible to cutbacks, due to fewer fixed costs, than institutional corrections. Imagine you are the administrator of a large community corrections agency and are required to make substantial cutbacks to next year's budget. Where would you try to save money and why? How might you save money in those areas? What services would you consider essential? What arguments would you make to protect resources for those activities?

KEY WORDS

boot camps
community supervision
conditions of supervision
day reporting centers
diversion programs
electronic monitoring
expiration of sentence
halfway houses
home confinement

intensive supervision
    probation
intermediate sanctions
net widening
new-offense violations
parole supervision
presentence investigation
prisoner reentry
probation

residential community
    correctional program
shock incarceration
special conditions
standard conditions
supervised release
supervision violations
technical violations

SUGGESTED READINGS

Carter, R., Cocks, J., and Glaser, D. (1996). "Community service: A review of the basic issues." In T. Ellsworth (Ed.), *Contemporary community corrections*, 266–278. Prospect Heights, IL: Waveland Publishing.

Cole, G. (1992). "Monetary sanctions: The problems of compliance." In J. Byrne, A. Lurrigo, and J. Petersilia (Eds.), *Smart sentencing: The emergence of intermediate sanctions*, 142–151. Newbury Park, CA: Sage Publications.

Commonwealth of Pennsylvania. (2004). "Community reentry workbook." Retrieved April 20, 2005, from http://www.portal.state.pa.us/portal/server.pt/community/department_of_corrections/4604.

Hillsman, S., and Greene, J. (1992). "The use of fines as an intermediate sanction." In J. Byrne, A. Lurrigo, and J. Petersilia (Eds.), *Smart sentencing: The emergence of intermediate sanctions,* 123–141. Newbury Park, CA: Sage Publications.

McDonald, D. (1992). "Punishing labor: Unpaid community service as a criminal sanction." In J. Byrne, A. Lurrigo, and J. Petersilia (Eds.), *Smart sentencing: The emergence of intermediate sanctions*, 182–193. Newbury Park, CA: Sage Publications.

Morash, M., and Rucker, L. (1990). "A critical look at the idea of boot camp as a correctional reform." *Crime and Delinquency* 36:204–222.

Office of Justice Programs. (2005). "Learn about reentry." Available from http://www.reentry.gov/learn.html.

Petersilia, J. (Ed.) (1998). *Community corrections: Probation, parole, and intermediate sanctions.* New York: Oxford University Press.

State of Michigan. (2004). "Michigan prisoner reentry initiative." Available from http://www.michigan.gov/corrections/0,1607,7-119-9741_33218—,00.html.

State of Ohio. (2002). "The Ohio plan for productive offender reentry and recidivism reduction." Available from http://www.drc.ohio.gov/web/ReentryFinalPlan.pdf.

Willing, R. (2005, February 3). "U.S. prisons to end boot-camp program." *USA Today.* Retrieved February 4, 2005, from http://www.usatoday.com/news/nation/2005-02-03-boot-camps_x.htm. ✦

CHAPTER 7

The Juvenile Justice System

CHAPTER OUTLINE

Dealing with juvenile offenders poses unique problems for society, and an entire system has been established to address juvenile concerns and issues. Where it is possible to talk about a "criminal justice system" that attempts to coordinate the efforts of the police, courts, and corrections into a functional whole, the juvenile justice system is often viewed as only an appendage to that system. This is largely due to the fact that juvenile justice was founded on a different set of assumptions about the nature of juvenile misbehavior and the proper responses to deal with juvenile transgressors.

THE DEVELOPMENT OF JUVENILE JUSTICE

The history of juvenile justice is a relatively short one. Until the mid-1800s, there was no separate legal status of "juvenile," nor was there a separate system for dealing with youthful offenders. Throughout most of history, juveniles have been treated as either property or little adults. When very young, particularly under the age of five, juveniles could be bought or sold by the family, just as a cow or other belonging. Once youths turned five or six, they were expected to go to work in the field or a business—the same as any adult.

The general view that children were the same as adults extended to the realm of legal sanctioning. Children were viewed as adults and were subject to the same rules and regulations as adults. There was not a separate system for dealing with youthful offenders. Society could sanction youths in the same way as adults. The law made no distinction based on the age of the offender. In fact, youths could be sentenced to death for various criminal actions. It is not uncommon to read historical accounts of youths being severely sanctioned for even minor offenses. While harsh punishments were meted out, many sanctions were never actually imposed because of the age of the youthful offenders. There was a de facto process of nullification, or a refusal to enforce the law and sanctions against children. While many youths could have been sentenced to death, few received such a sentence and most of those who did were never put to death.

Changes in the status of youths emerged in the early 1800s. Interestingly, the beginnings of the juvenile justice system are found in policy changes directed at dealing with poverty. The 1800s in the United States and other Western countries witnessed industrialization and the rapid growth of cities as people from the country-side moved to urban areas. In the United States, this also included the immigration of many people from Europe. The result was a growing population of people who had little education, had few skills useful in the new factories, could not speak English, and had few, if any, economic resources. They came to the United States and the cities with nothing more than a desire to partake in the promise of a new life.

This situation led cities to look for ways of assisting the poor, while alleviating the potential threat they posed to society. Many communities sought ways to help the poor become productive members of society. A primary response undertaken by many communities and religious groups was to take the poor off the streets and provide religious and vocational training, with the expectation that they would eventually be released so they could assume jobs and care for themselves and their families. Many groups focused their attention on dealing with poor children, because they were viewed as better candidates for education and training.

The Growth of Juvenile Institutions

Various institutions were established to assist in this policy of helping the poor while protecting society. The earliest such institutions were the **houses of refuge,** the first of which was established in New York in 1825. This was quickly copied in Boston (1826) and Philadelphia (1828). These institutions handled both adults and juveniles in need of assistance. Central aspects in the handling of youths were education, skills training, hard work, religious training, and parental discipline. Unfortunately, the houses of refuge quickly became overcrowded and failed to provide the training and assistance they promised.

By the mid-1800s, the houses of refuge gave way to a new set of institutions—the **reformatories**. While the basic goal of the reformatories was the same as the houses of refuge, they differed in two important ways. First, reformatories handled only youths. The religious and community leaders who promoted the idea of taking youths off the street and providing them with guidance and training saw that mixing youths with adults could be counterproductive, and they believed that more success could be achieved if they focused exclusively on youths. Second, rather than establish large physical structures to house youths, the reformatories were set up to more closely resemble homes. Typically, reformatories appeared as a series of small cottages, each with a set of surrogate parents and a small number of youths. This was supposed to resemble a family setting where the parents would provide the love and care needed by the children. Unfortunately, the reformatories suffered from many of the same problems as the houses of refuge. What makes them important is the fact that they started to recognize the unique needs and issues surrounding the young people in society.

Throughout the development of these new institutions, there remained a single system for dealing with criminal behavior by individuals of all ages in society. Youths who broke the law were still taken before the same courts as adults and subjected to the same penal code as anyone else in society. While the houses of refuge and the reformatories handled youths sent to them by the courts, most youths still found themselves jailed with adults and punished in the same ways as adults.

The Juvenile Court

The development of the juvenile court followed the same logic as the establishment of the new institutions, namely that some individuals needed assistance rather than

---

BOX 7.1

The Role and Mission of the Juvenile Court

Julian W. Mack was one of the leaders of the movement to establish a juvenile court and served as a judge in the Chicago juvenile court for many years. He described the role and methods of the court as follows:

> Most of the children who come before the court are, naturally, the children of the poor. In many cases the parents are foreigners, frequently unable to speak English, and without an understanding of American methods and views. What they need, more than anything else, is kindly assistance; and the aim of the court, in appointing a probation officer for the child, is to have the child and the parents feel, not so much the power, as the friendly interest of the state; to show them that the object of the court is to help them to train the child right. (Mack 1909)

---

punishment to make them law-abiding, productive contributors to society. The first recognized individual juvenile court was established in Cook County (Chicago), Illinois, in 1899. The legislation that established the Illinois court reflected the general belief that juveniles needed assistance to overcome the disadvantages they faced in society and that they could be reformed through a system of benevolence, rather than one that punished problematic behavior (see Box 7.1). Besides responding to the concern over the poor and destitute, the new juvenile court also emerged as a result of the growth of scientific explanations for behavior, particularly psychology and sociology. These disciplines argued that the problems of youths could be addressed in ways other than by simple imposition of punishment by the criminal justice system.

The new juvenile court had jurisdiction over all youths aged 15 and younger, no matter what the issue. The court was also supposed to operate in a very informal manner and avoid any resemblance to the adult court. Specifically, due process, attorneys, juries, and other elements of the adult system were excluded from the new juvenile system. The juvenile court was supposed to approach juveniles in a very paternalistic manner and offer them help and assistance just like that found in a family. Another important part of the court was the reliance on probation, rather than incarceration, for problem youths. The actual procedures and workings of the juvenile court generally reflected the character of the different judges and individuals working in the court.

The Philosophy of the System

The new juvenile court conformed to a philosophy that was diametrically opposed to the existing tenets of the adult criminal system. Rather than assume that people acted out of free will and chose to commit criminal and antisocial acts, the juvenile system took the stand that youths were incapable of forming the intent to commit criminal acts. Instead, their deviant behavior was the result of forces that were beyond their control, or they were simply too immature to understand the consequences of their behavior. As such, a strict legal response to juvenile misbehavior, which would include concerns over the constitutional rights of youths and the need to prove guilt and to require punishing the guilty, would be inappropriate. The appropriate alternative response would be to nurture, protect, and train the youths so that they could make decisions and avoid problems. This philosophy is known as **parens patriae.**

Parens patriae, or the state as parent, grew out of the English Chancery Court, which was tasked with looking after the property rights of orphaned children, among other things. The new juvenile court adopted this philosophy as the guiding force for its operations. The court was to act as a parent to those juveniles who were in need of assistance. Parens patriae opened the door to increased involvement in the lives of juveniles and their families. This is probably best exemplified in the passage of statutes specifically outlining status offenses. For example, the original Illinois statute establishing the juvenile court addressed criminal activity, dependency, and neglect. By 1903, however, the state added incorrigibility, curfews, and other status offenses to the court's mandate.

The parens patriae philosophy was not new to the juvenile court. Indeed, it had been used in an early court case in which a young girl was incarcerated against the wishes of her father. In *Exparte Crouse* (1838), a woman asked the court to incarcerate her daughter because she was incapable of taking care of her. The father objected and argued it was illegal to incarcerate a child without the benefit of a trial. The Pennsylvania Supreme Court, however, rejected the father's argument, stating that when a parent is incapable of doing his or her job, the state has a duty, under parens patriae, to step in and take action for the betterment of both the juvenile and the community (see Box 7.2). More importantly, the court noted that the rights of the parents are superseded by the rights and interests of society. This stance was reaffirmed after the initiation of the juvenile court in

---

BOX 7.2

Excerpt From *Ex parte Crouse* Decision

May not the natural parents, when unequal to the task of education, or unworthy of it, be superseded by the *parens patriae*, or common guardian of the community? It is to be remembered that the public has a paramount interest in the virtue and knowledge of its members, and that of strict right the business of education belongs to it. That parents are ordinarily entrusted with it, is because it can seldom be put in better hands; but where they are incompetent or corrupt, what is there to prevent the public from withdrawing their faculties, held as they obviously are, at its sufferance? The right of parental control is a natural, but not an inalienable one. It is not excepted by the declaration of rights out of the subject of ordinary legislation (*Ex parte Crouse* [1838]).

Commonwealth v. Fisher (1905). In this case, the Pennsylvania Supreme Court noted that when the objective of the state is not to punish or simply restrain a youth, but rather to provide care and protection, the state has a right and duty to step in and take custody of a youth. In essence, if the intent is to help the youth, parens patriae allows the juvenile court wide latitude to intervene in the life of the youth and the family.

The parens patriae philosophy remained the dominant view in the juvenile justice system throughout the twentieth century. Indeed, it was not until 1966 that the philosophy was seriously questioned in *Kent v. U.S.* While the U.S. Supreme

---

BOX 7.3

Juvenile Court General Purpose Clauses

Balanced and Restorative Justice Clauses:

- juvenile court is to focus on balancing the needs of the youth, the victim, and public safety
- typically includes an emphasis on treatment, care, and guidance of the youths
- found in 17 states

"Standard Juvenile Court Act" Clauses:

- emphasis on "care, guidance and control" to ensure the welfare of the youth
- offer care similar to that which would normally be supplied by the parents
- found in 9 states

"Legislative Guide" Clauses:

- provide care, protection, supervision, and rehabilitation to children
- maintain children in the home if at all possible
- provide institutional protection to youths
- found in 6 states

Punishment, Deterrence, Accountability, and/or Public Safety Clauses:

- criminal court orientation
- focus on community safety and offender accountability
- found in 6 states

Traditional Child Welfare Clauses:

- emphasis on welfare and best interests of child
- focus on *parens patriae* philosophy
- found in 3 states

SOURCE: Adapted by authors from Griffin, P., L. Szymanski, and M. King (2006) "National overviews." State Juvenile Justice Profiles. Pittsburgh: National Center for Juvenile Justice. http://www.ncjj.org/statepro files. Accessed: 6/29/08

Court did not rule specifically on the philosophy of the juvenile justice system, Justice Abe Fortas argued that:

> there may be grounds for concern that the child receives the worst of both worlds: that he gets neither the protections accorded to adults nor the solicitous care and regenerative treatment postulated for children. (*Kent v. U.S.* [1966])

Justice Fortas was suggesting that the philosophy allowed the juvenile court unfettered involvement in the lives of juveniles without granting them due-process rights, despite the fact that the court was also failing to provide the help and care that the philosophy mandated. Changes in the juvenile justice system over the past 30 years show a gradual diminution of parens patriae in juvenile proceedings.

Today, *parens patriae* is only one of the philosophical rationales underscoring juvenile justice, although it remains the key philosophy underlying juvenile courts in the United States. An analysis of state statutes reveals five general categories of juvenile court "purpose clauses" (see Box 7.3). In only one of the five categories (Punishment, Deterrence, Accountability, and/or Public Safety) is *parens patriae* largely excluded and the emphasis shifted to an adult court/criminal law orientation for the juvenile court. The other four categories maintain *parens patriae* as at least a key component in addressing problem youths.

Critical Thinking Exercise

Research the general purpose clause for the juvenile court in your state.

DEFINING DELINQUENCY

The development of a separate system for handling problem youths also meant that a new set of laws and terminology was not far behind. Certainly, the new juvenile justice system was meant to be different from the adult system. Nowhere was this more apparent than in the fact that "delinquency" replaced "crime" as the focus of the juvenile court.

It is important to note that "delinquency" did not exist prior to the establishment of the juvenile court. That does not mean that youths did not break the law or come to the attention of legal authorities. Rather, it means that handling youths under a different set of laws and policies emerged when the juvenile court was established. The advent of the juvenile justice system brought with it a new vocabulary, including "delinquency," "status offense," and (interestingly) "juvenile."

Delinquency can take a variety of different meanings. One way to define delinquency is to simply point to the criminal law definition of crime and apply it to juvenile behavior. In other words, a delinquent is any juvenile who violates

BOX 7.4

Age Criteria for Juvenile Court Processing by States

Ages of Criminal Court Jurisdiction

16	3 states
17	10 states
18	37 states and the District of Columbia

****

Lower Age Limits of Juvenile Court Jurisdiction

6	1 state
7	3 states
8	1 state
10	11 states

no specified age   35 states and DC

****

Maximum Age of Juvenile Court Jurisdiction

18	7 states
19	2 states
20	32 states and DC
21	1 state
22	1 state
24	4 states

no specified maximum   3 states

****

Minimum Age for Transfer to Adult Court

10	2 states
12	3 states
13	6 states
14	16 states
15	1 state

no specified minimum   22 states and DC

SOURCE: King, M., and L. Szymanski (2006) "National overviews." State Juvenile Justice Profiles. Pittsburgh: National Center for Juvenile Justice. http://www.ncjj.org/stateprofiles. Accessed: 6/13/08.

Critical Thinking Exercise

Look up the delinquency and status offense statutes for your state and compare them to those of Ohio that appear in Box 7.5. How are they similar and different?

BOX 7.5

Criminal Law Definition and Status Offense Definitions of Delinquency

Ohio defines a "delinquent child" as:

1) Any child, except a juvenile traffic offender, who violates any law of this state or the United States, or any ordinance of a political subdivision of the state, that would be an offense if committed by an adult;
2) Any child who violates any lawful order of the court. . .;
3) Any child who violates [prohibitions against purchasing or owning a firearm or handgun (Section 2923.21.1)];
4) Any child who is a habitual truant and who previously has been adjudicated an unruly child for being habitually truant;
5) Any child who is a chronic truant.

Ohio Chapter 2151.02.2 defines an "unruly child" (i.e., status offender) as:

(A) Any child who does not submit to the reasonable control of the child's parents, teachers, guardian, or custodian, by reason of being wayward or habitually truant;
(B) Any child who is an habitual truant from school and who previously has not been adjudicated an unruly child for being an habitual truant;
(C) Any child who behaves in a manner as to injure or endanger the child's own health or morals or the health of morals of others;
(D) Any child who violates a law . . . that is applicable only to a child.

Source: Ohio Revised Code. (2005). Sections 2151.02.2 and 2152.02.

---

the criminal code. Thus, a juvenile who commits a robbery, burglary, assault, or any other criminal offense is considered a delinquent. This definition is used throughout the United States. Delinquency is also defined in terms of actions that are illegal only for juveniles. This is usually referred to as a **status offense** definition. That is, only a person of a certain status can violate the code. Typical status offenses for juveniles include the use of alcohol or tobacco, curfew violations, truancy, disobeying one's parents, running away, or swearing. Adults who participate in any of these actions are not subject to sanctions by the criminal or juvenile justice systems. A status offender may be referred to under a variety of different names depending on the jurisdiction. Common terms one sees are "incorrigible," "unruly," "dependent," "PINS" (person in need of service), or "CHINS" (child in need of service). Some of these terms refer both to juveniles who have done something wrong and to youths who have been subjected to poor parenting or are victims of a crime and are in need of protection.

In defining delinquency, it is important also to note that the definition of a juvenile varies from jurisdiction to jurisdiction. In 37 states and the District of Columbia, a juvenile is anyone under the age of 18. Three states define juveniles as individuals under age 16, while 10 states define juveniles as those under age 17. While these ages set an upper limit for juvenile court jurisdiction, many states also set a minimum age for handling cases in the juvenile system. That age is typically between ages 6 and 10. Besides the minimum age, there are often provisions whereby the juvenile system can retain jurisdiction over an individual who was adjudicated in the system but has since passed the age of majority. States accomplish this under what are generally known as **youthful offender statutes.**

A special set of provisions that allows for the state to handle juveniles as adults in the criminal justice system are known as **transfer or waiver** provisions. Transfer, or waiver, is a process whereby someone who is legally a juvenile is determined to be beyond the help of the juvenile justice system. Thus, there is a need to invoke the adult criminal process to handle the youth and protect society. Most jurisdictions set a minimum age at which transfer can be invoked.

It should be evident that defining delinquency is not a straightforward endeavor. The definition varies greatly based on the age of the youth and the jurisdiction. This situation also leads to variation in the measurement of youthful misbehavior, since the level of delinquency varies according to how the problem is defined.

Critical Thinking Exercise

Explore your state's statutes and find the definitions and guidelines for juveniles and transfer/waiver used by your state. How do they compare with what is presented here? Randomly pick one or two other states and compare those results to your state.

MEASURING DELINQUENCY

There are a number of different ways to measure delinquency, each of which produces a different picture of the delinquency problem. The various methods for measuring delinquency result in different absolute levels of delinquency as well as different information on offenses, offenders, and victims. The two primary approaches to measuring delinquency are the use of official records and the administration of self-report surveys.

Official Arrest Records
As noted earlier in this book, the Uniform Crime Reports (UCR) are the most common official source of information on offending and offenders. Unfortunately, due to the fact that only a fraction of all crimes are cleared by arrest each year, little

information is known about the offenders in most crimes. Some idea about the participation of juveniles in delinquent/criminal behavior, however, can be gathered from an inspection of those cases where an offender can be identified or arrested. Arrest data by age for 2007 reveal that approximately 15 percent of those arrested were juveniles under the age of 18. A closer inspection of the arrest data reveals that youths comprised 16 percent of the arrests for the violent crimes of murder, rape, robbery, and aggravated assault. More striking is the fact that youths were arrested for almost 320,000 property offenses, approximately one-third of all property offenses arrests in 2007. Perhaps more importantly, these data show that youths are arrested at a higher rate than their representation in the population. Specifically, youths aged 10–17 are responsible for 15 percent of all arrests, but make up only about 11 percent of the total U.S. population (Office of Juvenile Justice and Delinquency Prevention 2001).

The use of arrest data for measuring youthful offending is problematic mainly due to the focus on the Part I crimes listed in the UCR. These arrest data miss a great deal of juvenile misbehavior due to the minor nature of many juvenile transgressions, such as status offenses. As such, there is a very skewed view of juvenile behavior if the focus is placed solely on crimes for which they have been arrested. What is missing are the many forms of misbehavior that are not reflected in the UCR.

Critical Thinking Exercise

Examine the UCR data at http://www.fbi.gov/ucr/cius2007/index.html for information on age, sex, race/ethnicity, and other factors related to offending. Also look at the juvenile court and http://www.ncjrs.gov/pdffiles1/ojjdp/202885.pdf.

Self-Report Measures

Self-report measures attempt to gauge the level of delinquency by asking individuals to admit to their participation in deviant activity. Where official measures reflect information on those offenses that have been reported to the authorities or where an individual has been arrested, self-reports do not need any involvement of the criminal justice system.

Self-report surveys have a long history in juvenile justice. One of the earliest self-report surveys was developed by Short and Nye (1958) to tap the level of misbehavior by youths. Their survey asked youths to note the frequency with which they committed each of 23 items. The items in the scale were dominated by status and minor property offenses. Dentler and Monroe (1961) offered a similar self-report survey that focused on minor delinquent offenses.

Most self-report surveys uncover a great deal of delinquent activity. Indeed, various studies using scales such as that of Short and Nye show that virtually every juvenile is a delinquent. This is due to the many minor transgressions that appear in them. Defying parental authority or trying alcohol at some time are pretty universal activities for juveniles. Asking if the individual has "ever" committed an act contributes to the high levels of positive responses. Compared to official counts of delinquency, such self-reports show a great deal more deviance.

More recent self-report surveys, such as the Monitoring the Future (MTF) survey, include many more serious offenses that elicit significantly fewer positive responses. The MTF survey includes questions on hitting teachers, group fighting, use of weapons, robbery, and aggravated assault. Data from these projects reveal that few youths commit the more serious offenses.

Critical Thinking Exercise

What measure of delinquency is the best, and why?

Like official data, self-report measures are not without fault. As already noted, many survey instruments tend to err on the side of recording numerous minor criminal acts and status offenses, but often fail to tap into more serious actions. Exceptions to this problem, such as the National Youth Survey and the Monitoring the Future project, which include serious criminal acts, find results much more in line with those revealed in official arrest statistics. A second major problem with self-report data is the fact that most surveys are one-time efforts, which makes it difficult to know what changes (if any) are taking place over time.

THE JUVENILE COURT PROCESS

Most youths come to the juvenile court by way of the police. In any given year, the police refer roughly 85 percent of the juveniles appearing in juvenile court. The remaining 15 percent are referred to the court by parents, schools, or other agencies and individuals. Once a juvenile is referred to court, the case can follow a range of different paths through the system. Cases can be petitioned to court and handled in a formal capacity or not petitioned and subjected to informal

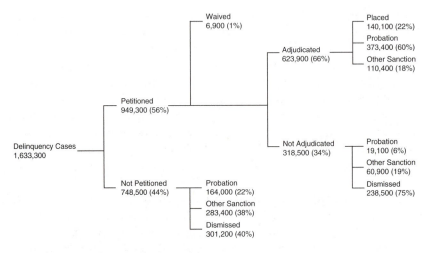

Figure 7.1 Juvenile Court Processing, 2005
SOURCE: Puzzanchera and Sickmund (2008).

interventions. Estimates of the number of cases and the movement of cases through the various alternative processes for 2005 appear in Figure 7.1.

No matter how youths reach the court, the process and decision points are the same. In general, there are five key stages in juvenile court processing: the detention decision, intake, transfer (or waiver), adjudication, and disposition. Within each stage, various issues and processes arise.

Detention

The initial decision to be made by juvenile court personnel is whether to hold a youth in custody or allow the youth to go home until further action is taken. A **detention** decision is the counterpart to the bail decision in adult court. Where an adult bail decision considers whether the individual will appear at a later date and whether the person is a threat to others, the detention decision also considers whether the juvenile is in danger himself. That is, detention is considered for the good of society *and* the good of the juvenile. Detention decisions are initially made by probation officers or special detention workers, although the final decision on whether to continue detention is up to the juvenile court judge. Most state laws require that a detention hearing be held within a specified period of time, typically 36 or 48 hours. A key concern is whether detention should be used to hold youths who are at high risk for committing further offenses, even in the event that no imminent danger to another person can be demonstrated. Critics of detaining youths for this cause generally claim that many youths who are held do not really constitute a threat and, therefore, the detention is a violation of their rights. Such preventive detention, however, has been declared constitutional by the U.S. Supreme Court (*Schall v. Martin* [1984]). Only about 20 percent of the youths brought to the attention of the court are held in detention. The remaining youths are released to their families.

The youths who are not released to their parents or guardians are placed into either secure or nonsecure detention facilities. Secure detention is the equivalent of the local jail for adults. This does not mean that the youths are put into cells alongside adult offenders. Indeed, it is illegal to do so. Juveniles must be isolated from adults, both physically and audibly. That is, youths are not supposed to be able to see or hear confined adults. In nonsecure detention, the youths may be placed in group homes, halfway houses, foster care, or other community-based alternatives to a secure facility. Youths in these facilities may still attend their normal schools and other functions as allowed by the court. Both secure and nonsecure detention facilities must provide food, a place to sleep, health care, educational programming, and appropriate treatment programs. Both the educational and treatment components respond to the parens patriae doctrine of helping youths rather than punishing them. It is not unusual, therefore, for detention centers to hold school classes during the week and to offer some form of treatment programming. These activities are especially important if the youths spend a prolonged period of time in detention prior to a final court disposition.

Because of the relatively short periods that most youths spend in detention, treatment interventions within the detention facilities are often very simplistic and do not address the underlying needs of the youths. Instead, the interventions tend to address the need to keep order in the facility. A very common form of detention programming is referred to as **boob tube therapy.** This is nothing more than parking youths in front of televisions all day long. Another common intervention used in detention facilities is the implementation of a **token economy.** Under this approach, youths receive points or tokens for acting appropriately and lose them for inappropriate behaviors. The tokens are good towards extra privileges or purchases from a store or vending machine. Other interventions, such as counseling and vocational training, may appear in some facilities, but are not very common due to the relatively short stay for many youths.

The cost involved in housing youths and providing for their constant care while in detention has led many jurisdictions to seek out alternative modes of supervision. One option, **day–evening centers,** provide educational programming, treatment programs, or other activities during the day, but send the youths home at night. This alleviates the need to provide beds, clothing, and three meals a day. The parents/guardians provide oversight at night. A second option is to utilize home detention, which involves ordering youths to remain at home at all times, unless given permission by the court to leave the premises. Youths are monitored by probation or court personnel through frequent visits, phone contacts, or even electronic monitoring devices. This is a cost-effective alternative to the use of a detention facility. A final alternative to detention is to allow youths to post bail as in adult court. This is a seldom-used alternative, due mainly to the inability of most youths and their families to raise the required funds. Nevertheless, some jurisdictions have successfully used bail to handle even serious cases.

The Intake Decision

The second major decision point in the juvenile court is intake. The **intake decision** is the juvenile system's counterpart to filing charges or a grand jury indictment in the adult system. It is at intake that the decision is made to file a petition with the court to hear the case or to handle the youth in another way. The petition alleges that a child is either delinquent, neglected, abused, incorrigible, dependent, or otherwise in need of court intervention. This decision to file a petition is typically made by a probation officer or intake officer. The decision usually comes after the probation or intake officer has reviewed the facts of the case, met with and talked to the youth and his or her family, gathered background information about the youth (including prior offending, school records, etc.), and considered other alternatives to formal court processing. In recent years, many jurisdictions have begun to mandate that all decisions to file or deny a petition be reviewed by a prosecutor in order to ensure that there is legal standing for the court to take action and guarantee that serious juvenile offenders are not moved out of the system. Despite the move to include prosecutorial oversight, 43 percent of all juvenile cases reaching the intake stage were *not* petitioned to the court in 1999 (Puzzanchera et al. 2003).

Youths who are not petitioned to court are not simply let go by intake. Most of the time some form of **informal adjustment** is mandated by the intake or probation office. An informal adjustment means that the youths will be required to participate in something short of a court procedure. Interestingly, in 1999, one-third of youths who were not petitioned to court were still placed on some form of probation, although often this is unsupervised (Puzzanchera et al. 2003). Other alternatives may be as simple as making restitution to a store for a theft or a homeowner for vandalism or as involved as attending a series of counseling or treatment programs. It is not unusual for such informal adjustments to require the participation of the parents and other family members, especially if counseling or treatment is mandated. These informal adjustments are an important part of the juvenile justice system and clearly fit the parens patriae philosophy of the court.

The Transfer (or Waiver) Decision

One possible option available to the juvenile court when faced with a serious juvenile offender is to transfer or waive the youth to the adult system for processing. This is an important decision, since the transfer means that the youth will be subjected to both the due-process concerns of the adult court and the same penalties imposed on adult offenders. In essence, the youth will be dealt with as an adult and will incur an adult criminal record if convicted. A criminal record may have serious ramifications for future employment opportunities, whereas a juvenile record is typically confidential and not subject to later disclosure.

While the traditional and most common method for waiving a juvenile was to petition the juvenile court to pass jurisdiction over to the adult court, today there are several different types of waiver (see Box 7.6). Judicial waiver, the traditional approach, is typically made at a hearing analogous to a preliminary hearing in

---

BOX 7.6

Forms of Transfer or Waiver

Judicial Waiver	Requires a waiver hearing in front of a judge who determines the suitability of removing the case to the adult court.
Prosecutorial Waiver	The decision to try a juvenile in the adult court is made by the prosecutor, who has sole discretion in the matter.
Legislative Waiver/Statutory Exclusion	The legislature has dictated, through a statute, that certain youths must be tried in the adult court—the juvenile court is excluded from hearing the case.
Once/Always	Once a youth has been adjudicated in adult court, the youth is permanently under the adult court's jurisdiction.
Demand Waiver	Youths demand a transfer to adult court, possibly to ensure greater due-process protections.

---

adult court. At this hearing the prosecutor asks the juvenile court judge to transfer the youth to the adult court for processing. The prosecutor must show probable cause that the juvenile committed the alleged offense. He or she must also convince the judge that the youth is not amenable to treatment in the juvenile system—that the juvenile justice system is not capable of helping the youth. This is typically demonstrated through past failures of the juvenile system to correct a problem or the particularly heinous nature of the offense.

Concern over the increasing number and seriousness of juvenile crimes, particularly since 1990, has led to a greater reliance on two other types of transfer—prosecutorial waiver and legislative waiver. Prosecutorial waiver refers to the ability of prosecutors to decide in which court (juvenile or adult) to file charges. That is, the prosecutor can use his or her discretion to take a youth straight to adult court by filing charges at that level. The prosecution is not totally free to make such a decision and is generally bound by state statutes that outline which offenses and which circumstances can be used to send a juvenile to the adult system. The statutes, however, do not mandate transfer of the case to adult court. Rather, the prosecutor can keep the case in juvenile court if he or she so desires. The last form of transfer is referred to as legislative waiver or statutory exclusion. Legislative waiver means that the state legislature has determined that certain offenses or circumstances warrant invoking the adult criminal process and mandates that the case be heard in the adult court. The case is excluded from juvenile court processing by statute. The typical cases addressed by legislative waiver are serious personal offenses, such as murder, or those involving serious repeat offenders. Once/ always provisions stipulate that once a youth is adjudicated as an adult, he or she will remain under the jurisdiction of the adult court for any future transgressions. Finally, some jurisdictions allow for youths to demand waiver to adult court.

Critical Thinking Exercise

Waiver protocols vary from jurisdiction to jurisdiction, and many jurisdictions allow for more than one type of waiver. The use of different forms of waiver by state can be found at the links provided on the textbook website (http://www.oup.com/us/labessentials). Examine this information and discuss what it tells you about the use of waiver.

Only a small portion of all youths are transferred to adult court; however, a significant number of youths find themselves facing adult sanctions. There has been a clear policy shift in juvenile justice to call for harsher sanctioning of violent youths. This was particularly evident in the late 1980s and early 1990s, when many legislators were calling for "get-tough" crime-control policies. It was then that many legislatures enacted exclusionary statutes or opened the way for prosecutors to make the decision to file charges in adult court. Nevertheless, in 1999, less than 1 percent of all juveniles petitioned to court were transferred to the adult court. This represents approximately 7,500 cases. The number of cases waived to the adult court increased greatly in the mid- to late 1980s and early 1990s, largely due to increases in the number of homicides and assaults related to the crack-cocaine epidemic. Recent reductions in the number of waivers, however, have not matched the increases in the early 1990s and the number of youths waived still exceeds that seen in the late 1980s.

The impact of transferring youths to adult court on subsequent offending and crime rates is not clear. There is some evidence that youths handled in adult court have a greater chance of receiving probation rather than being incarcerated or are released earlier than they would have been if kept under juvenile court jurisdiction (Fagan 1995). This may be due to the lack of appropriate places of confinement for youths who are convicted under adult statutes. They cannot simply be placed into adult correctional facilities with adults, but are not under the jurisdiction of the juvenile correctional system. There is also no strong evidence that youths handled in the adult courts recidivate at lower levels than those processed in the juvenile system (Fagan 1995). These results suggest that transferring youths to the adult system is not a panacea for the problem of youth crime.

Adjudication
Actual hearings in the juvenile court are referred to as the **adjudication** stage. During adjudication, the judge must determine whether there is enough evidence

to support the petition and what remedy to use with the juvenile. This is comparable to finding guilt or innocence and sentencing in the adult court.

The adjudication stage in the juvenile court is supposed to look a great deal different from what is seen in an adult court. Under parens patriae, there is not supposed to be a determination of guilt or innocence. The actual fact that a crime may have been committed is secondary to the needs of the youth and his or her family. Due-process considerations of the admissibility of evidence, the use of hearsay evidence, the presence of attorneys, and similar issues are secondary to determining what is in the best interests of the child. The entire setting of a juvenile courtroom is often configured to suggest a nonadversarial proceeding. Indeed, during the early days of the juvenile court, attorneys were rarely included in the proceedings, with only the judge, the youth, his or her parents, and perhaps a probation or intake officer in attendance. Today, many hearings are held around a large conference table and the judge does not even wear judicial robes. It is common for the judge to ask all the questions, and the probation or intake officer offers most of the evidence.

This ideal process of juvenile procedure has undergone several changes over the past 30 years. Today, there is a greater emphasis on procedural rights in many cases, particularly those dealing with serious offenses. As a result, both prosecuting and defense attorneys are becoming more commonplace in juvenile court proceedings. The determination of guilt or innocence has also become more common. Many courts have adopted the trappings of adult court, with a judge's bench, judicial robes, defense and prosecution tables, and concern for the due-process rights of the youth. This movement may be due to the increasing levels of serious offending by youths.

The emergence of due-process concerns and the participation of attorneys in the juvenile court process is not without its problems. First, many youths are not represented by attorneys because they do not understand their rights and often waive their right to representation out of ignorance of the law. Second, as in adult cases, a large number of youths rely on the overburdened public defenders' office. Puritz and her colleagues (1995) point out that many youths feel they receive poor representation from indifferent public defense attorneys. Third, when attorneys are present, they often fail to act as advocates for their youthful clients, opting instead to help the youths like concerned parents (Feld 1999). This may be perceived by some clients as inadequate and not in their best interest. Finally, there is conflicting evidence on the effectiveness of defense attorneys in the juvenile court. While some research suggests that attorneys are effective at obtaining dismissals and keeping youths out of detention (Fabricant 1983), other research reports that youths are more likely to be removed from their homes and placed in residential facilities when they are represented by attorneys (Feld 1988). The participation of attorneys in the juvenile court setting, therefore, may not be beneficial for many youths.

One consequence of increased concern over due-process rights and the inclusion of attorneys in the courtroom has been an increase in the amount of plea bargaining in juvenile court cases. One analysis notes that plea bargaining is now the norm in the majority of juvenile court cases (Puritz et al. 1995). The growth of plea bargaining in an adversarial juvenile court has led the Institute of Judicial Administration-American Bar Association (IJA-ABA) (1980) to offer several recommendations about its use. First, plea bargaining should be acknowledged in the court and the process should be made visible to observers. Second, judges should not be involved in the process, except to require that any agreement be made public and that they have the right to either accept or reject the recommendations. In cases where judges reject agreements, youths should have the chance to withdraw their guilty pleas and proceed to trial. Finally, in all plea bargains, judges should consult with youths' parents or guardians about the agreements and make certain that they approve (IJA-ABA 1980).

Disposition

Once the court has determined that the facts of the petition are sufficiently supported, a **disposition** (the equivalent to a sentence in an adult court) is determined. Most often, the disposition reflects the parens patriae philosophy and seeks interventions and treatments that address the needs of the youth and the family. The judge pays a great deal of attention to the recommendations of the probation officers, social workers, psychologists, and others who have examined the youth. Counseling, educational programming, and treatment programs dominate most dispositions, and most of the time there is a strong desire to send youths home for treatment within the community. Indeed, the vast majority of youths are placed on some form of probation.

Many jurisdictions have moved to more punitive sanctions in recent years. This trend has been mandated in many places by legislative attempts to "get tough" on juvenile offenders by setting minimum sanctions that the juvenile courts must impose for some crimes. It is not unusual for jurisdictions to impose these harsher dispositions on older youths who have been involved in repeat offenses. A good deal of the concern is that these youths will continue their offending once they become adults and are no longer under the juvenile court's jurisdiction. Indeed, many jurisdictions have developed a system of **blended sentencing** as a means of addressing the loss of jurisdiction by the juvenile court before youths can be adjudicated or before treatment can be completed. Under blended sentencing, the court imposes dispositions that rely on both the juvenile and adult systems. For example, a 17 year old who is adjudicated in juvenile court may begin his or her disposition in a juvenile facility. Instead of simply releasing the individual when he or she turns 18 and the juvenile facility is no longer appropriate, however, the individual automatically transfers to an adult facility and supervision by the adult court. Another possibility is for the 17 year old to be sent directly to adult supervision from the juvenile court. The opposite can also occur. A youthful adult offender (say age 19) may be found guilty of a crime in adult court, but the court feels the offender would be better served in a facility or program run by the juvenile court and sends him or her to the juvenile system for help. Such blended sentencing is becoming more commonplace as society grapples with offenders who do not quite fit into one or the other system.

DUE PROCESS FOR JUVENILES

Starting in the 1960s, challenges to the parens patriae philosophy began to have an impact on providing due-process protections to youths. These challenges to how youths were being handled in the juvenile justice system stemmed from various sources. One key issue was the fact that the crime rate was steadily increasing during the 1960s and early 1970s, and a large part of that increase was attributable to juvenile misconduct. The court, therefore, was faced with increasing case loads, more serious offenders, and a public demand to do something about crime. A second factor was the report of the President's Commission on Law Enforcement and the Administration of Justice (1967), which raised serious questions about the juvenile court's handling of youths, its ability to deal with the increasing caseload, and the need to protect both the youths and society. During this period, the U.S. Supreme Court and state courts began to take a more active look at the operations of the juvenile justice system. Consequently, youths are now afforded some of the same constitutional rights that adults have when facing the criminal justice system. At the same time, the courts still recognize the parens patriae doctrine as the driving force when dealing with juveniles and have been reluctant to award full constitutional protections to youths in the juvenile justice system.

As noted earlier, the first case to seriously question the parens patriae doctrine and the lack of due-process rights for juveniles was *Kent v. U.S.* (1966). In *Kent*, the U.S. Supreme Court was asked to examine the rights of a juvenile faced with transfer to the adult court. Kent was a 16-year-old male accused of rape who had been waived to the adult court without benefit of a hearing, the assistance of counsel, or an explanation of why he was waived. The Supreme Court decided that the juvenile court judge had erred. Specifically, the court should have allowed Kent's attorney to review the evidence and be present at a hearing in order to refute the evidence and offer a counterargument to the court. The denial of counsel was a violation of Kent's Sixth Amendment rights. Further, the Supreme Court ruled that the judge needed to set forth in writing the specific reasons why he transferred the case to the adult court. The *Kent* case is important for two reasons. First, it outlined the procedure by which transfer decisions must be made. No such procedure existed prior to this time. Second, and most important, the case established some due-process protections for the first time in juvenile procedures. While the protections only applied to transfer decisions, they opened the way for further challenges to parens patriae.

The year after the *Kent* decision, the U.S. Supreme Court ruled in the case *In re Gault* (1967). In this case, a 15-year-old youth was accused of making obscene phone calls and was subsequently sentenced to the state training school until he became an adult. In essence, Gault was given a six-year sentence for a crime that, for an adult, could only bring a $50 fine and two months in jail. The appeal, however, was not over the sentence. Instead, the questions raised dealt with the procedure followed when imposing the sentence. Gault was taken into custody by the police without any notice being given to his mother. He was detained until his hearing one week later, at which he was denied the right to counsel, no specific charges were ever filed, the person making the accusation was not required to appear, and no transcripts of the proceedings were kept. The Supreme Court ruled that, when there is a possibility of confinement, a juvenile does have certain rights, including the right to an attorney, the right to know the charges against him or her, the right to confront his or her accuser, and the right to remain silent (*In re Gault* [1967]). The Court specifically noted that the inclusion of due-process rights in juvenile court would not hinder the court's ability to act in the best interests of the child.

The rights of juveniles to due process were further enhanced in 1970 in the case *In re Winship.* In this case, a 12-year-old boy was confined to the state training facility for allegedly stealing $112 from a woman's purse. During the juvenile court hearing, the court adjudicated the youth delinquent using a "preponderance of evidence" criterion. The appeal dealt with whether this standard of proof was sufficient for incarcerating a juvenile. The U.S. Supreme Court noted that the higher standard of "beyond a reasonable doubt" as used in the adult court must also be used in juvenile proceedings when there is the possibility of committing a youth to a locked facility (*In re Winship* [1970]). The Court also questioned the use of "preponderance of evidence" based on its lack of accuracy and openness to interpretation.

Despite the growth of due-process considerations in juvenile court, not all constitutional rights afforded to adults are applicable to juveniles or the juvenile court. This was made evident only one year after *Winship* in the case *McKeiver v. Pennsylvania* (1971). In this case, the juvenile was denied the right to a jury trial and appealed to the U.S. Supreme Court for relief. The Supreme Court, however, sided with the lower courts and denied the appeal. It did this for several reasons. First, the Court ruled that there is no need for a jury trial to ensure fairness. Bench trials are just as capable of ensuring fairness as a jury trial. Second, the Court did not want to turn the juvenile courts into an adversarial setting, and a jury trial would be much more adversarial. Third, the Court pointed out that the juvenile court was capable of fulfilling its mandate without giving full due-process rights to juveniles. Finally, while it did not mandate jury trials in juveniles cases, the Court did note that a jurisdiction could allow for juries if it desired to do so (*McKeiver v. Pennsylvania* [1971]).

These four cases are typically considered the most important cases for the juvenile justice system. They opened the door to review of the actions of the juvenile court and offered some constitutional protections to youths. At the same time, they limited the extent of those constitutional rights and reaffirmed the basic philosophical mandate underlying the juvenile system. Since these cases were decided, many other challenges have been mounted on behalf of juveniles. Some of those cases further refine the rights of juveniles in the juvenile and criminal justice systems. Other cases address larger constitutional issues, such as juveniles' rights to free speech, privacy rights in schools, abortion rights, and many others (see Box 7.7 for a list of other rulings).

BOX 7.7

Court Rulings Impacting Juvenile Justice

***Breed v. Jones* (1975)**	Attached double jeopardy to cases in which youths are adjudicated in juvenile court and then waived to adult court for processing.
***Fare v. Michael C*. (1979)**	The Court ruled that a youth does not have a right to speak to his probation officer after an arrest; a youth only has a right to speak to counsel.
***Schall v. Martin* (1984)**	Preventive detention is permissible if there is adequate concern that further crimes will be committed, although the juvenile has a right to a hearing on the detention.
***New Jersey v. T.L.O.* (1985)**	The warrantless search of a student's purse by school authorities is permissible based on reasonable suspicion of violating school rules.
***Doe v. Renfroe* (1981)**	The use of dogs to sniff students and their possessions for drugs at school is not a violation of their rights.
***Qutb v. Strauss* (1993)**	Juvenile curfews are not a violation of an individual's rights if they serve a compelling state interest.
***Board of Education of Independent School District No. 92 v. Lindsay Earls et al.* (2002)**	Random drug tests required of students participating in extracurricular activities are permissible.

Critical Thinking Exercise

Should juveniles be given full constitutional protections? What would be the consequence of doing so? What would be the consequence of not doing so?

Throughout the court cases, there is an attempt to balance the rights of juveniles as individuals and citizens with the family and societal needs to protect and raise children to be law-abiding citizens. The growth of litigation over the rights of youths can be considered a direct result of changes in both the behavior of youths and societal responses to that behavior. As society and the juvenile justice system have taken new steps to address youthful misbehavior, particularly in terms of more adversarial proceedings and harsher forms of punishment, the courts have stepped in to outline appropriate safeguards for the rights of youths. In essence, the courts have established policy through the rulings they have handed down.

INSTITUTIONAL CORRECTIONS

Juvenile corrections takes a variety of forms, ranging from institutional and residential settings to probation and community-based alternatives. The primary goal throughout juvenile corrections is to help youth overcome the problems leading to misbehavior. The history of many correctional initiatives today date back to founding principles of the juvenile system. The early houses of refuge and reformatories set the stage for today's residential institutions, while probation has been a cornerstone of dealing with juveniles since before the first juvenile court was established.

Critical Thinking Exercise

What impact has the introduction of due-process rights into the juvenile justice system had on problem youths and the operations of the system?

Institutional and Residential Interventions

According to a one-day count taken in 2003, there were over 96,000 youths being held in some form of residential facility, with more than one-third of those being held for offenses against persons (Snyder and Sickmund 2006). Seven out of 10 youths were in public facilities. The vast majority of these facilities are considered secure facilities that are locked down to keep the youths from escaping.

The equivalent of adult prisons in the juvenile system are **state training schools**. Youths who are considered to be a risk to themselves and the community and who are beyond the help of community-based interventions are sent by the court to training schools for help. The actual set-up of training schools varies greatly from place to place. Some training schools closely resemble adult prisons, with high walls, fences, barbed wire, locked cells, and heavily regimented activities. At the other extreme are training schools built on the cottage design of the early reformatories. These institutions may be totally open, meaning that there are no fences or locked doors to keep juveniles from escaping. The "guards" in these facilities may actually act more like parents than jailers. The most important part of training schools is the degree of programming that is supposed to take place. Not all training schools are huge institutions located in a centralized location. Today, many institutions resemble the basic ideas of a training school but are much smaller and are much closer to the home of the youths they serve. Indeed, even detention centers that house postadjudicated, long-term youths mirror many aspects of training schools.

Most training schools offer some combination of academic education, vocational training, and behavior modification. As in detention, the youths must attend school during the academic year, just as any other child would outside the institution. Older youths who have either completed school or who are no longer required to go to school may be offered the chance to undergo training in some vocational skill that may be useful for finding employment later in life. Besides the typical educational programming found in any school, institutions may also offer remedial education and training and life-skills development.

Behavior modification is used ostensibly to teach youths about proper behavior through a system that rewards positive behavior and punishes poor behavior. Most institutions use a very formalized point system, or token economy. Youths receive points or tokens for the proper display of behavior and for following rules, which can be used towards special activities or to purchase goods from a "store." Similarly, youths can lose points or tokens for acting out or refusing to follow directions. The assumption is that the youths will come to recognize that good behavior is rewarded and that they will carry this lesson with them after they leave the institution. A more cynical view of behavior modification is that it simply serves to control the youths while in the institution and any long-term behavioral change is an added bonus. No matter the rationale underlying the use of behavior modification, it is almost universally found in residential institutions.

Beyond these three interventions, institutions may implement a wide range of additional programming. Individual, group, and family counseling are popular interventions used in institutions, along with drug or alcohol programs, work release, vocational counseling, and job placement. Many training schools use **guided group interaction** as a main form of counseling. This approach relies on the youths to identify problem behaviors, confront one another about their past actions, offer acceptable alternatives to deviant responses, and provide peer pressure to change the behavior of group members (Bartollas 1985). The counselor or leader tries to remain neutral in the sessions and only guides the discussion with a minimum of input. There is a wide range of other treatment modalities used in institutions. What is important to note is that, with very few exceptions, the emphasis is on helping youths overcome the problems and situations that lead to delinquent activities.

A key issue facing institutional programming is its effectiveness at reducing recidivism and helping the youths become productive members of society. Unfortunately, the evidence on effectiveness is mixed (see Whitehead and Lab 2009). The reason for this is not entirely clear, although a large part of the problem may entail the degree to which the intervention is appropriately implemented and carried out. That is, did the institution deliver the treatment as it was meant to be delivered and at a level sufficient to bring about a positive change? Many studies have failed to find any positive impact of institutional programs in the aggregate. This means that, when considering changes across a large number of youths, there is little evidence of improvement. At the same time, there may be some individuals who benefit from the programming, but they are not in the majority and do not influence the overall results. One group of advocates for correctional interventions notes that, if the right treatment is applied to the appropriate individuals in the sufficient dosage, treatment is effective (Andrews et al. 1990). The problem is that most interventions, as implemented, do not meet those requirements and, thus, fail to have an impact on many individuals.

Alternative Residential Interventions

Questions over the efficacy of correctional institutions have led to the development of various alternatives in recent years. Three such alternatives—boot camps, wilderness experience, and scared-straight programs—are considered here. **Boot camps** have become a popular alternative to traditional training schools. Also known as a type of **shock incarceration**, boot camps are short-term programs that are supposed to handle first-time, non-violent offenders. The camps are operated on a military model, with strict rules and discipline, physical training and conditioning, and counseling and education. The camps are supposed to show youths that, with hard work and self-discipline, they can succeed in life and do not need to turn to delinquent or criminal behavior. The impact of juvenile boot camps on recidivism, however, is not good, with most evaluations showing little or no change in delinquent behavior (Peters, Thomas, and Zamberlan 1997). Despite this fact, boot camps remain a popular alternative, possibly because they take a tough stance and mix physical punishment with treatment activities. They clearly fit the "get tough on crime" movement in the United States over the past 15 years.

Another approach is **wilderness programming**, in which youths are placed in situations where they must learn survival skills and rely on one another to succeed. These programs can be either short term or long term and can take a variety of different forms, including sailing trips, wagon trains, or back-country camps. The underlying idea is to build self-esteem and show the youths that hard work and perseverance pay off. Implicit in the approach is that the skills and self-esteem developed in the program can be transferred back into the daily lives of the youths. While research on these approaches is relatively limited, Lipsey and Wilson (1998) argue that wilderness experience programs have little or no impact on recidivism rates and that youths who participate in these interventions recidivate at comparable levels to those who experience processing through other juvenile correctional programs. In addition, these programs can be very costly, and there have been problems including serious injuries and even death.

One popular and widely known alternative intervention is the so-called **scared-straight programs.** These programs involve intensive confrontation between inmates and pre- and early delinquents. The assumption is that this confrontation will literally scare the youths away from further offending and into law-abiding behavior. This approach gained a great deal of attention from a film documentary based on the Juvenile Awareness Project at Rahway State Prison in New Jersey. In these programs, youths are sent by the juvenile court to spend time in prison with (typically) long-term, adult offenders. During the stay, the prisoners try to impress on the youths the reality of prison life and the fact that the continued offending by the youths will eventually see them end up in prison. The prisoners typically spell out in gory detail the deprivations, assaults, and indignities of prison life in an effort to deter youths from future offending. While initial reports on the Rahway program claimed reduced recidivism, more in-depth analyses of this and similar programs failed to find any deterrent effect of program participation (see Lundman 1993).

Deinstitutionalization

One of the strongest policy recommendations made by the President's Commission in 1967 was to deinstitutionalize many of the youths held in secure juvenile facilities. One underlying rationale for this suggestion was the fact that many incarcerated youths were there for status offenses and not violations of the criminal law. A second argument was that there was little evidence that institutionalization was effective at correcting the problems of youths. Perhaps the strongest argument favoring **deinstitutionalization** was the belief that involvement in the formal justice system was criminogenic, meaning that youths would be more prone to criminal behavior after system intervention than before. Youths labeled as delinquent or criminal would act in accordance with the label. The solution to these problems would be to keep youths out of institutions as much as possible.

The move towards deinstitutionalization was codified in the 1974 Juvenile Justice and Delinquency Prevention Act. A major part of this legislation was to remove status offenders from any form of secure confinement. The rationale for this was twofold. First, mixing status offenders and serious delinquents has the potential of causing the status offenders more harm than good. Second, status offenders have committed no transgressions against other individuals. Rather, they have exhibited behavior that may lead to further problems. Given the possible criminogenic effects of system intervention, it would be in the best interests of the youth to keep them out of any institutional placement. Interestingly, this legislation could not directly force states to deinstitutionalize status offenses, since the status have the legislative authority over this matter. In order to influence the states, however, the legislation mandated withholding federal monies from jurisdictions that failed to deinstitutionalize status offenders. Today, less than 5 percent of all youths held in residential facilities are there for status offenses (Sickmund 2002).

The most widely cited example of deinstitutionalization in action took place in Massachusetts in the 1970s. Under the leadership of Jerome Miller, Massachusetts closed all of its state-run training schools. What emerged was a system of community-based programs and the placement of serious offenders in private residential settings. Other states, including Maryland, Pennsylvania, and Utah, followed suit and moved to less-secure methods for handling problem youths. Most of the alternative placements used by these states are run by private agencies under contract with the state authorities. What residential programs remain typically house few youths (often fewer than 30) and hold the youths for relatively short periods of time (Krisberg and Austin 1993).

The deinstitutionalization in Massachusetts and other states exhibited mixed outcomes. In terms of cost efficiency, the alternatives used in place of residential placement are significantly cheaper. The impact on recidivism, however, is not as positive. Various evaluations show that the recidivism rate has not significantly changed as a result of deinstitutionalizing youthful offenders (Krisberg and Austin 1993). While the move towards deinstitutionalization has been effective at reducing the numbers of youths in confinement, particularly status offenders, the move has not resulted in the promise of lower recidivism.

COMMUNITY INTERVENTIONS

At the outset of the juvenile justice system in 1899, community interventions were the preferred method for dealing with youths in need of assistance. There were no residential institutions under the control of the court, and the court relied on probation as the primary means of dealing with youths in need of help. Keeping juveniles at home and in the community was considered the best way of helping children.

Probation

Today, community interventions can take a variety of forms, although the most common remains probation. Almost two-thirds of all youths processed through the juvenile court end up being placed on probation. In addition, many more youths handled informally are also placed under some form of probation supervision.

Probation departments are active throughout the juvenile system and often fulfill the duties of intake, staff and administer local detention facilities, run informal intervention programs, develop social-history reports (i.e., the juvenile system equivalent of a presentence investigation), and make recommendations to the judge on dispositions, as well as supervising and working with youths placed on probation. Much of the supervision revolves around making certain that the youths remain in school, obey the law, become involved in prosocial activities, as well as fulfill any orders to complete counseling, make restitution, or participate in other treatment programs. In general, probation in the juvenile justice system mirrors the process in the adult system. The biggest difference, however, should be a greater emphasis on providing treatment and aid to youths and a reduced interest in simply monitoring and enforcing rules.

Aftercare

Juvenile justice also has a form of parole, commonly referred to as **aftercare**. Aftercare differs from probation mainly by the fact that youths in aftercare have spent some amount of time in secure facilities and are being released back into the community. Many of the rules, regulations, and programming available in aftercare are identical to those found in probation, with supervision being the most important component. Due to the similarity between probation and aftercare, in many communities, aftercare is provided by the probation department. Both probation and aftercare use many of the same treatment ideas, including reality therapy, behavior modification, an emphasis on educational achievement, and vocational training.

Issues in Supervision

While supervision appears to be a straightforward idea, there are a number of competing factors that make it a very difficult task for both probation and aftercare. The traditional view of supervision in the juvenile justice system has emphasized the parens patriae goals of providing benevolent assistance to youths and their families. Supervision is supposed to help youths identify problematic behavior and to uncover means to overcome the problems and issues that push or pull them into delinquency. This approach is sometimes referred to as a "social worker" approach that works to find solutions to the problems underlying the behavior.

At the same time, there is a growing tendency to "get tough" with the youths. Rather than work to help youths, supervision becomes a means of watching for violations and sanctioning youths for additional transgressions. Supervision, therefore, is little more than another method used under a punitive model of juvenile justice. Probation officers and aftercare workers act as extensions of the police and seek to justify ways of placing youths into secure residential institutions.

An emerging middle ground for supervision is the balanced approach. Under this approach, probation or aftercare workers are responsible for addressing youths' needs while simultaneously taking the safety and security needs of the larger community into account. Typical responses under the balanced approach include restitution, community service, counseling, rehabilitation, and punishment. Officers are expected to identify the correct mix of the competing philosophies (parens patriae, retribution, restorative, etc.) to use with each youthful offender.

While it may appear reasonable to use elements of a wide range of philosophies and approaches when addressing juvenile misconduct, this situation causes a great deal of anxiety for system workers. What is the correct approach to use with each individual juvenile? What interests are to be emphasized and when (e.g., youth or society)? What training is the most appropriate for the job? What does the community really want (e.g., retribution or rehabilitation)? How should the impact of supervision be evaluated (i.e., arrests, convictions, number of counseling sessions, improved grades in school, etc.)? These and many other questions and issues form the basis for role confusion and discontent for many probation officers and aftercare workers.

Questions of the effectiveness of community interventions are similar to those found with institutional interventions. Many programs have exhibited positive results for some youths, especially when the program has been properly implemented and the proper amount of intervention has been applied. What has not been found is any one program that works all the time. In general, programs tend to be time and place specific.

SPECIAL TOPICS

The juvenile justice system must deal on a regular basis with a wide range of issues and topics related to youthful misbehavior. Some of the more prevalent issues are gang behavior, restorative justice, and capital punishment. There have also been calls to eliminate the juvenile justice system. While space does not permit a full discussion of these issues, each is briefly addressed in the following paragraphs.

Gangs

The prevalence and role of gangs have a long history in the juvenile justice system. A major reason for this is the observation that youths tend to commit offenses when in the company of other youths. Some authors have suggested a **group hazard hypothesis**, which claims that society responds to group transgressions more than to individual violations (Erickson 1973).

The study of juvenile gangs dates back to work done in Chicago in the 1930s. Since that time, a wide range of definitions for a gang have emerged, and writers have not settled on a single definition. Typical definitions include reference to a group that identifies itself as a gang, has a name, is recognized by outsiders as a gang, participates in criminal activity, and has some degree of permanence. Curry and Decker (1998) offer six elements as common to most definitions of a gang (see Box 7.8). While all gangs do not look alike, there are some common features of most gangs. Most gangs draw youths from the lower classes, are racially homogeneous, offer their members a sense of belonging and status, and are dominated by youths in their late teens. The degree of organization and the behavior of gangs vary considerably, although most gangs are involved in some type of criminal activity. Physical aggression or the willingness to use physical force has long been a cornerstone of gang activity, although in recent years this aggression has increasingly used firearms and resulted in the death of combatants. Drive-by shootings, or forays, have become a recognized part of gang violence in many cities.

BOX 7.8

Typical Elements of a Gang Definition

Group	Usually a specified minimum number of members, certainly more than two.
Symbols	Clothes, hand signs, colors, and so on that serve to indicate membership.
Communication	Verbal and nonverbal forms, such as made-up words, graffiti, hand signals, and so forth.
Permanence	Gangs must persist over time, generally at least one year.
Turf	Territory claimed and/or controlled by the gang (not as common in many definitions).
Crime	Involvement in criminal behavior.

SOURCE: Compiled from Curry and Decker (1998).

The extent of gang membership is also difficult to assess. Since 1995, the National Youth Gang Center (NYGC) has conducted annual surveys to assess the extent of gang membership and gang activity. According to the NYGC survey, there are 26,100 gangs with 785,000 members operating in U.S. cities.

Critical Thinking Exercise

Information on gangs and characteristics of gang members are routinely gathered by the National Youth Gang Center. Examine the information from the National Youth Gang Survey at http://www.nationalgangcenter.gov/About/Surveys-and-Analyses.

Interventions with gangs have taken a variety of forms. At one extreme are strong law enforcement responses, such as the Los Angeles Police Department's Community Resources Against Street Hoodlums program, which sought to disrupt the daily activity of gangs, make arrests, and incarcerate gang members. Legislatures also tend to take a heavy-handed approach and pass laws that make membership in gangs a crime, such as California's Street Terrorism Enforcement and Prevention Act of 1988 (the STEP Act). At the other extreme are efforts to interject workers into the daily activity of gangs in the hope of redirecting the gang's activities. The best-known effort of this kind was the Detached Worker Program. Unfortunately, there has been little evidence that any of these approaches have had an appreciable impact on gang participation in the United States (Lundman 1993). One of the most recent attempts to address gangs has been to try to reach youths before they become gang members and provide them with the tools to resist the lure of gangs. The Gang Resistance Education and Training (GREAT) program involves using police officers to teach antigang, antiviolence lessons in middle schools (see Box 7.9). Early evaluations of the program show some promising results, although it is not clear if the program has a significant long-term impact on gangs (Esbensen and Osgood 1997).

Unfortunately, the evidence on the effectiveness of interventions with gangs and gang members does not suggest strong positive results. Most methods appear to have little impact on criminal and deviant behavior. Some of the failure may be attributable to the fact that many programs fail to target the key causes of gangs and gang behavior and are poorly implemented. Indeed, most interventions tend to try to suppress gang behavior through arrest and prosecution, rather than attacking the underlying causes of gangs and gang activity: the lack of social opportunities, the lack of jobs, poor education, and other key factors.

Restorative Justice

Given the recent debate over the proper goal of the juvenile justice system, whether to emphasize rehabilitation or punishment, it is not surprising that the idea of

---

BOX 7.9

G.R.E.A.T. Middle School Curriculum

1. Welcome To G.R.E.A.T.
   - Program Introduction
   - Relationship Between Gangs, Violence, Drugs, and Crime
2. What's the Real Deal?
   - Message Analysis
   - Facts and Fiction About Gangs and Violence
3. It's About Us
   - Community
   - Roles and Responsibilities
   - What You Can Do About Gangs
4. Where Do We Go From Here?
   - Setting Realistic and Achievable Goals
5. Decisions, Decisions, Decisions
   - G.R.E.A.T. Decision-Making Model
   - Impact of Decisions on Goals
   - Decision-Making Practice
6. Do You Hear What I Am Saying?
   - Effective Communication
   - Verbal vs. Nonverbal
7. Walk In Someone Else's Shoes
   - Active Listening
   - Identification of Different Emotions
   - Empathy for Others
8. Say It Like You Mean It
   - Body Language
   - Tone of Voice
   - Refusal-Skills Practice
9. Getting Along Without Going Along
   - Influences and Peer Pressure
   - Refusal-Skills Practice
10. Keeping Your Cool
    - G.R.E.A.T. Anger Management Tips
    - Practice Cooling Off
11. Keeping It Together
    - Recognizing Anger in Others
    - Tips for Calming Others
12. Working It Out
    - Consequences for Fighting
    - G.R.E.A.T. Tips for Conflict Resolution
    - Conflict Resolution Practice
    - Where to Go for Help

13. Looking Back
- Program Review
- "Making My School a G.R.E.A.T. Place" Project Review

SOURCE: Bereau of Justice Assistance (2005)

restorative justice is becoming more popular. The apparent competing concerns of finding an alternative to the system for some offenses, assisting victims, and intervening with offenders suggests that any new intervention needs to serve a broader audience. The concept of **restorative (reparative) justice** seeks to use interventions that return victims, offenders, and communities to their preoffense states (Bazemore and Maloney 1994).

The three most common forms of restorative justice practices are Victim-Offender Mediation (VOM), Family Group Conferencing (FGC), and Circle Sentencing. The basic premise of VOM is that crime is the result of complex factors that are beyond the ability of the criminal code to address on its own. VOM seeks to identify for offenders the types and levels of harm suffered by the victims as a result of the crimes. Victims are given the opportunity to express their concerns about the crimes and their losses, while offenders can explain why they committed the acts. The intent is to repair the harm done to victims, help victims heal, restore communities to their precrime states, and reintegrate offenders into society.

FGC came to prominence in 1989 when New Zealand adopted the idea to address the increasing numbers of Maori youths being handled in the formal justice system. The Children, Young Persons, and Their Families Act removed all youths aged 14–17 from formal court processing and mandated that they be diverted to family group conferencing (Kurki 2000). The primary difference between FGC and VOM is the inclusion of family members, close friends, and other support groups of the victims and offenders in the conferences. Facilitators lead the participants through a discussion of the facts of the cases, the impact of the events on all parties, the feelings of all participants towards the actions and the offenders, and the development of mutually agreed-upon resolutions.

The third type of restorative justice program, Circle Sentencing, is based on Canadian First Nation practices and began formal operation in the early 1990s. Circle sentencing invites community members to participate in determining appropriate sanctions for offenders. Since this is a sentencing procedure, the process typically occurs after cases are concluded and the offenders are found guilty in court. Participants in sentencing circles typically include all of the parties found in FCGs, as well as general community members who wish to be included.

In addition, the circles may function either as a part of the court or separate from the court. Outcomes from the circles can include apologies, restitution, community service, treatment or rehabilitation programs, and recommendations for institutionalization (Van Ness and Strong 2002).

Evaluations of restorative justice show some promising results, particularly in terms of satisfaction with the program and some reduction in recidivism. Unfortunately, few evaluations exist and a great deal of additional research is needed on the impact of restorative justice programs on juvenile offending. This is especially true for FGC and Circle Sentencing programs. The growing interest in using restorative justice approaches across the United States and other countries indicates that there is a great need to adequately assess the potential of this approach.

Capital Punishment and Juveniles

The appropriateness of capital punishment for juveniles has been a matter of debate for several years. This is particularly true since the rise in lethal violence by youths in the late 1980s and early 1990s. Between 1973 and 2000, almost 200 individuals were sentenced to death for crimes committed when the offender was a juvenile, and 15 offenders were age 15 at the time of the crime (Streib 2000). At the outset of 2005, 23 states permitted the imposition of the death penalty for those who committed their crimes while juveniles. Statutes allowing the imposition of the death penalty for individuals who committed their crimes when aged 16 or 17 were permissible under the U.S. Supreme Court ruling in *Stanford v. Kentucky* (1989).

The legal status of the death penalty for youthful offenders was overturned in the case *Roper, Superintendent, Potosi Correctional Center v. Simmons* (2005). In the majority opinion, the Court noted that the "evolving standards of decency that mark the progress of a mature society" clearly indicate that imposing death on juveniles constitutes "cruel and unusual punishment" in violation of the Eighth Amendment. The Court noted that most states did not allow for the death penalty for juvenile cases, the majority of states with death penalty statutes for youthful offenders do not carry out the executions, and the prevailing international opinion is against the use of the death penalty for youths (*Roper v. Simmons* [2005]). After many years of debate, the death penalty is no longer an issue in relation to juvenile offenders.

Calls to Eliminate the Juvenile System

The most extreme suggestion made for the future of the juvenile justice system is to eliminate it. Proponents of this move call for the adult criminal system to assume responsibility for all juvenile transgressions. The underlying reason for this movement is the growth of serious juvenile crime and the inability of the juvenile system to rehabilitate serious offenders. In essence, the call is to return to the same system that was abandoned in 1899.

In some respects, there has been a steady erosion of the parens patriae approach in recent years. The use of transfer has increased and states have made transfer mandatory for some offenses. There has been a move to the use of mandatory incarceration for some offenders and blended sentences are being used with more frequency. The police are now permitted to fingerprint and photograph youthful offenders, and these records are now kept for future reference. Juvenile records are even available to adult courts for consideration in future cases, something that was unheard of 20 years ago.

Critical Thinking Exercise

What impact would eliminating the juvenile justice system have on the adult criminal system? What impact would it have on youths?

Despite these changes, there remains a belief in the need to help youths rather than punish them. Consequently, eliminating the juvenile justice system makes little sense. The adult system would have to make drastic changes if it were to assume responsibility for juvenile offenders. Many of the changes would probably mirror the current activities of the juvenile system. What is needed is a system that has the flexibility to provide the due-process rights needed to protect the accused and the power to use whatever intervention is in the best interests of both offenders and society. Clearly, the juvenile justice system will continue to undergo change, and that change may include moving closer to the adult system.

CONCLUSION

Juvenile offending raises special problems for society and agents of social control. Indeed, a separate system of justice has been in existence for over 100 years to deal with problem youths. This system operates under a different philosophical base from the criminal justice system, although many people have challenged the parens patriae philosophy in recent years. The juvenile system generally assumes that youths are in need of help rather than punishment and operates from the premise that the proper intervention can remove the causes of misbehavior. Unfortunately, rising levels of delinquency have called into question the effectiveness of the juvenile justice system, and many critics call for a move towards a more punitive response to offending youths. Those calls have not gone unheeded, as evidenced by the move to waive more youths to the adult court, the use of more punitive sanctions, and an increasing emphasis on the safety of the community. Despite these changes, it does not appear that the juvenile system is in danger of being abolished. Instead, it will continue to adapt to the competing demands being placed on it from various societal constituencies.

KEY WORDS

adjudication

aftercare

behavior modification

blended sentencing

boob tube therapy

boot camps

day–evening centers

deinstitutionalization

delinquency

detention

disposition

group hazard hypothesis

guided group interaction

houses of refuge

informal adjustment

intake decision

Monitoring the Future
  Survey

parens patriae

reformatories

restorative (reparative)
  justice

scared-straight programs

shock incarceration

state training schools

status offense

token economy

transfer or waiver

wilderness programming

youthful offender statutes

SUGGESTED READINGS

Empey, L. (1982). *American delinquency: Its meaning and construction*, Chapters 2–4. Homewood, IL: Dorsey Press.

Sickmund, M. (1994). *How juveniles get to criminal court: Juvenile justice bulletin.* Washington, DC: U.S. Department of Justice.

Torbet, P., Gable, R., Hurst, H., Montgomery, I., Szymanski, L., and Thomas, D. (1996). *State responses to serious and violent juvenile crime.* Washington, DC: Office of Juvenile Justice and Delinquency Prevention.

Feld, B. (1993). *Justice for children: The right to counsel and the juvenile courts.* Boston, MA: Northeastern University Press. ✦

CHAPTER 8

Conclusion

CHAPTER OUTLINE

Criminal Justice and Discretion
Criminal Justice and Policy
Criminal Justice as a Processing System

CRIMINAL JUSTICE AND DISCRETION

The criminal justice system is multidimensional, so it can be thought about in different ways. For example, the system can be viewed as a series of interrelated discretionary decision points where citizens and criminal justice system actors make decisions about reported crimes and the future of suspects/defendants/ offenders. For example, crime victims decide if they will report their victimization, police officers decide if they will arrest a suspect, prosecutors decide if (and how) to prosecute, and so on.

These decisions are made at different levels. At an individual level, each actor decides how to act, given a range of possible actions. There are usually multiple choices available to actors. Judges sentencing convicts usually choose from a range of supervision types (probation, intensive supervision probation, boot camps, or prison), the length of supervision, and the conditions (e.g., will the convict be required to attend substance abuse treatment as a condition of supervision?).

Discretionary decisions also occur at an organizational or aggregate level. Some jurisdictions rely upon different balances of actions and options than do other jurisdictions and some jurisdictions may not have some options available (e.g., boot camps, a secure detention facility for juveniles). For example, one jurisdiction may rely heavily upon community corrections options, such as probation and parole, to a greater extent than other jurisdictions. One court jurisdiction may plea bargain more cases than another.

Discretionary decision making by actors is not without constraints. Both policy and substantive law limit and guide how these discretionary decisions are made by system actors. Decisions are also constrained and molded by local norms of appropriate behavior for actors. For example, in some jurisdictions police officers resort to physical force more often than in other jurisdictions. Most organizations exhibit informal, unwritten occupational norms of conduct for their employees, such as the police subculture. Because these norms and subcultures are unwritten, they are hard to change via formal methods, such as changing a law, crafting a written organizational policy, or holding formal training programs. Although hard to see and hard to change, these informal norms impose powerful influence over system actors. At the end of the day, there is still significant latitude in discretionary decison making despite the constraints imposed by policy, law, and local norms.

CRIMINAL JUSTICE AND POLICY

The system can also be viewed as an arena where facts and information about crime and offenders are implemented as policy and where policies are crafted to respond to information about crime. There are benefits and problems with much of the information available for criminal justice decision makers, such as the ways in which crime is measured. Despite these limitations, society must still make decisions about how the system should operate. Ideally these decisions are based upon good information and the eventual outcomes of these decisions are later analyzed to determine if they were truly wise decisions. Regardless of whether decisions about policy fit this ideal or not, however, the policy cycle begins with information about crime and criminal justice. Policy represents our attempts to respond to social problems.

For example, since the early 1990s many states and the federal courts have implemented three-strikes laws. The laws are a policy response to crimes committed by hardened repeat offenders and should decrease overall crime by incapacitating some serious offenders and deterring others. The research on three-strikes laws reveals that most either do not decrease crime or the crime decreases are so small that they are negligibly beneficial (Worrall 2006).

Each step in this policy process involves thinking logically about what we know, crafting a policy that will address the problem, and then studying how well the policy works in real-world conditions. As with discretion, policies are implemented at all steps in the system and in organizations, as well as states, and the nation as a whole. Like discretionary decison making, policy permeates the criminal justice system.

CRIMINAL JUSTICE AS A PROCESSING SYSTEM

The system can also be viewed as a system of interrelated organizations and entities that process each others' outputs, crimes, victims, and offenders. Taking a system perspective can be helpful because it highlights the interrelated nature of the different steps in the process. Chapters 3, 4, 5, and 6 describe the steps in this process model.

This process model represents society's attempts to control crime. How society controls crime is suggested by the different philosophies of criminal justice. These philosophies sometimes contradict each other, and most policies are usually a balance of different philosophies. Such contradiction is unavoidable in a democracy, but discretionary decision making allows criminal justice actors to implement these sometimes competing policies while at the same time the system still functions. Usually these philosophies are enacted by legislators as substantive laws. Procedural laws prescribe the methods by which governmental bodies may enact laws and are important because they limit many of the government's powers and thus dictate and constrain the creation and implementation of criminal justice policy. Lawmaking is in turn influenced and constrained by local politics, the media, and public sentiments and voting patterns.

Citizens are the true gatekeepers of the criminal justice system. When they choose to report crimes, their actions serve as the inputs for the police. Citizens also serve a vital role as sources of information for the system as witnesses and informants and when they vote and voice their expectations of what the system should do.

The police handle a wide range of duties beyond processing criminal suspects, but for the rest of the system, the police serve as the input source for arrestees. Police officers and the more than 18,000 agencies in the United States make discretionary decisions concerning what laws to focus on and when to arrest. This decision making by police officers and agencies is in turn influenced by the communities they serve and by laws and policies.

The court system is composed of multiple courts and different jurisdictions; thus, there are differences in the policies that are created and enacted. Prosecutors may decide to release an arrestee without charge or to press charges. Prosecutors also decide if, when, and how they might plea bargain. The process of prosecution involves other system actors such as judges and defense attorneys, all of whom embody their different backgrounds and institutional allegiances, which influence their decision making.

Convicted defendants become the inputs for the corrections system. Prisons, jails, and community corrections are also arenas where actors exercise discretionary decision making and where policies are enacted. Here too some of these policies and decisions are influenced by the philosophies of criminal justice (such as the value of rehabilitation as opposed to incapacitation). The resulting policy implications of these philosophies compete with each other for resources and sometimes contradict each other. Compromises often result as actors carry out competing mandates in their day-to-day work.

In the end what we view as the criminal justice system is a complex web of social interactions among a myriad of system actors and the thousands of criminal justice organizations, as the system pursues multiple, competing, and sometimes contradictory goals. Philosophies are crafted into laws and policies, and system actors strive to implement these laws and policies via their discretionary decisions.

Glossary

A

actus reus The "act" of a crime, usually an overt act or act of omission.

adjudication In the juvenile court, the counterpart to finding guilt or innocence and sentencing in the adult court.

administrative law Law that is created and enforced by administrative bodies.

adversarial system A system, like the criminal justice system, in which two opposing parties (prosecution and defense) work with a neutral body (the judge) to determine the outcome of a case.

aftercare The juvenile justice system equivalent to adult parole.

alternative dispute resolution An alternative to the traditional criminal court, in which victims, offenders, and others work together to settle disputes outside of the criminal justice system.

anonymity In self-report surveys, a condition where the identity of respondents is not known by the researchers or others, so that information from a respondent cannot be traced back to an individual. Note that anonymity is different from **confidentiality.**

appeal The opportunity for defendants to challenge their convictions, sentences, and other issues in order to ensure that their cases were handled properly.

appellate jurisdiction Courts with this jurisdiction hear cases on appeal from lower courts; they do not hold trials.

arraignment Stage of a criminal case where defendants are required to enter pleas to the formal charges against them, usually after a **preliminary hearing** or **grand jury hearing.**

assembly-line justice Term used to describe the fast and efficient movement of cases in and out of the court system.

assigned counsel A court-appointed attorney paid on a case-by-case or hourly basis to act as defense counsel.

B

background checks   A standard part of the hiring process in any law enforcement agency. Telephone and in-person contacts with references, criminal history checks, and the like are made to assure that candidates have the appropriate ethics, mentality, and skills to perform a job and to verify that all information provided by the candidates' applications is accurate.

bail   A system requiring a guarantee by defendants to return for court dates. Judges decide whether defendants must pay a certain amount of money to be released prior to trial or must be detained due to flight risk, public safety, and so forth.

bailiffs   Typically, law enforcement officers who maintain order in the courtroom.

beat integrity   The philosophy and administrative priority of assigning specific officers to specific beats for long periods of time, to develop a comprehensive knowledge of the area and establish positive working relationships with the residents and merchants there; replaced an older system that moved officers around to many beats, frequently or haphazardly, in order to reduce the opportunities for corruption.

beats   Formally defined areas of patrol. A specific officer or group of officers is responsible for answering calls and dealing with any police-related matters occurring within the boundaries of the beat. Also may be called by other terms, such as "district."

behavior modification   A system that rewards positive behavior and punishes poor behavior as a means of changing or controlling behavior; typical approach used in institutions.

bench trial   A trial without a jury, in which a judge hears the evidence and renders a verdict in a criminal case.

bills of attainder   Policies that allow the imposition of punishment without a trial. This type of policy is unconstitutional according to the U.S. Constitution.

blended sentencing   A disposition that relies on both the juvenile and adult systems, such as when a youth begins his or her disposition in a juvenile facility and is automatically transferred to an adult facility after reaching the age of majority.

blue wall of silence   The term for the refusal of police officers to report misconduct of other officers, usually out of a misguided sense of solidarity or a fear of social ostracism and denial of assistance ("backup") on duty. The blue wall is usually composed of nonoffending officers who know of elements of the misconduct, but refuse to "rat" on or testify against other officers, regardless of the seriousness of the offense, thus thwarting effective investigation of police misconduct and crimes committed by police officers.

"Bobbies"   The English police; an affectionate term that draws upon the name of the founder of the Metropolitan London Police, Sir Robert Peel.

boob tube therapy   A term used to describe allowing youths in detention facilities to watch television all day long in lieu of providing other, more meaningful activities and programming.

boot camps   Sometimes called **shock incarceration**, boot camps are short-term programs that are supposed to handle first-time, nonviolent offenders. They operate on a military model, with strict rules and discipline, physical training and conditioning, and counseling and education.

Boston Police Strike of 1919   A labor action by more than three-quarters of the Boston police department, seeking higher wages; riots resulted and the militia was called in; the strikers were fired, and attempts to unionize the police were effectively quashed until the mid-1960s.

Broken Windows   An informal theory of police responsibility for controlling low-level disorders and the relationship of disorder to more serious crime. First advanced by James Q. Wilson and George Kelling in an article in *The Atlantic Monthly* in 1982, the hypothesis asserted that order maintenance should be the primary police focus, not serious felony crime; reductions in serious crime would follow the reestablishment of civil order in the neighborhoods.

burden of proof   Level of proof needed to find a defendant guilty of a crime, to issue search warrants, and so forth (for example, to obtain a conviction, a prosecutor must prove his or her case "beyond a reasonable doubt").

C

campus-based academies   Police recruit training facilities that function like college campuses and are frequently located on such campuses. The academies may be self-contained, giving instruction only to new police officers, or may be part of an academic degree course of study, typically a two-year associate's degree. The instructional curriculum is similar to that of stress academies, but without the military boot-camp trappings.

case attrition   Cases disappearing from the criminal justice system by being dropped, dismissed, and so forth.

case law   Law created by judges through their interpretation of other types of laws.

chain of command   A term referring to the command and supervision of the police organization. It is the sequence through which orders are given and information is relayed.

challenge for cause   A method of removing jurors during jury selection for a legally prescribed cause (for instance, being a relative of the victim).

citizen patrols   An activity organized under police auspices, in which citizens of a neighborhood supplement police patrols by walking through the area to discourage unlawful activities and by notifying the police of developing situations.

civil rights movement   A long-standing attempt by the African-American community to overturn the legal and social restrictions of "Jim Crow" segregation and the social attitude prevalent among whites that blacks were inferior (a legacy of slavery). While the movement has been ongoing since the end of Reconstruction, it was most visible and powerful in the 1950s and 1960s, when televised conflicts with white police galvanized both the movement and attempts to reform the police.

civilian review   A special process of handling complaints against police officers by having civilian boards, or mixed police and civilian boards, review the facts and adjudicate the complaint; highly unpopular with police officers. Civilian review boards (CRBs) may work in concert with Internal Affairs or independent of it; the scope of authority given to a CRB is determined locally through the political process. CRBs emerged from strong feelings of dissatisfaction with police internal review of complaints against "their own."

Classical school   Eighteenth-century philosophy that contends that humans possess free will and are rational and thus make choices about how to behave. Advocates consider behavior a process whereby people weigh the costs of their actions and the benefits they expect to receive.

classification   Assessment made by corrections personnel whereby the needs and risks of offenders are evaluated to determine their best placement within the prison system.

clerks of court   Individuals who are responsible for maintaining case files.

close security   A security classification representing a middle ground between **maximum** and **medium security**. Facilities with this classification may be used for individuals convicted of violent offenses who do not require a maximum-security setting or disruptive inmates who do not pose as great a physical threat to inmates or staff.

collateral attack   A type of appeal that allows a prisoner to challenge a conviction or sentence after the first appeal is over.

common law   English-based law that was known throughout the country and applied by local judges through the use of precedent.

community-oriented policing   The term devised for a reform movement that arose in the mid-1980s to ease racial tensions and increase police effectiveness in minority neighborhoods. The thrust of the movement was to break down old prejudices by placing officers in regular contact with citizens in nonemergency settings, building better information about community events and conditions, building mutual trust, and creating effective problem solving. The community-policing movement incorporates a wide range of tactical deployments, from walking beats to crime-prevention activities to community organizing. One of the features that distinguishes community policing from traditional law enforcement is a focus on a range of noncrime problems broadly known as "quality-of-life issues," in which police advocacy and leadership play more important roles than law enforcement.

Community Policing Era   The current "era" of American policing, placing crime control on an equal footing with forging community partnerships and allowing communities greater ability to control their own affairs, incorporating crime prevention and crime analysis into an overall community effort to reduce crime and disorder.

community supervision   A general term to denote a variety of circumstances and sanctions requiring an offender to abide by specific conditions in order to remain in the community rather than being placed in an institutional setting.

CompStat   A management initiative of the New York City Police Department under Commissioner Bill Bratton in the 1990s. Named for a column in a crime statistics database, CompStat involved the use of up-to-date crime information to reinvigorate the NYPD's command staff's commitment to crime reduction. It was also criticized for the sometimes adversarial nature of the central administration's challenges to the precinct commands. The term CompStat has become synonymous with data-driven approaches to crime control and police accountability.

conditions of supervision   The specific requirements imposed by a court or correctional authority that an offender must agree to and abide by to remain in the community.

confidentiality   In self-report surveys, a condition where the identity of a respondent is known by the researcher, but the researcher does not reveal that individual's identity. In confidential situations the information from a respondent can be traced back to an individual. Note that confidentiality differs from **anonymity.**

consent decrees   Formal contracts between the U.S. Department of Justice and local agencies or corporate entities to correct unlawful conditions. Usually an alternative to civil rights suits, consent decrees set out timetables and corrective measures to bring the agencies in line with acceptable practices.

constable   An ancient English office of local police authority, with mandatory service on a rotating, annual basis under the 1285 Statute of Winchester; in contemporary America, a local office often attached to the court for service of papers and other writs; in modern-day England, a form of address to a police officer.

constitutional law   Law that is found in the U.S. Constitution and the various state constitutions.

contract system   A form of appointed counsel where private attorneys or law firms issue bids to represent indigent defendants; the court usually selects the lowest bid.

convict leasing   A Southern development that spread throughout the United States, where inmates were contracted out to work in the stone quarries and coal mines during the industrial era of punishment.

COP   *See* **community-oriented policing.**

correctional officers   Individuals who supervise inmates in an institutional setting, sometimes referred to as guards.

corruption   Generically, the misuse of a position of authority for personal gain. Police corruption in particular takes a variety of forms, from passive acceptance of gratuities to actively seeking bribes to accepting money from crime figures to destroy evidence or reveal police information. A subset, "corruption of noble cause," has emerged to describe the use of illegal means to achieve a legitimate crime-control end, with no personal benefit to the officers.

court administrators   Individuals who supervise court staff and assist judges with budgets and personnel.

court reporters   Employees of the court who record what transpires during court proceedings.

courtroom workgroup   The collection of people who work in and around courthouses. The term *workgroup* is used because these people are employed by different organizations (prosecutor's offices, public defender's offices, probation, corrections, etc.) and the membership changes often, usually from one defendant's case to another.

crime-control model   Philosophy of criminal justice that contends that the most important goal of the criminal justice system is to suppress crime. This goal is best achieved via the aggressive and quick apprehension, trial, and processing of criminals.

crime prevention   A series of related actions, often promoted by the police, that reduce individual or collective risk of crime victimization. Target hardening through the use of locks or barriers, personal self-defense, property-marking records that reduce the resale value of stolen goods, collective actions such as Neighborhood Watch or other community organizing, educational programs in schools, and many more all fall under the crime prevention label.

crime rate   The number of crimes committed (or reported to authorities), usually expressed as the number of events per 1,000 or 100,000 people (or residents) per year.

D

diversion programs   Programs available for some first-time, youthful, and/or nonviolent offenders that temporarily stop the prosecution of their cases in exchange for participation in preapproved programs. Upon successful completion of a program, the original charges are dismissed.

double jeopardy   Constitutional provision that prohibits multiple prosecutions for the same offense.

drug courts   Courts that focus on rehabilitation and treatment for drug offenders instead of criminal punishment.

dual court system   Represented by the various state court systems and the federal courts. Individuals may be prosecuted by either state or federal courts (and sometimes both).

dual-disorder inmates   Inmates who can be classified as having both substance abuse and mental-health problems.

dual-entry tracks   A term most often applied to progressive sheriffs' departments that hire separately for jail deputies and for patrol (road) deputies. It replaces the older "single-entry" system where all deputies began their careers as jail deputies and then moved up to patrol. *See also* **single-entry tracks**.

due-process model   As opposed to the **crime-control model**, a model of criminal justice that emphasizes procedures and guidelines that the government must follow in order to adjudicate defendants.

due-process revolution   Term applied to a series of famous court cases that provided criminal suspects protections from the government. The due-process revolution began in the early 1960s.

E

electronic monitoring   Use of technology to monitor offenders who are released into the community before trial or as a condition of a home-confinement sentence.

en banc proceeding   A court proceeding, typically at the appellate court level, in which all judges of the court are present.

ex post facto   A retroactive law that is prohibited by the U.S. Constitution.

excessive bail   Unreasonably high bail, prohibited by the Eighth Amendment to the U.S. Constitution.

excessive fines   Financial punishment deemed to be disproportionate to the offense, prohibited by the Eighth Amendment to the U.S. Constitution.

exclusionary rule   A constitutional protection for citizens against unlawful police actions; the rule requires that any evidence obtained illegally must be excluded from criminal trials. Originally a federal-level rule only, it was applied to the states and to local police departments in the landmark 1961 Supreme Court decision *Mapp v. Ohio*.

expiration of sentence   The full completion of a correctional sentence without any continuing conditions imposed by the state.

F

felony   Term applied to the most serious of crimes (including murder, robbery, and rape). Felonies usually carry a possible prison term of greater than one year.

Field Training (Officers and Programs)   A process by which a newly hired police recruit makes the transition from academy learning to the street, under the tutelage and observation of an experienced police officer. Most programs involve a gradual increase in responsibilities, a formal grading process, and a series of tests on duty to determine whether the new officer is in fact an appropriate hire for the agency or should be dismissed because of conditions not revealed by the initial hiring process.

fines   Punishment that requires payment of a monetary sum to the court. Usually used in conjunction with probation.

first responders   Public employees in the emergency services who are the first to be called to the scene of an emergency, including Fire and EMS (Emergency Medical Services, ambulance and first-aid workers). Police patrol officers are considered first responders, while detectives and other investigators are not.

Flint (Michigan) Neighborhood Foot Patrol Program   A 1982 field experiment comparing the effectiveness of foot patrol to motorized patrol; while crime levels remained the same, citizen and police satisfaction were greater in foot patrol areas; the experiment provided an early justification for increased community contacts in the then-developing community policing philosophy.

force continuum A training guide for police use of force, linking police levels of force to specific actions by the citizens.

FTO Field Training Officer. *See* **Field Training (Officers and Programs)**.

G

general deterrence A subtype of deterrence theory that predicts that those contemplating the commission of a crime will be influenced by their understanding of the certainty and severity of the punishment and the speed at which that punishment will be administered. General deterrence contends that when laws entail sufficient certainty and severity and the punishment is quickly meted out, potential criminals will not commit crimes.

grand jury A proceeding featuring citizens who assess a prosecutor's evidence in order to determine if there is enough evidence to proceed to trial.

group hazard hypothesis The claim that society responds to group transgressions more strongly than to individual violations; thus, youth gangs are singled out for intervention more often than individual offenders.

guided group interaction Form of counseling that relies on individuals to identify problem behaviors, confront one another about their past actions, offer acceptable alternatives to deviant responses, and provide peer pressure to change the behavior of group members.

H

habeas corpus Protection that allows defendants to challenge the legality of their confinement or incarceration.

halfway houses A term usually used to describe facilities that house recently released inmates or inmates in the transition process of approaching full release and that assist with their transition back into the community. May be privately operated or state-run.

harassment A common complaint against the police by youths and minority groups, who resent being the subject of police attention—which they consider extralegal attention—while going about their law-abiding business. Also, sometimes used by the police in sardonic fashion to describe their focused attention on known criminals and crime-producing locations.

HAZMAT An acronym for "hazardous materials," a broad category of harmful substances ranging from toxic chemicals to explosives to nuclear waste. First responders who respond to HAZMAT emergencies require special equipment and training.

home confinement The restriction of offenders to their residences except for preapproved activities. May be enforced by the use of various electronic monitoring equipment that can assist officials in knowing offenders' whereabouts. Also known as "house arrest."

houses of refuge Early institutions handling youths in need, particularly the poor, which focused on education, skill training, religious training, hard work, and discipline.

hue and cry   A comedy team in medieval England; a formal responsibility of English citizens, under common law and especially the 1285 **Statute of Winchester**, to assist the constable or sheriff in the apprehension of a thief or other lawbreaker. The classic "Stop ! Thief!"is the modern equivalent.

hung jury   The term used when a trial jury cannot come to a unanimous verdict.

I

impartial trial   Protection that hopes to ensure an unbiased and neutral jury at trial.

importation model   Suggests that the skills, experiences, and attributes that individuals bring with them into a prison environment affect the prison culture and the ability of an individual to adjust to that environment.

incapacitation   A philosophy of criminal justice that argues that the role of the criminal justice system is to separate or segregate criminals from the rest of society in order to protect it. If known criminals are removed from society, advocates argue, there will be less crime. Unlike **retribution**, incapacitation does not see segregation as a form of punishment. Rather, incapacitation also differs from **rehabilitation** in that it does not necessarily advocate treating offenders.

incarceration rate   The number of incarcerated persons for every 100,000 persons in the population.

incorporation   The process of requiring states to adopt the protections found in the federal Bill of Rights.

indeterminate sentencing   A sentencing scheme that is characterized by a range of punishments; the exact amount of time served is determined by the parole board.

industrial era   The period in correctional history when inmates spent their confinement involved in private and state industry craft- or factory-oriented labor, worked on state-run canal and road projects, and even constructed prisons.

informal adjustment   Decision to handle youths in a manner that does not involve full formal court processing.

informal social control   One of two methods by which society and the other individuals that make up society influence behavior (the other method is called *formal social control*). Examples of informal social control include staring, scorn, the cold shoulder, shunning, and telling people that they are doing something wrong. Societies rely very heavily upon informal social control to keep people in conformity.

initial appearance   The first appearance of a defendant before a judge after arrest, when the defendant is notified of the charges against him or her, a bail decision, and the right to counsel. Also known as *first appearance*.

intake decision   The juvenile system's counterpart to filing charges or a grand jury indictment in the adult system; at intake the decision is made to file a petition with the court to hear the case or to handle the youth in another way.

intensive supervision probation   A form of probation (or parole) that requires more frequent contacts between offenders and their supervising officers than regular probation and typically involves more conditions of supervision.

intermediate sanctions   A general term used to describe a variety of sanctions that fall between regular probation and jail or prison in severity.

Internal Affairs   A special investigative unit within a police department, charged with investigating complaints against police officers. The current trend is toward redefining the unit as an "Office of Professional Responsibility" or similar title; other, less printable names are applied to it by police officers under investigation.

J

jails   Facilities designed to hold a variety of offenders for a relatively brief period of time, usually less than one year.

john details   A form of sting operation directed against street prostitution in which undercover police officers pose as prostitutes to arrest "johns," men who solicit prostitutes for sex.

judges   Individuals who are considered neutral figures among the courtroom workgroup. They make a number of decisions ranging from issuance of warrants to sentencing defendants.

judicial review   The power of courts to declare laws unconstitutional.

jurisdiction   The authority of a court to hear a case; for instance, appellate courts have jurisdiction over appeals, but not trials.

jury trial   *See* **trial by jury**.

just deserts   Appropriate punishment for a crime; an element of retribution.

justification   A defense to criminal liability that states that an offender was justified in committing a crime (for example, self-defense).

K

Kansas City Preventive Patrol Experiment   The first randomized test of police patrol's effectiveness as a deterrent of crime; preliminary results indicated that the number of police officers had little or no impact on crime or citizens' perceptions; subsequent developments in the field, notably the Minneapolis Hot Spots of Crime experiment, have refocused the issue with different results.

L

law compliance   The voluntary observance by citizens of the requirements of law.

law enforcement   The application of deterrence, rapid response, investigation, arrest, and prosecution against those who would or do violate the criminal law. Also applied to violators of traffic laws and local ordinances.

Law Enforcement Assistance Administration   A federal effort to improve the quality of police services in America. Funded by the 1968 Omnibus Crime Control and Safe Streets Act, the Law Enforcement Assistance Administration poured billions of dollars into the training, education, and equipping of the police during the 1970s.

Law Enforcement Education Program   A part of the Law Enforcement Education Program efforts to improve policing that funded college education for American police officers and those seeking to be police officers.

legal aid   A form of appointed counsel that is considered non-profit and is usually found in larger cities.

M

mala in se   Behaviors that are considered inherently bad and must be prohibited and punished (for example, murder).

mala prohibita   Behaviors that are considered problematic, but not necessarily bad (for example, gambling).

master jury list   A list of individuals in the community deemed eligible for jury service, usually those who are registered voters or who possess drivers' licenses.

maximum security prisons   A prison classification that represents the highest level of security in many states, typically holding the most violent and disruptive prisoners in those jurisdictions without supermax facilities. Movement within such facilities is limited.

medium security prisons   A classification of prisons that hold a diverse inmate population and can have a variety of architectural styles. Inmates may have some degree of movement within the institutions during certain times of the day and participate in a range of activities.

mens rea   The intent or "guilty mind" behind the commission of a crime.

mental capacity   A defense to criminal liability in which offenders' mental states can reduce or absolve them of liability (for example, insanity).

mental-health courts   Courts that work with corrections officials and the community to assist defendants who suffer from mental illness.

merit selection   A from of judicial appointment in which a state governor selects a judge to serve a specified amount of time (usually one year) and asks voters to either retain or replace the judge at the end of that period.

Metropolitan London Police   The first modern police force, established in England by an Act of Parliament in 1829 to reduce crime and the potential for riots. The force was organized along military lines, but with civilian control at the national level, in the Home Office. Also called The New Police and later the "**Bobbies.**"

minimum security prisons   A prison classification representing the most open and least restrictive type of institution. These facilities can house prisoners convicted of nonviolent offenses, those who pose a minimal security risk, and those nearing final release and allow the greatest freedom of movement for housed inmates.

misdemeanor   A class of less serious crimes, usually involving punishment of less than one year in prison. Misdemeanors often have different levels of seriousness (such as misdemeanor one, misdemeanor two, etc.).

Monitoring the Future Survey   A self-report survey that includes many more serious offenses than earlier self-report surveys and elicits significantly fewer positive responses. It includes questions on hitting teachers, group fighting, use of weapons, robbery, and aggravated assault.

Multi-Jurisdictional Task Forces Composite organizations made up of representatives of law enforcement personnel from many agencies across a wide geographical area that may include representatives from state and federal agencies. Task forces concentrate on crime problems that extend far beyond the jurisdictional boundaries of any single agency, such as organized crime, drug distribution networks, and counterterrorist intelligence work. Sometimes called *Regional Task Forces, Multi-Jurisdictional* is the current preferred term, recognizing federal and state participation.

mutual aid Formal agreements between and among police agencies to assist each other in times of need. A system of legal compacts that provide law enforcement authority and civil protection to officers who are called upon to assist in jurisdictions other than their own.

N

Neighborhood Watch A national program to organize communities around anticrime activities.

net widening Term used to describe circumstances in which a correctional program is inadvertently used for a larger or different population than the one originally intended.

new-generation jails (NGJs) Newer facilities, often built to replace or modify existing jails, that house fewer inmates in what are known as pods or modules that contain anywhere from 16 to 30 separate cells with one or two inmates per cell.

new-offense violations Criminal offenses that violate offenders' community-supervision sanctions.

nonpartisan election A method of electing state judges in which candidates do not indicate a party affiliation on the ballot.

O

official statistics One of three types of data society gathers on crime. Official statistics are gathered by or from criminal justice institutions and usually involve crimes brought to the attention of these institutions. The most famous of these official statistics are the FBI's Uniform Crime Reports (UCR), which record the number of crimes reported to the police and the number of arrests police make. *See also* **self-report statistics** and **victimization studies**.

order maintenance A form of police activity that targets conduct that is less serious than predatory crime, but still disturbs the quality of life of citizens; generally low-level police interventions encourage law compliance, but law enforcement techniques may be used when necessary, to ensure general compliance with expected forms of conduct: "local rules" about the use of parks, loud music, self-expression through graffiti, and a wide range of other social expectations and violations.

original jurisdiction   Jurisdiction in which a court serves as the entry point for cases, typically for initial appearances, trials, and so forth.

P

pains of imprisonment   Deprivations faced by inmates to varying degrees while imprisoned, such as the loss of liberty, deprivation of goods and services, barring of heterosexual relations, limitations on autonomy, and concerns over personal security.

parens patriae   Basic philosophy of the juvenile court emphasizing a role of the state as parent. The philosophy grew out of the English Chancery Court, which was tasked with looking after the property rights of orphaned children, among other things.

parole supervision   The supervision of offenders who have been released from correctional institutions prior to the completion of their maximum terms of incarceration and must abide by their conditions of supervision to remain in the community. Used in jurisdictions with indeterminate sentencing.

partisan election   A method of electing state judges in which candidates indicate a party affiliation on the ballot.

patrol   A form of police deployment that puts officers on the streets as a visible presence, both to deter criminals and reassure law-abiding citizens and to discover crimes and unsafe conditions that require police intervention; although most patrolling is done in police cars, other types of patrol such as motorcycles, bicycles, and foot patrols are common.

patronage (system)   An entrenched form of corrupt government in American cities of the 1800s. All holders of city jobs owed their positions (and thus their livelihood) to their "patrons," the mayors and ward heelers who ran the cities and decided who worked and who did not.

penitentiary era   The period in correctional history when a formal penal system was developed that relied heavily on incarceration as punishment.

peremptory challenge   A method of removing jurors from the jury pool in which the prosecutors or defense attorneys do not specify reasons for the removal.

plea bargain   An agreement between the prosecutor and defense attorney, approved by the judge, in which a defendant pleads guilty to a charge in hopes of lenient treatment.

police academy   The "boot camp" for new or prospective police officers. A formal training setting in which the basic knowledge, skills, and responsibilities of police service are taught through formal instruction. Two models exist: **stress-based academies**, which emulate many features of the military boot camp, and **campus-based academies**, in which the training regimen is often integrated into an associate's degree program on the campus.

Police Activity League   A national program, but operated by local police agencies, that offers a wide range of after-school activities for children, from sports to science to chess clubs; originally the Police Athletic League, the contemporary version offers a broader range of options than just sports.

police brutality The illegal or excessive use of force by police, whether to effect a lawful goal or to achieve a corrupt one. In contemporary references, particularly those involving conflicts of race and ethnicity, the term also extends to embrace "disrespect" even if no physical force is employed.

police subculture An outgrowth of studies of police in the 1960s, the concept of a "police subculture" assumes a broad allegiance to various philosophical beliefs and common concerns: danger, challenges to authority, political conservation (reactionary, in the 1960s), and the general division of the world into good and bad, with the police as a "thin blue line" separating tax-paying civilization from the anarchy of the criminal classes. In light of wholesale changes in the police occupation, including the inclusion of women and minorities and the changes in philosophy of **community-oriented policing** and **problem-oriented policing**, the assumptions of this notion are now being challenged.

Political Era A reference to the nineteenth-century climate under which the American police developed in the cities. Also known as the "Patronage Era" because of its corrupt politics. Notable for the low quality of police recruits and for the general absence of crime control as a police duty.

Positivist school The Positivist school of criminal justice contends that human behavior is influenced by external conditions and situations that are beyond individuals' control; things such as poverty and abusive parenting influence the likelihood that a child will grow up poor and abusive as well.

postconviction review A form of appeal undertaken after the first appeal of right in which defendants challenge the constitutionality of the case process.

power shifts Special time slots, usually spanning the late evening and early morning hours, when additional police officers are on duty to handle expanded call load. Power shifts are often volunteer slots, selected by officers because of the greater likelihood of activity. They tend to be permanent or semipermanent hours, although some flexibility is possible in many agencies.

precedent The judicial practice of relying on previous decisions to make current ones, in order for the law to be stable and consistent.

precincts Administrative division of police agencies containing multiple beats and patrol areas; refers to both a specific geographical area and the police personnel assigned to it. A feature of larger communities where central command is cumbersome, precinct organization allows for more responsive policing services and a tighter chain of command for everyday operations. Both patrol and investigative services may be precinct based, though support services and some investigative units may operate from a single, central command center.

preliminary hearing The stage in a criminal case in which a judge determines if there is enough evidence against a defendant to proceed to trial. Used in place of a grand jury if a grand jury is not convened.

presentence investigation A report produced at the request of the court to assist in determining the most appropriate sentence for a particular offender.

preservice training   In some states, individuals are permitted to seek their police-officer certification by putting themselves through a police-training academy before being hired by an agency; completion of the training does not give them police powers, however, which are only bestowed once they are hired by a municipality or other jurisdiction.

President's Commission on Law Enforcement and the Administration of Justice   A widespread investigation of the deficiencies and needs of the criminal justice system in America ordered by President Johnson. Its February 1967 report, *The Challenge of Crime in a Free Society*, galvanized reform efforts and contributed to the passage of the 1968 Omnibus Crime Control and Safe Streets Act and to the creation of the **Law Enforcement Assistance Administration**.

preventive detention   Detention of a defendant pending trial because of a perceived risk to public safety.

principle of legality   A principle of law that requires the existence of a law that prohibits conduct before a person can be found guilty of it.

prison   A facility designed to hold offenders who have been convicted and sentenced to more than one year of incarceration of felony offenses.

prison programs   Organized instruction designed to help offenders with rehabilitation, educational, and vocational needs and to guide the structure and activities involved in inmates' daily routines.

prison violence   Coercive actions, threats made, and physical assaults against and between those living and working in prison.

prisoner reentry   A general term used to denote a prisoner's transition from an institutional setting and the challenges in that process.

private police   Uniformed security services that function as police protection for local interests. Some employ officers who have completed state-mandated police certification; others do not. The authority for private police typically derives from the property rights of their employers, but there are special legal provisions in some cases. Campus police officers serving colleges and universities, the Port Authority Police of New York and New Jersy Port Authority, railroad police, and others operate under particular legislative authorization.

private prison   A correctional facility that is managed and operated by a private corporation.

pro bono   A form of legal representation in which attorneys volunteer their time without compensation.

pro se   A form of legal representation in which defendants serve as their own attorneys in court proceedings.

probation   A form of community supervision in which an offender is allowed to remain in the community but must abide by certain restrictions, such as finding employment or obstaining from alcohol use.

problem-oriented policing   An informal theory of police effectiveness first articulated by Herman Goldstein in 1979, which criticizes the police efforts at crime control as incident-based and emphasizing the means over the ends. It proposes the use of broader analysis to link multiple events that stem from common sources, redefining them as "problems" and bringing a wide spectrum of police and community resources to bear on the sources of the problem. The tactical equivalent is known as "problem solving," and both are united under the acronym POP.

procedural law The "how" of the law that outlines procedures that government officials must follow when adjudicating defendants.

Professional Era A reference to the period of American police history from the late 1800s to the middle or late 1900s, during which police autonomy from local political control was sought; selection and promotion by merit were employed for personnel; scientific investigation of crime was advanced; and crime control was selected as the primary police mission. The professional model places great emphasis on police efficiency in the deterrence of crime by visible patrol, rapid response to reports of crime and intensive investigation of crimes not solved at the scene. It came under fire in the 1960s and 1970s for failing to meet its own professed goals and is in the process of being replaced by the community-policing model.

property marking An organized anticrime activity, usually conducted under police auspices, to mark personal property with a unique identification number in order to aid in its recovery and reduce its value on the black market for stolen goods.

prosecutors Attorneys who represent the state against the accused in criminal cases and are responsible for charging defendants and presenting evidence of their guilt.

public defender A type of appointed counsel who provides indigent defense services only.

public trial Criminal proceeding open to the public, which acts as a "watchdog" over government practices. The right to a public trial is guaranteed by the Sixth Amendment to the U.S. Constitution.

punishment Response given to those who violate group norms, rules, and laws.

R

racial profiling A contested practice, denied by the police but asserted by minority comunities, in which police aggressively stop black and Hispanic motorists for trivial reasons in order to view and try to search their cars for drugs. It is premised upon an unsupported belief that minorities are more involved in the illegal drug trade than whites.

reform era The period in correctional history when a more humanitarian approach to the practice of incarceration was advocated. Practices such as purposeful labor, vocational and educational training, early release, and rewards for good behavior were utilized.

reformatories Early institutions for handling youths that largely supplanted houses of refuge. They focused on education, religious training, hard work, and discipline.

Regional Task Forces *See* **Multi-Jurisdictional Task Forces**.

rehabilitation A philosophy of criminal justice that views criminals as "broken" and seeks to "repair" them by reformation and treatment. According to supporters of rehabilitation, once reformed, criminals will no longer engage in crime. Examples of rehabilitation include drug treatment, mental-health counseling, and job training.

rehabilitation era   The period in correctional history that focused on the needs of individual offenders and relied less on prisons to carry out criminal sanctions. The medical model of treating offenders as if their offending was an illness that could be cured predominated the thinking of this era.

residential community correctional program   A general term used to describe a facility that houses offenders (typically for six months or less) who were either sentenced to or placed in the program as a condition of their community supervision. There is a considerable diversity in the populations served by these programs, the types of programs available, and the freedom of movement afforded residents.

restorative (reparative) justice   Programs that use interventions to return victims, offenders, and communities to their preoffense states. They generally involve the voluntary participation of offenders, victims, and community members in seeking an outcome acceptable to all parties. Also known as *reparative justice*.

retribution   A philosophy based on the belief that criminals should be punished because they have violated the law and that the criminal justice system exists to punish wrongdoers. Punishment should be commensurate with the harm committed by the criminal (an "eye for an eye"), which is in accord with the beliefs of those who follow the Classical school. Retribution, however, does not punish in order to prevent potential criminals from committing crime. Rather, advocates of retribution argue that punishment is the proper and just thing for a society to do, regardless of its effectiveness in preventing crime.

retributive era   The period in correctional history when the response to law violators was more severe penalties and decreasing support for rehabilitative efforts, including lengthier prison sentences, more punitive sanctions such as "three strikes, you're out," and attempts to limit the discretion of judges and correctional administrators who make decisions on sentence lengths.

right to counsel   Protection guaranteed by the Sixth Amendment to the U.S. Constitution that allows certain defendants the right to have attorneys assist them in their defense.

rotating shifts   A means of providing around-the-clock police coverage in a manner that is fair to all employees. The burden of working the difficult hours of the midnight shift and weekends, and the benefits of working days, are equally distributed by assigning officers to work each shift in turn for a set period of time, then "rotating" or moving to another shift: days to evenings to midnights and then back to days to begin the cycle again. Rotating shifts tend to be defined in terms of weeks or months (usually no more than three months at the longest). Disruption of the "internal clock" of the body's circadian rhythm is one of the negative effects of rotating shifts. The alternative is **steady shifts** of longer duration.

S

safe havens A nationally organized project to identify and prominently mark homes and businesses where children can go for help if they feel threatened or scared.

scared-straight programs Programs involving intensive confrontation between inmates and pre- and early delinquents, with the goal of literally scaring the youths away from further offending and into law-abiding behavior.

school resource officers Sworn police officers who are assigned to schools or networks of schools, on either a full -or part-time basis. School resource officers usually work in uniform and monitor safety situations in the schools in addition to performing community-relations work with school-age children and with other school groups.

self-incrimination Protection found in the Fifth Amendment to the U.S. Constitution that specifies that an individual cannot be forced to confess to involvement in criminal activity.

self-report statistics One of three types of data collected on crime. Self-report statistics are gathered by asking people to report the number of times they have committed a crime during a set period of time. Self-report statistics are often better at discovering unreported crimes, victimless crimes, less serious crimes, and crimes where arrest is unlikely. *See also* **official statistics** and **victimization studies**.

sentencing guidelines Sentencing structures utilized in some states to determine sentences based on the offenses commited, the defendants 'prior records, and other information in order to create more fairness and equity in sentencing.

service An umbrella term for a wide range of police assistance to citizens (e.g., directions, emergency transportation, escorts of funeral processions, etc.) that do not fall under either **law enforcement or order maintenance**.

sheriff The chief law enforcement officer of a country. Also, an ancient office, first developed in England. Also, an elected position and an office established in the state constitution of many states. Sheriffs' departments provide general policing services, court security and services, and correctional facilities of the country jail, although not all sheriffs' departments provide all three services.

shift A division of police patrol and occasionally of investigative units. The term has two complementary meanings: (1) a specific time on duty, such as day shift, evening shift, or night shift (sometimes called "watch"), and (2) the complement of police officers assigned to work during that time period. Fixed shifts, or **steady shifts**, are permanent or semipermanent assignments (e.g., 6- or 12-month tours), while **rotating shifts** change their hours regularly on a known schedule, typically monthly or weekly, going from days to evenings to nights and back to days again in cycle. *See also* **power shifts**.

shock incarceration Something used interchangeably with **boot camps**, but can also refer to a program in which judges or correctional authorities are given the authority to grant early conditional release (often after less than 180 days' incarceration) to low-risk offenders who had been originally sentenced to a term of incarceration and place them on a form of community supervision for the remainder of their sentences.

single-entry tracks   A phrase referring to the practice of starting all sworn employees of an agency at the same level: patrol officer in police departments and frequently jail officer in sheriffs 'departments. *See also* **dual-entry tracks**.

special conditions   Conditions of community supervision that are tailored to the risks or needs of particular offenders and that are not used for all offenders in a jurisdiction. Common examples include drug treatment, work towards obtaining a GED, sex-offender counseling, and the payment of restitution to a victim.

specialized prisons   Facilities that primarily house inmates with specific characteristics that pose unique challenges to institutions, such as substances abusers, sex offenders, and mentally handicapped or psychiatric prisoners.

specific deterrence   One of the two types of deterrence. Specific deterrence refers to the deterring effect of punishing a particular offender and argues that offenders who are punished for a crime will be less likely to commit that crime again because they will remember the punishment they received the first time. *See also* **general deterrence**.

speedy trial   Protection found in the Sixth Amendment to the U.S. Constitution that guarantees that defendants have their trials commence within a certain amount of time after arrest.

standard conditions   Conditions of community supervision that are required for all offenders placed on community supervision in a given jurisdiction. Common examples include remaining law abiding, reporting to their supervising officers as directed, and notifying their officers of changes in residence.

state training schools   The juvenile justice system alternative to adult institutions.

status offense   An action that is illegal only for juveniles. Typical status offences include the use of alcohol or tobacco, curfew violations, truancy, disobeying one's parents, running away, and swearing.

Statute of Winchester   A national law passed in England in 1285 to formally impose responsibilities upon the citizenry for their own defense against crime. It required all citizens to maintain weapons and to assist the sheriff or constable when the hue and cry were raised to pursue lawbreakers and imposed mandatory, unpaid service on all male adults to serve in the Watch and to take a year-long turn as **constable**.

statutory law   The most common type of law, created by legislative bodies. Crimes and punishments are examples of statutory law.

steady shifts   A means of providing around-the-clock police coverage that allows the body to adjust to shift work over longer periods, typically from six months to a year. Shift assignments are usually voluntary or assigned on a seniority-based lottery system. Officers spend a longer time on one shift.

sting operations   Anticrime tactics in which police officers pose as criminals in order to arrest other criminal actors and discredit criminal market areas. Sting operations include officers posing as drug dealers in known drug locations, posing as prostitutes in areas known for street prostitution or gay cruising, posing as fences for stolen property, and impersonating other market-driven criminal enterprises.

stress-based academics   Police recruit training facilities that function in a fashion similar to military boot camps, with a heavy emphasis on physical training, regimented military style discipline, and residental settings. The instructional curriculum is similar to that of the alternate model, **campus-based academics**, which forgo the boot-campstyle of inducing stress in favor of other values.

strict liability   Crimes that do not require **mens rea**, or intent, for an individual to be held liable.

substantive law   The "what" of the law. Describes what the law is rather than how the law should be enforced (i.e., **procedural law**).

supermax prisons   The most restrictive and secure prisons in the country, generally reserved for the most incorrigible and dangerous prisoners in a correctional system.

supervised release   A term of supervision following a prisoner's mandatory release from prison. While similar to parole, it is used in jurisdictions with **determinate sentencing** and does not involve a discretionary release by the parole authority.

supervision violations   Violations of a condition of supervision. Depending on the seriousness of the violations, may result in consequences ranging from informal warnings to eventual revocation of offenders' community supervision and possible prison sentences.

SWAT   Special Weapons and Tactics. Special training for high-risk situations such as hostage-taking incidents and active shooters.

T

technical violations   Violations of conditions of supervision that do not involve the commission of new criminal offenses. Common examples include failure to pay financial conditions, failure to attend required treatment programs, or drug tests that indicate the use of illegal or prohibited substances.

token economy   Method for controlling or rewarding behavior in juvenile facilities. Youths receive points or tokens for acting appropriately and lose them for inappropriate behaviors. Tokens are good towards extra privileges or purchases from a store or vending machine.

transfer or waiver   Process whereby youths are sent to the adult court for processing. It may take various forms, including judicial waiver, prosecutorial waiver, statutory exclusion/legislative waiver, or demand waiver.

trans-institutionalization   Process whereby the mentally ill were first placed in secure confinement in a hospital setting, released, and then reconfined under the authority of the criminal justice system (i.e., prisons).

trial by jury   Criminal proceedings heard by a jury made up of a defendant's peers. The right to a trial by jury is guaranteed by the U.S. Constitution, but only applies to defendants facing six months' or more incarceration.

trial courts of general jurisdiction　Usually, courts that handle felony trials.

trial courts of limited jurisdiction　Courts that handle the early stages of criminal cases, such as first appearances, bail hearings, and so forth, as well as other cases such as traffic violations and minor civil actions.

troops　Administrative divisions of a state police or state patrol agency, corresponding to "precincts" in local police departments. It refers to both a specific geographical area and the police personnel assigned to it.

U

use of force　A general power of the police, used to gain compliance when other measures such as persuasion and direction fail. Use of force is a broad term covering any physical contact initiated by police against a resisting citizen, from a guiding hand to a firm restraining grip, to the application of chemical sprays, stun guns, or impact weapons like the nightstick, to the use of firearms. Use of firearms and some applications of impact weapons fall under the special category of **deadly force**, that which can produce death or serious bodily injury.

V

venire　A group of individuals called for jury duty. After receiving a summons in the mail, these individuals must report to court for jury selection.

victim advocates　Individuals who work with victims of crime to voice victims' concerns and to guide victims through criminal cases. They usually serve as liaisons between victims and prosecutors.

victimization studies　One of the three types of crime data collected. Victimization studies ask people if they have been victims of a crime during a certain time period, and they mitigate some of the problems encountered by **official statistics** and **self-report statistics**.

victimless crime　Class of crime in which there is no individual directly victimized, including crimes such as illegal drug use or underage drinking.

vigilantes　Historically, groups of citizens on the American frontier who acted in concert to protect life and property against outlaws in the absence of formal law enforcement. In modern use, a pejorative term for those who "take the law into their own hands" rather than assisting authorized law enforcement.

voir dire　The questioning of potential jurors during jury selection to screen out those who may not be appropriate (for example, those who may be biased against the defendant or who may be relatives of the victim).

W

Watch　Historically, a group of citizens charged with ensuring the security of the town or precinct at night, usually against fire and vagabonds, which was made mandatory by the 1285 Statute of Winchester. In nineteenth-century American policing, a 12-hour shift for the earliest police departments. Now incorporated into "Neighborhood Watch" and "Block Watch" as a citizen responsibility.

Wickersham Commission A 1931 commission to investigate charges of police brutality and other allegations of police corruption.

wilderness programming Programs in which youths are placed in situations where they must learn survival skills and rely on one another to succeed. Can be either short-term or long-term and can take a variety of different forms, including sailing trips, wagon trains, or back-country camps. The underlying idea is to build self-esteem and show the youths that hard work and perseverance pay off.

Y

youthful offender statutes Provisions whereby the juvenile justice system can retain jurisdiction over individuals who were adjudicated in the system but have since passed the age of majority.

Z

zero tolerance An informal theory of police operations that emphasizes arrests for all low-level offenses without exception. An offshoot of the **Broken Windows** hypothesis that emphasizes only **law enforcement**, not **order maintenance**. ✦

Bibliography

Abadinsky, H. (1997). *Probation and parole: Theory and practice,* 6th ed. Upper Saddle River, NJ: Prentice Hall.

Adams, K. (1992). "Adjusting to prison life. "In M. Tonry (Ed.), *Crime and justice: A review of research,* 275–360. Chicago, IL: University of Chicago Press.

Aday, R. (2003). *Aging prisoners: Crisis in American corrections.* Westport, CT: Praeger.

Albanese, J. (2002). *Criminal justice.* Boston MA: Allyn and Bacon.

Alemagno, S., E. Shaffer-King, P. Tonkin, and R. Hammel. (2004). *Characteristics of arrestees at risk for co-existing substance abuse and mental disorder.* Washington, DC: National Institute of Justice.

American Law Institute. (1962). *Model penal code.* Philadelphia, PA: American Law Institute.

Anderson, J. (2003). *Public policymaking: An introduction.* Boston: Houghton Mifflin.

Andrews, D.A., and J. Bonta. (2006). *The psychology of criminal conduct.* Cincinnati: Anderson Publishing.

Andrews, D., I. Zinger, R. Hoge, J. Bonta, P. Gendreau, and F. Cullen. (1990). "Does correctional treatment work? A clinically relevant and psychologically informed meta-analysis." *Criminology* 28:369–404.

Antiterrorism and Effective Death Penalty Act. (1996). Retrieved January 15, 2005, from http://www.gpoaccess.gov/congress/index.html.

Applegate, B., R. Surette, and B. McCarthy. (1999). "Detention and desistance from crime: Evaluating the influence of a new generation jail on recidivism." *Journal of Criminal Justice* 27:539–548.

Argersinger v. Hamlin, 407 U.S. 25 (1972).

Arnold, E., P. Valentine, M. McInnis, and A. McNeece. (2000). "Evaluating drug courts: An alternative to incarceration." In L. Mays and P. Gregware (Eds.), *Courts and justice: A reader,* 419–431. Prospect Heights, IL: Waveland Press.

Austin, J., and J. Irwin. (2001). *It's about time: America's imprisonment binge,* 3rd ed. Belmont, CA: Wadsworth Thompson.

Barron v. Baltimore, 32 U.S. 243 (1833).

Bartollas, C. (1985). *Correctional treatment: Theory and practice.* Englewood Cliffs, NJ: Prentice Hall.

Batson v. Kentucky, 476 U.S. 79 (1986).

Bayens, G., J. Williams, and J. Smykla. (1997). "Jail type makes a difference: Evaluating the transition from a traditional to a podular, direct supervision jail across ten years." *American Jails* 11:32–39.

Bazemore, G., and D. Maloney. (1994). "Rehabilitating community service: Toward restorative service sanctions in a balanced justice system. "*Federal Probation* 58:24–35.

Beck, A., and L. Maruschak. (2001). *Mental health treatment in state prisons, 2000.* Washington, DC: Bureau of Justice Statistics.

Belknap, J. (2001). *The invisible woman: Gender, crime, and justice.* Belmont, CA: Wadsworth.

Bernfeld, G.A., D.P. Farrington, and A.W. Leschied. (Eds.). (2001). *Offender rehabilitation in practice: Implementing and evaluating effective programs.* New York: John Wiley and Sons.

Bittner, E. (1970). *The functions of the police in modern society: A review of background factors, current practices, and possible role models.* Cambridge, MA: MIT Press.

Black, D. (1981). *The manners and customs of the police.* New York: Academic Press.

Blackstone, W. (2002). *Commentaries on the laws of England.* Chicago, IL: University of Chicago Press.

Blumstein, A., (1995). "Crime and punishment in the United States over 20 years: A failure of deterrence and incapacitation?" In P. Wikstrom, R. Clarke, and J. McCord (Eds.), *Integrating crime prevention strategies: Propensity and opportunity,* 123–140. Stockholm, Sweden: National Council for Crime Prevention.

Blumstein, A., and A. Beck. (1999). "Population growth in U.S. prisons." In M. Tonry and J. Petersilia (Eds.), *Prisons,* 17–62. Chicago, IL: University of Chicago Press.

Blumstein, A., J. Cohen, and D. Nagin. (1978). *Deterrence and incapacitation: Estimating the effects of criminal sanctions on crime rates.* Washington, DC: National Academy of Sciences.

Board of Education of Independent School District No. 92 v. Lindsay Earls et al., 536 U.S. 822 (2002).

Bond, B. (2001). "Principals and SROs: Defining roles." *Principal Leadership* (April):51–55.

Bottomley, K. (1990). "Parole in transition: A comparative study of origins, developments, and prospects for the 1990s." In M. Tonry and N. Morris (Eds.), *Crime and justice: A review of research,* 319–374. Chicago: University of Chicago Press.

Bottoms, A. (1999). "Interpersonal violence and social order in prisons." In M. Tonry and J. Petersilia (Eds.), *Prisons,* 205–282. Chicago: University of Chicago Press.

Breed v. Jones, 421 U.S. 519 (1975).

Brinegar v. U.S., 338 U.S. 160 (1949).

Brown, M.K. (1981). *Working the street: Police discretion and the dilemmas of reform.* New York: Russell Sage Foundation.

Brown, R.M. (1969). "The American vigilante tradition." In H.D. Graham and T. Gurr (Eds.), *Violence in America: Historical and comparative perspectives.* A report submitted to the National Commission on the Cause and Prevention of Violence, 121–169. Washington, DC: USGPO.

Bureau of Justice Statistics. (2000). *Correctional populations in the United States, 1997.* Washington, DC: U.S. Department of Justice.

——. (2004a). *Prisoners in 2003.* Washington, DC: U.S. Department of Justice.

——. (2004b). *Correctional populations in the United States, 2003.* Washington, DC: U.S. Department of Justice.

——. (2004c). *State prison expenditures, 2001.* Washington, DC: U.S. Department of Justice.

——. (2004d). *Prison and jail inmates at mid-year 2003.* Washington, DC: U.S. Department of Justice.

——. (2004e). *Felony sentences in state courts, 2002.* Washington, DC: U.S. Department of Justice.

——. (2004f). *Correctional populations in the United States, 2002.* Washington, DC: U.S. Department of Justice.

——. (2008a). Number of sentenced inmates incarcerated under state and federal jurisdiction per 100,000, 1980–2007. Retrieved from http://www.ojp.usdoj.gov/bjs/glance/corr2.htm.

——. (2008b). *Probation and parole in the United States, 2007: Statistical tables.* Available from http://www.ojp.usdoj.gov/bjs/abstract/ppus07st.htm.

Burke, P. (1995). *Abolishing parole: Why the emperor has no clothes.* Lexington, KY: American Probation and Parole Association.

Byrne, J. (1996). "Reintegrating the concept of community into community-based corrections." In T. Ellsworth (Ed.), *Contemporary community corrections,* 422–448. Prospect Heights, IL: Waveland Publishing.

Byrne, J., A. Lurigo, and J. Petersilia (Eds.). (1992). *Smart sentencing: The emergence of intermediate sanctions.* Newbury Park, CA: Sage Publications.

Caher, J., and M. Riccardi. (2000, March 15). "Coalition of lawyers protests low assigned counsel fees." *New York Law Journal,* 1. Retrieved April 2, 2005, from Lexis-Nexis Academic database.

California Penal Code. (2005). Retrieved May 5, 2006, from http://www.leginfo.ca.gov.

California State Constitution. (2005). Retrieved January 15, 2005 from http://www.leginfo.ca.gov/const-toc.html.

Carp, R., and R. Stidham. (1990). *Judicial process in America.* Washington, DC: Congressional Quarterly Press.

Carroll, L. (1974). *Hacks, blacks, and cons.* Lexington, MA: Lexington Books.

Center for Substance Abuse Treatment. (2005). *Substance abuse treatment for adults in the criminal justice system.* Treatment Improvement Protocol (TIP) Series 44. Rockville, MD: Substance Abuse and Mental Health Services Administration.

Clear, T., and H. Dammer. (2003). *The offender in the community.* Belmont, CA: Thompson Wadsworth.

Clear, T., P. Harris, and S. Baird. (1992). "Probationer violations and officer response." *Journal of Criminal Justice* 20:1–12.

Cohen, S. (1985). *Visions of social control.* Cambridge, MA: Polity Press. *Commonwealth v. Fisher,* 213 Pa. 48 (1905).

Conley, J. (1980). "Prisons, production, and profit: Reconsidering the importance of prison industries." *Journal of Social History* 14:257–275.

Cooper v. Pate, 378 U.S. 546 (1964).

Crank, J.P. (1998). *Understanding police culture.* Cincinnati, OH: Anderson.

Crime and Justice Institute. (2004, April 24). *Implementing evidence-based practice in community corrections.* Retrieved June 1, 2009, from National Institute of Corrections website at http://www.nicic.org/pubs/2004/019342.pdf.

Cruz v. Beto, 405 U.S. 319 (1972).

Curry, G., and S. Decker. (1998). *Confronting gangs: Crime and community.* Los Angeles, CA: Roxbury Publishing.

Dentler, R.A., and L.J. Monroe. (1961). "Social correlates of early adolescent theft." *American Sociological Review* 26:733–743.

Digital History. (2007). *Progressive Era.* Retrieved April 28, 2007, from http://www. digitalhistory.uh.edu/modules/progressivism/index.cfm

Ditton, P.M. (1999). *Mental health and treatment of inmates and probationers.* Washington, DC: U.S. Department of Justice. Available from www.ojp.usdoj.gov/bjs/pub/pdf/mhtip.pdf.

Doe v. Renfroe, 631 F.2d 91, 92–93 (7th Cir. 1981).

Donziger, S. (Ed.). (1996). *The real war on crime.* New York: HarperPerennial.

Egley, A., and A. Major. (2004). *Highlights of the 2002 national youth gang survey: OJJDP fact sheet #1.* Washington, DC: Office of Juvenile Justice and Delinquency Prevention.

Ellsworth, T. (1996). "The emergence of community corrections." In T. Ellsworth (Ed.), *Contemporary community corrections,* 3–12. Prospect Heights, IL: Waveland Publishing.

Erickson, M. (1973). "Group violations and officials delinquency: The group hazard hypothesis." *Criminology* 11:127–160.

Esbensen, F., and D. Osgood. (1997) *National evaluation of G.R.E.A.T.: NIJ Research in Brief.* Washington, DC: National Institute of Justice.

Ex parte Crouse, 4 Wheaton (Pa.) 9 (1838).

Ex parte Hull, 312 U.S. 546 (1941).

Fabricant, M. (1983). *Juveniles in the family courts.* Lexington, MA: Lexington Books.

Fagan, J. (1995). "Separating men from the boys: The comparative advantage of juvenile versus criminal court sanctions on recidivism among adolescent felony offenders." In J. Howell, B. Krisberg, J. Hawkins, and J. Wilson (Eds.), *A sourcebook: Serious, violent, and chronic juvenile offenders,* 238–260. Thousand Oaks, CA: Sage Publications.

Faiver, K. (1998). *Health care management issues in corrections.* Lanham, MD: American Correctional Association.

Fare v. Michael C., 442 U.S. 707 (1979).

Federal Bureau of Investigation. (1999). CJIS: A *Newsletter for the Criminal Justice Community. NIBRS Edition.* Vol. 4, No. 1. Clarksburg, WV: U.S. Department of Justice, FBI.

——. (2004). *Crime in the United States, 2003.* Washington, DC: U.S. Department of Justice.

Feld, B. (1988). "*In re Gault* revisited: A cross-state comparison of the right to counsel in juvenile count." *Crime and Delinquency* 34:393–424.

——. (1999). *Bad kids: Race and the transformation of the juvenile court.* New York: Oxford University Press.

Fletcher v. Peck, 10 U.S. 87 (1810).

Fyfe, J.J., J.R. Greene, W.F. Walsh, O.W. Wilson, and R.C. McLaren. (1997). *Police administration,* 5th ed. New York: McGraw–Hill.

Gaes, G., T. Flanagan, L. Motiuk, and L. Stewart. (1999). "Adult correctional treatment." In M. Tonry and J. Petersilia (Eds.), *Prisons,* 361–427. Chicago, IL: University of Chicago Press.

Gaes, G., and W. McGuire. (1985). "Prison violence: The contribution of crowding versus other determinants of prison assault rates." *Journal of Research in Crime and Delinquency* 22:41–65.

Garofalo, J., and M. McLeod. (1989). "The structure and operations of Neighborhood Watch Programs in the United States." *Crime and Delinquency* 35(3):316–344.

Gideon v. Wainwright, 372 U.S. 335 (1963).

Godttfredson, M., and D. Gottfredson. (1988). *Decision making in criminal justice: Toward the rational exercise of discretion.* New York: Plenum Press.

Gowdy, V. (2001). "Should we privatize our prisons: The pros and cons." In E. Latessa, A. Holsinger, J. Marquart, and J. Sorenson (Eds.), *Correctional contexts: Contemporary and classical readings,* 198–208. Los Angeles, CA: Roxbury Publishing.

Gray, M.K., M. Fields, and S.R. Maxwell. (2001). "Examining probation violations: Who, what, and when." *Crime and Deliquency* 47(4):537–557.

Guyot, D. (1979). "Bending granite: Attempts to change the rank structure of American police departments." *Journal of Police Science and Administration* 7(3):253–284.

Haas, K., and G. Alpert. (1989) "American prisoners and the right of access to the courts: A vanishing concept of protection." In L. Goodstein and D. MacKenzie (Eds.), *The American prison: Issues in research and policy*, 65–87. New York: Plenum.

Hagan, J., and R. Dinovitzer. (1999). "Collateral consequences of imprisonment for children, communities, and prisoners." In M. Tonry and J. Petersilia (Eds.), *Prisons*, 121–162. Chicago, IL: University of Chicago Press.

Hammett, T. (1998). *Public health/corrections collaborations: Prevention and treatment of HIV/AIDS, STDs, and TB*. Washington, DC: National Institute of Justice.

Harer, M., and D. Steffensmeier. (1996). "Race and prison violence." *Criminology* 34:323–355.

Harland, A. (1998). "Defining a continuum of sanctions: Some research and policy development implications." In J. Petersilia (Ed.), *Community corrections: Probation, parole, and intermediate sanctions*, 70–79. New York: Oxford University Press.

Harmelin v. Michigan, 501 U.S. 957(1991).

Harris, M. (1996). "The goals of community sanctions." In T. Ellsworth (Ed.), *Contemporary community corrections*, 13–33. Prospect Heights, IL: Waveland Press.

Harrison, P., and A. Beck. (2004). *Prisoners in 2003*. Washington, DC: U.S. Department of Justice, Office of Justice Programs.

Hawkins, R., and G. Alpert. (1989). *American prison systems: Punishment and justice*. Englewood Cliffs, NJ: Prentice Hall.

Hemmens, C., J. Worrall, and A. Thompson. (2004). *Significant cases in criminal procedure*. Los Angeles: Roxbury Publishing.

Henry, V.E. (2002). *The CompStat paradigm: Management accountability in policing, business, and the public sector*. Flushing, NY: Looseleaf.

Hindelang, M., T. Hirschi, and J. Weis. (1979). "Correlates of delinquency: The illusion of discrepancy between self-report and official measures." *American Sociological Review* 44:995–1014.

Innes, Martin. (2006). "Policing Uncertainty: Countering Terror through Community Intelligence and Democratic Policing. The Annals of the American Academy of Political and Social Science, Vol. 605, May 2006: 222–241.

In re Gault, 387 U.S. 1 (1967).

In re Winship, 397 U.S. 358 (1970).

Institute of Judicial Administration-American Bar Association (IJA-ABA). (1980). *Juvenile justice standards: Standards relating to adjudication*. Cambridge, MA: Ballinger.

Internet Newsletter. (2004, September 10). "Net news: Feds cracking down on cybercrime." Retrieved January 15, 2005, from Lexis Nexis Academic database.

Irwin, J. (1980). *Prisons in turmoil*. Boston, MA: Little, Brown.

Jacobs, J. (1976). "Stratification and conflict among prison inmates." *Journal of Criminal Law and Criminology* 66: 476–482.

——. (1982). "Sentencing by prison personnel: Good time." *UCLA Law Review* 30:217–270.

James, D.J., and L.E. Glaze. (2006). *Mental health problems of prison and jail inmates*. Washington, DC: U.S. Department of Justice.

Johnson, H., and N. Wolfe. (1996). *History of criminal justice*, 2nd ed. Cincinnati, OH: Anderson Publishing.

Johnson, R. (2002). *Hard time: Understanding and reforming the prison.* Belmont, CA: Wadsworth.

Joyce, N. (1992). "A view of the future: The effects of policy on prison population growth." *Crime and Delinquency* 38:357–368.

Justice Center. (2008). *Mental health courts: A primer for policy makers and practitioners.* New York: Justice Center/Council of State Governments. Available from the National Institute of Corrections website at http://www.nicic.org.

Kelling, G.L., and M.H. Moore. (1988). *The evolving strategy of policing.* National Institute of Justice, *Perspectives on policing,* 4. Washington, DC: National Institute of Justice.

Kent v. U.S., 383 U.S. 541 (1966).

Klockars, C. (1985). *The idea of police.* Newbury Park, CA: Sage Publications.

Krisberg, B., and J. Austin (1978). *The children of Ishmael.* Palo Alto, CA: Mayfield.

———. (1993). *Reinventing juvenile justice.* Newbury Park, CA: Sage Publications.

Kurki, L. (2000). "Restorative and community justice in the United States." In M. Tonry (Ed.), *Crime and justice: A review of research,* vol. 27. Chicago, IL: University of Chicago Press.

Kyllo v. U.S., 533 U.S. 27 (2001).

Lab, S.D. (2004). *Crime prevention: Approaches, practices, and evaluations.* Cincinnati, OH: Anderson/LexisNexis.

Lane, R. (1967 [1975]). *Policing the city: Boston, 1822–1885.* Boston, MA: Atheneum. Originally published by Harvard University Press.

Langan, P., and D. Levin. (2002). *Recidivision of prisoners released in 1994.* Washington, DC: Bureau of Justice Statistics.

Latessa, E.J., and F.T. Cullen. (2002). "Beyond correctional quackery: Professionalism and the possibility of effective treatment." *Federal Probation* 66:43–49.

Latessa, E., and L. Travis. (1992). "Residential community correctional programs." In J. Byrne, A. Lurrigo, and J. Petersilia (Eds.), *Smart sentencing: The emergence of intermediate sanctions,* 166–181. Newbury Park, CA: Sage Publications.

LEMAS Data Sets: Law Enforcement. (2006). Retrieved November 27, 2006, from http://www.la.utexas.edu/crimedata/lemas.html.

Lipsey, M., and D. Wilson. (1998). "Effective intervention for serious juvenile offenders: A synthesis of research." In R. Loeber and D. Farrington (Eds.), *Serious and violent juvenile offenders: Risk factors and successful interventions.* Thousand Oaks, CA: Sage Publications.

Lowenkamp, C., and E. Latessa. (2002). *Evaluation of Ohio's community based correctional facilities and halfway house programs: Final report.* Retrieved April 1, 2005 from http://www.drc.ohio.gov/web/reports/UCReportsFinal.pdf.

Lowenkamp, C.T., and E.J. Latessa. (2005). "Increasing the effectiveness of correctional programming through the risk principle: Identifying offenders for residential placement." *Criminology and Public Policy* 4(2):263–290.

Lundman, R.J. (1993). *Prevention and control of juvenile delinquency,* 2nd ed. New York: Oxford University Press.

Lurigio, A., and J. Petersilia. (1992). "The emergence of intensive probation supervision programs in the United States." In J. Byrne, A. Lurrigo, and J. Petersilia (Eds.), *Smart sentencing: The emergence of intermediate sanctions,* 3–18. Newbury Park, CA: Sage Publications.

Mack, J.W. (1909). "The juvenile court." *Harvard Law Review* 23: 104–119.

MacKenzie, D.L. (2000). "Evidence-based corrections: Identifying what works." *Crime and Delinquency* 46:457–471.

Maguire, E.R., and W.R. King. "Federal-Local Coordination in Homeland Security." Chapter forthcoming in Security and Justice in the Homeland: Criminologists on Terrorism. Edited by Brian Forst, Jack Greene, and James Lynch.

Maguire, K., and A. Pastore (Eds.). (2002). *Sourcebook of criminal justice statistics* [Online]. Retrieved February 22, 2005, from http://www.albany.edu/sourcebook/.

Maltz, M. (1999). *Bridging gaps in police crime data: A discussion paper from the BJS Fellows Program.* Washington, DC: U.S. Department of Justice.

Mancini, M. (1978). "Race, economics, and the abandonment of convict leasing." *Journal of Negro History* 63:339–340.

Mans, L. (2004). "Liability for the death of a fetus: Fetal rights or women's rights?" *Florida Journal of Law and Public Policy* 15:295–312.

Mapp v. Ohio, 367 U.S. 643 (1961).

Marbury v. Madison, 5 U.S. 137 (1803).

Martinson, R. (1974). "What works?—Questions and answers about prison reform." *The Public Interest* 42:22–54.

Maruna, S., and R. Immarigeon (Eds.). (2004). *After crime and punishment: Pathways to offender reintegration.* Portland, OR: Willan Publishing.

Maruschak, L. (2004). *HIV in prisons, 2001.* Washington, DC: Bureau of Justice Statistics.

Mastrofski, S.D., J.B. Snipes, and A.E. Supina. (1996). "Compliance on demand: The public's response to specific police requests." *Journal of Research in Crime and Delinquency* 35(3):269–305.

Mauer, M. (1997). *American behind bars: U.S. and international use of incarceration, 1995.* Washington, DC: National Institute of Justice.

McBride, D., and C. VanderWaal. (1997). "Day reporting centers as an alternative for drug using offenders." *Journal of Drug Issues* 27:379–397.

McCleary, R. (1992). *Dangerous men: The sociology of parole,* 2nd ed. New York: Harrow and Heston.

McCollister, K., M. French, M. Prendergast, E. Hall, and S. Sacks.(2004). "Long-term cost effectiveness of addiction treatment for criminal offenders." *Justice Quarterly* 21:559–679.

McCulloch v. Maryland, 17 U.S. 316 (1819).

McDevitt, J., and R. Miliano. (1992). "Day reporting centers: An innovative concept in intermediate sanctions." In J. Byrne, A. Lurrigo, and J. Petersilia (Eds.), *Smart sentencing: The emergence of intermediate sanctions,* 152–165. Newbury Park, CA: Sage Publications.

McGuire, J. (2002). *Offender rehabilitation and treatment: Effective programs and policies to reduce re-offending.* New York: John Wiley and Sons.

McKeiver v. Pennsylvania, 403 U.S. 528 (1971).

McMann v. Richardson, 397 U.S. 759 (1970).

Miller, W. (1975). *Violence by youth gangs and youth groups as a crime problem in major American cities.* Washington, DC: National Institute for Juvenile Justice and Delinquency Prevention.

Miranda v. Arizona, 384 U.S. 436 (1966).

M'Naughten's Case, 8 Eng. Rep. 718 (1843).

Morgan, K. (1996). "Factors influencing probation outcome: A review of the literature." In T. Ellsworth (Ed.), *Contemporary community corrections,* 327–340. Prospect Heights, IL: Waveland Press.

Morris, N., and D. Rothman. (1995). *The Oxford history of the prison*. New York: Oxford University Press.

Morris, N., and M. Tonry. (1990). *Between prison and probation: Intermediate punishments in a rational sentencing system*. New York: Oxford University Press.

Morrissey v. Brewer, 408 U.S. 471 (1972).

National Institute of Justice. (2003). *Correctional boot camps: Lessons from a decade of research*. Washington, DC: U.S. Department of Justice.

Neubauer, D. (2004). *America's courts and the criminal justice system*. Belmont, CA: Wadsworth Publishing.

New Jersey v. T.L.O., 468 U.S. 1214 (1985).

Newman, S.A, J.A. Fox, E.A. Flynn, and W. Christeson. (2000). *America's after-school choice: Prime time for juvenile crime, or enrichment and achievement*. Washington, DC: Invest in Kids.

Niederhoffer, A. (1967). *Behind the shield: The police in urban society*. New York: Doubleday & Company.

Office of Juvenile Justice and Delinquency Prevention. (2001). Statistical briefing book. Retrieved March 15, 2005, from http://ojjdp.ncjrs.org/ojstatbb/corrections/.

Ohio Department of Rehabilitation and Corrections. (2007). *Best practices tool-kit: Sex offender assessment and treatment*. Retrieved June 1, 2009, from ORDC website at http://www.drc.state.oh.us/web/iej_files/SO_AssessmentTreatment.pdf.

Ohio Revised Code. (2005). Retrieved May 5, 2006, from http://codes.ohio.gov/.

O'Neal v. Vermont, 144 U.S. 323 (1892).

Packer, H. (1968). *The limits of the criminal sanction*. Stanford, CA: Stanford University Press.

Palko v. Connecticut, 302 U.S. 319 (1937).

Peters, M., D. Thomas, and C. Zamberlan. (1997). *Boot camps for juvenile offenders: Program summary*. Washington, DC: U.S. Department of Justice.

Petersilia, J. (1997). "Probation in the United States." In M. Tony (Ed.), *Crime and justice: A review of research*, 149–200. Chicago, IL: University of Chicago Press.

——. (1998). "A crime control rationale for reinvesting in community corrections." In J. Petersilia (Ed.), *Community corrections: Probation, parole, and intermediate sanctions*, 20–28. New York: Oxford University Press.

——. (2002). "Community corrections." In J. Wilson and J. Petersilia (Eds.), *Crime: Public policies for crime control*, 483–508. Oakland, CA: Institute for Contemporary Studies.

——. (2003). *When prisoners return home: Parole and prisoner reentry*. New York: Oxford University Press.

Petersilia, J., A. Lurigio, and J. Byrne. (1992). "Introduction: The emergence of intermediate sanctions." In J. Byrne, A. Lurigio, and J. Petersilia (Eds.), *Smart sentencing: The emergence of intermediate sanctions*, ix–xv. Newbury Park, CA: Sage Publications.

Petersilia, J., and S. Turner. (1993). *Evaluating intensive supervision probation/parole: Results of a nationwide experiment. Research in brief: National Institute of Justice* (May 1993). Washington, DC: U.S. Department of Justice.

Pisciotta, A. (1994). *Benevolent repression: Social control and the American reformatory-prison movement*. New York: New York University Press.

Platt, A.M. (1977). *The child savers: The invention of delinquency*. Chicago, IL: University of Chicago Press.

Pollock, J. (2004). *Prisons and prison life: Costs and consequences.* Los Angeles, CA: Roxbury Publishing.

President's Commission on Law Enforcement and the Administration of Justice. (1967). *The challenge of crime in a free society.* Washington, DC: U.S. Government Printing Office.

Prins, S.J., and L. Draper. (2009). *Improving outcomes for people with mental illnesses under community supervision: A guide to research-informed policy and practice.* New York: Justice Center/Council of State Governments. Available from the National Institute of Corrections website at http://www.nicic.org.

Puritz, P., S. Burrell, M. Schwartz, M. Solar, and L. Warboys. (1995). *A call for justice: An assessment of access to counsel and quality of representation in delinquency procedings.* Washington, DC: American Bar Association.

Puzzanchera, C., A. Stahl, A. Finnegan, N. Tierney, and H. Snyder. (2003). *Juvenile court statistics.* Washington, DC: Office of Juvenile Justice and Delinquency Prevention.

Puzzanchera, C., and M. Sickmund. (2006). *Juvenile Court Statistics, 2005.* Pittsburgh, PA: National Center for Juvenile Justice.

Qutb v. Strauss, 11 F.3d 488, 492 (5th Cir. 1993).

Rantala, R. (2000). *Effects of NIBRS on crime statistics: Bureau of Justice Statistics special report.* Washington, DC: U.S. Department of Justice.

Reichel, P. (1997). *Corrections.* Minneapolis/St. Paul: West Publishing Company.

Reider, L. (1998). "Towards a new test for the insanity defense: Incorporating the discoveries of neuroscience into moral and legal theories." *UCLA Law Review* 46: 289–342.

Rembar, C. (1989). *The law of the land: The evolution of our legal system.* New York: Perennial Library.

Roe v. Wade, 410 U.S. 113 (1973).

Roper, Superintendent, Potosi Correctional Center v. Simmons, 543 U.S. 551 (2005).

Rose, D., and T. Clear. (2003). "Incarceration, reentry, and social capital: Social networks in the balance." In J. Travis and M. Waul (Eds.), *Prisoners once removed: The impact of incarceration and reentry on children, families, and communities,* 313–342. Washington, DC: The Urban Institute Press.

Rosenbaum, D.P (1987). "Theory and research behind Neighborhood Watch: Is it a sound fear and crime reduction strategy?" *Crime and Delinquency* 33(1): 103–134.

Rothman, D. (1971). *The discovery of the asylum.* Boston, MA: Little, Brown.

——. (1980). *Conscience and convenience: The asylum and its alternatives in progressive America.* Boston, MA: Little Brown.

Samaha, J. (2002). *Criminal procedure.* Belmont, CA: Wadsworth Publishing.

Schall v. Martin, 467 U.S. 253 (1984).

Scheb, J., and J. Scheb. (1999). *Criminal law and procedure.* Belmont, CA: Wadsworth Publishing.

Schwartz, B. (1992). *The great rights of mankind: A history of the American Bill of Rights.* Madison, WI: Madison House.

Scott v. Illinois, 440 U.S. 367 (1979).

Sellin, J. (1976). *Slavery and the penal system.* New York: Elsevier.

Sexton, G. (1995). *Work in American prisons: Joint ventures with the private sector.* Washington, DC: National Institute of Justice.

Sheldon, R. (2001). "Controlling the dangerous classes: An introduction to the history of criminal justice." Needham Heights, MA: Allyn and Bacon.

Short, J., and I. Nye. (1958). "Extent of unrecorded delinquency: Tentative conclusions." *Journal of Criminal Law, Criminology, and Police Science* 49:296–302.

Shy, Y. (2004). *Mandatory minimum sentencing in Massachusetts: Alternative approaches.* Retrieved November 2, 2004, from http://www.cjpc.org/dp_manmin_in_other_states.htm.

Sickmund, M. (2002), *Juvenile offenders in residential placement: 1997–1999. OJJDP Fact Sheet #07.* Washington, DC: Office of Juvenile Justice and Delinquency Prevention.

Silverman, E.B. (1999), *NYPD battles crime: Innovative strategies in policing.* Boston, MA: Northeastern University Press.

Skolnick, J.H. (1966), *Justice without trial: Law enforcement in democratic society.* New York: John Wiley and Sons.

Slate, R. (2000). "Courts for mentally ill offenders: Necessity or abdication of responsibility?" In L. Mays and P. Gregware (Eds.), *Crime and justice: A reader,* 432–450. Prospect Heights, IL: Waveland Press.

Smith, Brent L., and Gregory P. Orvis. (1993). America's response to terrorism: An empirical analysis of federal intervention strategies during the 1980s. *Justice Quarterly,* Vol. 10, No. 4: 661–681.

Smith, D., and C. Visher. (1981). "Street-level justice: Situational determinants of police arrest decisions." *Social Problem* 29:167–177.

Smith, S., and C. DeFrances. (1996). *Indigent defense.* Washington, DC: U.S. Department of Justice, Office of Justice Programs.

Snyder, H.H., and M. Sickmund. (2006). *Juvenile Offender and Victims: 2006 National Report.* Pittsburg PA: National Center for Juvenile Justice.

Stanford v. Kentucky, 492 U.S. 361 (1989).

Stinchcomb, J., and V. Fox. (1999). *Introduction to corrections.* Upper Saddle River, NJ: Prentice Hall.

Streib, V. (2000). *The juvenile death penalty today: Death sentences and executions for juvenile crimes, January 1, 1973–June 30, 2000.* Ada, OH: Ohio Northern University Claude W. Pettit College of Law.

Strickland v. Washington, 446 U.S. 668 (1984).

Sykes, G. (1958). *The society of captives.* Princeton, NJ: Princeton University Press.

Tennessee v. Garner, 471 U.S. 1 (1985).

Thompson, J., and G. Mays (Eds.). (1991). *American jails: Public policy issues.* Chicago, IL : University of Chicago Press.

Tonry, M. (1990). "Stated and latent functions of ISP." *Crime and Delinquency* 36:174–191.

Tonry, M., and M. Lynch. (1996). "Intermediate sanctions." In M. Tonry (Ed.), *Crime and Justice: A review of research,* 99–144. Chicago, IL: University of Chicago Press.

Trac Reports, *Criminal terrorism enforcement in the United States during the five years since the 9/11/01 attacks,* (2002), retrieved November 09, 2009, from http://trac.syr.edu/tracreports/terrorism/169/.

Travis, J., and M. Waul (Eds.). (2003). *Prisoners once removed: The impact of incarceration and reentry on children, families, and communities.* Washington, DC: The Urban Institute Press.

Trupin, E., H. Richards, D. Wertheimer, and C. Bruschi. (2001). *Seattle municipal court mental health court. Evaluation report 2001.* Retrieved January 15, 2005, from http://www.cityofseattle.net/courts/pdf/MHreport.pdf.

United States Constitution. (1789). Retrieved January 15, 2005, from LexisNexis Academic database.

U.S. v. Salerno, 481 U.S. 739 (1987).

U.S. Department of State. (2005). *Background on the Pendleton Act*. Retrieved April 27, 2007, from http://usinfo.state.gov/usa/infousa/facts/democrac/28.htm.

Vaas, A., and A. Weston. (1990). "Probation day centres as an alternative to custody." *British Journal of Criminology* 30:189–205.

Van Ness, D., and K. Strong. (2002). *Restoring justice*. Cincinnati, OH: Anderson Publishing.

Van Voorhis, P. (1994). *Psychological classification of the adult male prison inmate*. Albany, NY: University of New York Press.

Von Hirsch, A. (1998). "The ethics of community-based sanctions." In J. Petersilia (Ed.), *Community corrections: Probation, parole, and intermediate sanctions*, 89–98. New York: Oxford University Press.

Walker, S. (1993). *Taming the system: The control of discretion in criminal justice, 1950–1990*. New York: Oxford University Press.

White, T.F. (2005). *Re-engineering probation towards greater public safety: A framework for recidivism reduction through evidence-based practice*. Retrieved June 1, 2009, from the National Institute of Corrections website at http://www.nicic.org/downloads/pdf/misc/ReEngineeringProb_ct1105.pdf.

Whitehead, J., and S. Lab. (2009) *Juvenile justice: An introduction*, 3rd ed. Cincinnati: Anderson Publishing.

Wilson, D.B., D.L. MacKenzie, and F.N. Mitchell, (2005). *Effects of correctional boot camps on offending: A Campbell Collaboration systematic review*. Available at http://www.aic.gov.au/campbellcj/reviews/titles.html.

Wilson, J.Q. (1968). *Varieties of police behavior: The management of law and order in eight communities*. Cambridge, MA: Havard University Press.

Wilson, J.Q., and G.L. Kelling. (1982). "Broken windows: The police and neighborhood safety." *The Atlantic Monthly* (March): 29–38.

Wooldredge, J.D. (1994). "Inmate crime and victimization in a Southwestern correctional facility." *Journal of Criminal Justice* 22:367–381.

Worrall, J. (2006). *Crime control in America: An assessment of the evidence*. Boston, MA: Pearson.

Zalman, M., and L. Siegel. (1997). *Criminal procedure: Constitution and society*. Belmont, CA: Wadsworth Publishing.

Zimmer, L. (1986). *Women guarding men*. Chicago, IL: University of Chicago Press. ✦

Index